Melanie Blood

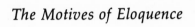

The Motives of Eloquence

The Motives of Eloquence

LITERARY RHETORIC IN THE RENAISSANCE

Richard A. Lanham

NEW HAVEN AND LONDON
YALE UNIVERSITY PRESS

Library of Congress catalog card number: 75-43323
International standard book number: 0-300-02002-3,
0-300-02985-3 (pbk.)

Designed by Sally Sullivan
and set in Palatino type.
Printed in the United States of America by
Vail-Ballou Press, Binghamton, New York.

3   5   7   9   11   10   8   6   4   2

Carolae coniugi rarissimae

If ever the passion for formal rhetoric returns, the whole story will have to be rewritten and many judgements may be reversed.

—C. S. Lewis

Contents

Acknowledgments

I've been thinking about this book, in one way or another, for some years, and my greatest debt is to the students with whom I first worked out my ideas. One of my UCLA graduate students, Carol Hartzog, has also acted as research assistant, typist, critic, and encourager, and to her very special thanks are owed.

I must also acknowledge a deep indebtedness to my friend Professor William C. Dowling, III, of the Department of English at the University of New Mexico. Few authors, surely, have been lucky enough to receive the kind of criticism he gave the draft of this book. Evidence of his good sense and critical acumen is to be found on every page which remains—and on the two hundred pages of detailed explication and contentious citation which, through his efforts, the reader has been spared. Finally, I would like to thank Ellen Graham and Lynn Walterick of the Yale Press for care and attention far beyond the call of duty.

The Research Committee at UCLA has generously supported my work, and the National Endowment for the Humanities, by awarding me a Senior Fellowship for 1973–74, gave me the time to write.

I should also record these earlier appearances: A version of part of chapter 1 was read at a Clark Library Seminar on 4 February 1972 and published in *To Tell a Story: Narrative Theory and Practice*, William Andrews Clark Library (Los Angeles, 1973). A version of chapter 3 originally appeared in *English Studies* 48 (1967).

R. A. L.
Los Angeles
January 1976

The Motives of Eloquence

1

The Rhetorical Ideal of Life

I

The discussion of verbal style in
the West has proceeded on the basis of a few simple premises
which it may help to hold before us. I shall call them *serious*
premises. They run something like this. Every man possesses a
central self, an irreducible identity. These selves combine into a
single, homogeneously real society which constitutes a referent
reality for the men living in it. This referent society is in turn
contained in a physical nature itself referential, standing "out
there," independent of man. Man has invented language to
communicate with his fellow man. He communicates facts and
concepts about both nature and society. He can also communicate a third category of response, emotions. When he is communicating facts or concepts, the success with which they are
communicated is measured by something we call *clarity*. When
he is communicating feelings, success is measured by something
we call *sincerity*, faithfulness to the self who is doing the feeling.
Against this ordinary use of language stands another kind of
use—literature. Literature creates a representation of society and
nature, imitates them. Success here is measured by the faithfulness of the imitation, although a very great deal of leeway must
be allowed in assessing such faithfulness. The nature presented
may be less seen than envisioned. The good style, for either
ordinary or literary utterance, will be the transparent style, the
style which is looked through rather than noticed, the style
which communicates most efficiently either facts, concepts, or
imitations of reality. The bad style will be the excessive style, the
style which shows.

Against this set of serious premises for the study of style, juxtapose the actual Western practice. Style has been studied intensively since the Greeks, and always, until very recent times at least, as part of a training in rhetoric. In its main outlines, scholars agree, the rhetorical paideia has not changed since the Greeks. What was it like to pass through it? Let me synthesize a generic portrait.

Start your student young. Teach him a minute concentration on the word, how to write it, speak it, remember it. Stress memory in a massive, almost brutalizing way, develop it far in advance of conceptual understanding. Let words come first as objects and sounds long before they can, for a child, take on full meaning. They are looked *at* before they can be looked through. From the beginning, stress behavior as performance, reading aloud, speaking with gesture, a full range of histrionic adornment. Require no original thought. Demand instead an agile marshaling of the proverbial wisdom on any issue. Categorize this wisdom into predigested units, commonplaces, *topoi*. Dwell on their decorous fit into situation. Develop elaborate memory schemes to keep them readily at hand. Teach, as theory of personality, a corresponding set of accepted personality types, a taxonomy of impersonation. Drill the student incessantly on correspondences between verbal style and personality type, life style. Nourish an acute sense of social situation. Let him, to weariness, translate, not only from one language to another, but from one style to another.

We think, Aristotle says, about those things which offer alternative possibilities. (βουλευόμεθα δὲ περὶ τῶν φαινομένων ἐνδέχεσθαι ἀμφοτέρως ἔχειν. *Rhetoric* 1357A.) Shape this habit into a doctrine of antilogy, the ability to argue with equal skill on either side of a question. Stress, too, the need for improvisation, ad-lib quickness, the coaxing of chance. Hold always before the student rhetoric's practical purpose: to win, to persuade. But train for this purpose with continual verbal play, rehearsal for the sake of rehearsal.

Use the "case" method. Let the student reenact fictional or historical situations: Nicias at Syracuse, Hannibal at Cannae, Socrates, hemlock-in-hand. Practice this re-creation always in an

agonistic context. The aim is scoring. Urge the student to go into
the world and observe its doings from this perspective. And urge
him to continue this rehearsal method all his life, forever rehearsing a spontaneous real life. Fill public life, agora, forum, court,
with men similarly trained. Make this intense training in the
word, in dramatic incarnation, the aristocratic paideia, the only
path to wealth and honor, union-card to public life. Downgrade
training in a subject, shoe making, business, generalship,
medicine—although as subjects for debate, all these may of
course become respectable. Training in the word thus becomes a
badge, as well as a diversion, of the leisure class. As such, attach
to it a whole range of snob values, of invidious comparisons,
with which it has no natural affinity.

What kind of world would such a training create? What kind of
man would *homo rhetoricus* be? What would "the rhetorical ideal
of life"[1] be like? Our composite picture suggests, as a first reflection, that rhetorical man must have felt an overpowering self-
consciousness about language. So far have we moved in the
opposite direction that the point bears emphasis. For rhetorical
man, what we think of as a natural verbal spontaneity was never
allowed to develop. Language, spoken or written, was naturally
premeditated. Attention would fall, first and last if not always,
on the verbal surface, on words not ideas. No matter about
detail, about whether you had been taught to order your oration
in seven parts, or five, four, three, or two; no matter whether you
felt reasoning by *epicheireme* a shaky endeavor or not; no matter
whether there were four levels of style, three, or two. Much more
important, you had been taught to look at language in a certain
way. You would be a nominalist to the end of your days. Whatever sins you might enregister, stylistic naivete would not be
one.

---

1. "There are two contrasting types of life, two *bioi*. One of them is built upon
the flattering quasi-arts—really not arts at all but copies of arts. We may call it,
after one of its main species of flattery, *the rhetorical ideal of life*. Its purpose is to
create pleasure and win approval. The other, its opponent, is the philosophical
life. It is based on knowledge of human nature and of what is best for it: so it is a
real techné, and it really cares for man, for the body as well as the soul." Werner
Jaeger, *Paideia*, 2:144. (Emphasis mine.)

Nor would the self be naive and bubbly. Rhetorical man is an actor; his reality public, dramatic. His sense of identity, his self, depends on the reassurance of daily histrionic reenactment. He is thus centered in time and concrete local event. The lowest common denominator of his life is a social situation. And his motivations must be characteristically ludic, agonistic. He thinks first of winning, of mastering the rules the current game enforces. He assumes a natural agility in changing orientations. He hits the street already street-wise. From birth, almost, he has dwelt not in a single value-structure but in several. He is thus committed to no single construction of the world; much rather, to prevailing in the game at hand. He makes an unlikely zealot. Nor is conceptual creativity, invention of a fresh paradigm, demanded of him. He accepts the present paradigm and explores its resources. Rhetorical man is trained not to discover reality but to manipulate it. Reality is what is accepted as reality, what is useful. So Protagoras's wonderful answer when asked if the gods exist: "I do not know whether they exist or not. It is a difficult question and life is too short." Nothing is aught till it is valued. Rhetorical man does not ask, "What is real?" He asks, "What is accepted as reality here and now?" He is thus typically present-centered. Past and future remain as possibility only, a paradigm he may some day have to learn. Until then, he does not sentimentalize them. No golden-ager, he, and no Utopian either.

Nor is he a Puritan, especially about language. He cannot be surprised ceaselessly *pushing through* language to a preexistent, divinely certified reality beyond. No such reality exists for him. He can play freely with language. For him it owes no transcendental loyalties. Rhetorical man will always be an unregenerate punster. He will be not so much dazzled by the delights of language, poisoned by roses, as a sophisticated connoisseur of them. Such a connoisseurship would form a predictable analogue to the emphasis on scoring.

The rhetorical view of life, then, begins with the centrality of language. It conceives reality as fundamentally dramatic, man as fundamentally a role player. It synthesizes an essentially bifurcated, self-serving theory of motive. We play for advantage, but we play for pleasure, too. Such a scheme is galvanized by the Gorgian prime mover, ἡδονή, pleasure. Purposeful striving is invigorated by frequent dips back into the pleasurable resources of pure play. Rhetoric is always ritualizing, stylizing purpose in order to enjoy it more. The rhetorical view thus stands fundamentally opposed to the West's bad conscience about language, revels in what Roland Barthes (in "Science vs. Literature") has called "the Eros of Language." *Homo rhetoricus* cannot, to sum up, be *serious*. He is not pledged to a single set of values and the cosmic orchestration they adumbrate. He is not, like the serious man, alienated from his own language. And if he relinquishes the luxury of a central self, a soul, he gains the tolerance, and usually the sense of humor, that comes from knowing he—and others—not only may *think* differently, but may *be* differently. He pays a price for this, of course—religious sublimity, and its reassuring, if breathtaking, unities.

The premises used in discussing style, I hope it is now apparent, have not been those actually operating when style was taught. Indeed, the two sets of premises, serious and rhetorical as I shall call them, stand diametrically opposed. The opposition, it seems to me, goes far to explain the two persistently puzzling facts about the history of rhetoric: why it has been so deplored and why it has so endured. It has been deplored because it has been discussed in serious terms, in terms, that is, not germane to its essence. If we consider rhetoric within serious premises, it will truly be the "grotesque bogey" which a distinguished historian of medieval Latinity, E. R. Curtius, thought it. It will be indeed the bogey that Plato conjured up under the banner of "sophist" and that has been plaguing us ever since. The only thing to be done with it will be to do away with it. So George Kennedy prefaces his definitive history of Greek rhetoric with an epigraph from the great Platonist Paul Shorey: "We are freed from rhetoric only by study of its history." But this long tradition of criticism, so apposite within its own serious terms, within rhetorical premises seems beside the point. Such criticism points to differences so fundamental they indicate a wholly different way of looking at the world.

The rhetorical view of life threatens the serious view at every point. Thus rhetoric's most perceptive serious students damn it utterly, find it in principle irredeemable. To find it a mixed blessing, like Aristotle and unlike Plato, is, at least at first, to underestimate its power, direction, and inner coherence. But would it not make far more sense to recognize the rhetorical ideal as a world view, a way of life as well as a view of life, a coherent counterstatement to "serious" reality? The recurring attempts to make rhetorical training respectable in serious terms all go astray. The contribution rhetorical reality makes to Western reality as a whole is greatest when it is most uncompromisingly itself, insists most strenuously on its own coordinates.

The Western self has from the beginning been composed of a shifting and perpetually uneasy combination of *homo rhetoricus* and *homo seriosus*, of a social self and a central self. It is their business to contend for supremacy. To *settle* the struggle would be to end the Greek experiment in a complex self. Those who seek for sensible compromise, like Aristotle, though they contribute more to a living balance, throw less light on the theoretical antithesis than those, like Plato, who wish the Western self to become entirely serious. The rhetorical half of the pairing has been described by Platonic philosophers, or by rhetoricians who did not—and most did not—see clearly the implications of their own proceedings.[2] They could not see their own authentic contribution to the larger task at hand, constructing the complex, creative, unstable, painful Western self. We find here the explanation for rhetorical training's paradoxical durability. To leave it out cuts man in half.

Thus, though the media stayed in serious hands, rhetorical training thrived long after the immediate needs it satisfied. It had, by that time, come to satisfy needs yet more fundamental and long-lasting. It provided a brilliant education in politics and the social surface. From the Sophists onward, it addressed itself

---

2. Thus the *Rhetorica ad Herennium*, for example, begins with a glancing apology for not studying philosophy instead, and Quintilian confesses that rhetorical training, if it fails to form the *moral* judgment, must be considered a failure (*Institutes* 12.1.1-4.)

to speaking and acting in the city's business (τὰ τῆς πόλεως καὶ λέγειν κ̀αὶ πράττειν). It provided a training in the mechanisms of identity, offered a selection of roles the adolescent could try out. It offered a training in tolerance, if by that we mean getting inside another's skull and looking out. It offered the friendliest of advices on how to tap into any and all sources of pleasure. It habituated its students to a world of contingent purpose, of perpetual cognitive dissonance, plural orchestration. It specialized less in knowledge than in the way knowledge is held, which is how Whitehead defines wisdom.

Perhaps the serious premises have thrived because they flatter us. The rhetorical view does not. The rhetorical view of life is satirical, radically reductive of human motive and human striving. Rhetoric's real crime, one is often led to suspect, is its candid acknowledgment of the rhetorical aspects of "serious" life. The concept of a central self, true or not, flatters man immensely. It gives him an identity outside time and change that he sees nowhere else in the sublunary universe. So, too, the theory of knowledge upon which seriousness rests. Here there is little to choose between a positivist reality and a Platonic, between realism and idealism. As Eric Havelock points out, "For Plato, reality is rational, scientific and logical, or it is nothing." How reassuring to arrive at essence, Eleatic Being. How flattering that we, at whatever brave cost to ourselves, penetrate to the way things are, look, at the end of our quest, upon the true face of beauty "itself, of and in itself, always one being" (αὐτὸ καθ᾽ αὑτὸ μεθ᾽ αὑτοῦ μονοειδὲς ἀεὶ ὅν [*Symposium* 211B]). How humiliating to be all this time only looking in a mirror.

At the heart of rhetorical reality lies pleasure. We personify for pleasure, we act for pleasure. And we clothe this pleasure with high-minded protestations, again for pleasure, as well as for advantage. The rhetorical view makes us all incorrigible sentimentalists. Again, how humiliating. We would prefer to dwell on our tragic fate, painful but heroic. To set ourselves off against the whole universe makes us, in a manner of speaking, as big as it is. *Homo rhetoricus* is flung into a meaningless universe too, of course. But unlike his serious—or existential—*doppelgänger*, he doesn't repine, bathe in self-pity because his world possesses no center. He can resist such centermentalism because he knows that his own capacity to make up comforting illusions is as infinite as the universe he is flung into. Naked into the world he may come, but not without resource.

Perhaps we can see now why the Western paideia has always been a mixed one. The Sophists cannot have founded it alone, nor the philosophers. The best education has always put the two views of life into profound and fruitful collision. Divorce and domination present equal dangers. The West has confused itself unnecessarily. Its education has until modern times been in the hands of rhetoricians, but the historians of education have been philosophers. So too in literary history. The poets have been rhetoricians, the critics serious philosophers. Best is collision: πόλεμος πατὴρ πάντων. Perhaps literature has always gravitated to the center of such a curriculum because it enshrines with greatest intensity and clarity the polemic Western self.

Shorey's dictum, then, taken as a description of the whole truth, may seriously mislead. The study of rhetoric does not free us from rhetoric. It teaches, rather, that we *cannot* be freed from it, that it represents half of man. If truly free of rhetoric, we would be pure essence. We would retain no social dimension. We would divest ourselves of what alone makes social life tolerable, of the very mechanism of forgiveness. For what is forgiveness but the acknowledgment that the sinner sinning is not truly himself, plays but a misguided role? If always truly ourselves, which of us shall scape hanging? To liberate man from his rhetorical dimension is to freeze him in the nightmarish prison of unchanging essence Plato so prayerfully invoked in the *Republic*. The *Republic* succeeds in abolishing politics, abolishing dramatic reality. What remains, though, is not essential reality but ontological vacuum, not freedom but political tyranny. For the central self depends on the social self. Platonic thought from first to last aims to defend the central self, "real" reality. It ends up imperiling both. The human self exists inasmuch as it continues to debate with itself. The struggle between social and central self is a—literally—self-generating, self-protective device. To free ourselves from rhetoric would be to shut that device down. To recommend such "freedom" invites us to think ourselves divine.

II

What else but just this struggle between two kinds of self, we might reflect, is incarnated in that narrative-speech-narrative-speech alternation so endemic to Western literary utterance? Here again a confrontation of style amounts to a confrontation of philosophies. Western literature has tried to build into itself just that fruitful clash between rhetorical and serious reality the complex Western self requires for sustenance. Such a stylistic pattern seems to antedate all other critical categories, generic or whatever. It occurs in plays and lyric poems as well as, most characteristically, in the major forms. Speeches are everywhere in classical narrative, not just in the historians. Almost half the *Iliad* and two-thirds of the *Odyssey* are taken up with formal speechifying. Lovers orate spontaneously in Hellenistic romance, and this practice continues unchanged up to Sidney's *Arcadia*. Formal orations dominated Elizabethan drama, especially historical drama, as they did Athenian tragedy, and Senecan tragedy still more. They supplied the focus for theories of language, the example for definitions of eloquence, the public occasions for political discourse. Such orations are fond of reporting what *ought to have been said*, τὰ δέοντα, a kind of high-class *esprit d'escalier*.

The first lesson here was taught by Thucydides, who uses speeches to illustrate the public world, the domain of professed purpose. We might look, for example, at chapter six of book one, wherein is described one of the rhetorical sparring matches which preceded the Peloponnesian War. The Corinthians try to convince the Spartan Assembly that the Spartans should, the Athenian envoys that they should not, go to war with Athens. Both speeches are good, the Corinthian—in its vivid delineation of the Athenian spirit—especially so. One really wonders what the Spartans will decide. But the wonder is irrelevant. And so, we soon learn, are the speeches. The Spartans decide for the

Corinthians "not so much," Thucydides tells us, "because they were influenced by the speeches as because they were afraid of the further growth of Athenian power."

The speeches, then, are purely for display, form only a counterpoint to the backstage reckonings of national interest. The speeches dramatize public conscience. Three city-states offer themselves and each other pious truisms about treaties, traditional obligations, gratitude for past service, all as a cloak for their inevitable pursuit of self-interest. Thucydides' story tells not only what people do and why they really do it, but why they think, and why they say, they do it. Or rather, it suggests that realistic motive is a combination, an interaction, of professed and expedient purpose. The speeches must be flowery and devious if they are to imitate accurately this deeper mixed motive. Thucydides wants us to see that these three city-states were fooling not only each other but themselves. He wants to show us how readily we hide behind fine words. He wants to make a statement about language and its role in human motive, and hence in true history. Are we to say, because the tape recorder had not yet been invented, that he was falsifying the event? Wasn't he really proceeding from a more sophisticated conception of event than "objective" history has yet come to?

Surely this is what he has in mind when, in the midst of the Mytilene debate in book three, he has Cleon taunt the Athenians with their love of rhetoric:

> In competitions of this sort the prizes go to others and the state takes all the danger for herself. The blame is yours, for stupidly instituting these competitive displays. You have become regular speech-goers, and as for action, you merely listen to accounts of it; if something is to be done in the future you estimate the possibilities by hearing a good speech on the subject, and as for the past you rely not so much on the facts which you have seen with your own eyes as on what you have heard about them in some clever piece of verbal criticism. Any novelty in an argument deceives you at once, but when the argument is tried and proved you

become unwilling to follow it; you look with suspicion on what is normal and are the slaves of every paradox that comes your way. The chief wish of each one of you is to be able to make a speech himself, and, if you cannot do that, the next best thing is to compete with those who can make this sort of speech by not looking as though you were at all out of your depth while you listen to the views put forward, by applauding a good point even before it is made, and by being as quick at seeing how an argument is going to be developed as you are slow at understanding what in the end it will lead to. What you are looking for all the time is something that is, I should say, outside the range of ordinary experience, and yet you cannot even think straight about the facts of life that are before you. You are simply victims of your own pleasure in listening, and are more like an audience sitting at the feet of a professional lecturer than a parliament discussing matters of state.[3]

Love of language, eloquence as motive, forms part of the story Thucydides has to tell. Rhetorical man claims his share of the tale.

He does so yet more obviously in another well-roasted chestnut, the famous debate at the beginning of *Metamorphoses* 13 between Ajax and Ulysses over the armor of Achilles. We must first notice that the debate is already a *topos*, having been taken from its Homeric context and made into a school exercise. Thus Ovid's reader sees it, first and foremost, as a famous rhetorical occasion. He is not likely, as is the modern reader, to wonder why the issue wasn't settled a little more briskly. The speeches are the point, not the armor. They are not, though, unrelated to Ovid's larger design. He is in the midst of the Troy story and—to summarize boldly and baldly—is concerned to show a change in the concept of hero as Troy moves west to found Rome. Ajax represents the old ideal, the *rudis et sine pectore miles*, Ulysses the new ideal, shrewd, political, above all verbal. Thus the topos

3. *History of the Peloponnesian War*, trans. Rex Warner (Penguin Classics, 1954), p. 182.

takes on mythic overtones and these work very much to Ovid's
purpose at this point in the poem. It also brings forward all the
arguments for and against the two conceptions of heroism. It
constitutes a philosophical digression in dramatic form. The
ultimate lesson the debate teaches is not that Ulysses deserves
the armor more than Ajax—Ovid's sympathies lean toward
Ajax—but that the best talker wins. The verdict is given almost
laconically:

> Mota manus procerum est, et quid facundia posset,
> re patuit, fortisque viri tulit arma disertus.

> The band of chiefs was persuaded, and what eloquence
> might do, now stood revealed. The eloquent man bore the
> arms of the brave.

Ovid doesn't bother to tell us directly who won, because the real
winner is not so much Ulysses as *Eloquence*. (The loser is not
specified either—does *fortisque viri* refer to Achilles or Ajax?—
and for the same reason. The loser is *Military Valor*.) The hero is
now talker not doer. The rhetorical occasion turns in upon itself;
the self-conscious style ends up not only using rhetoric but
talking about its uses.

Any speech set off like this, by narrative or stylistic discontinuity, tends to turn in on itself and meditate on the limits of
language. Historical narrative of the rhetorical sort thus contains
a built-in control over its own veracity, a perpetual reminder of
the boundary conditions language sets to truth. The rhetorical
interlude perpetually analyzes the kind of statement the narrative plot is allowed to make. It will not let us think we know more
than we do. By the side of it, "objective" history seems often a
trifle naive.

Context, then, is crucial in rhetorical literary documents. What
seems a sublime, if superficial, interruption may be a profound
comic corrective. Only a sense of context can show how the best
history builds into itself a dialogue between the two ways of
knowing. It is a sense of context which tells us that, for example,
Xerxes' war conference, as Herodotus describes it in book seven,
is a farce, that Sidney's *Old Arcadia* is a comedy; it is this sense

that relates the fourth book of *The Courtier* to the first three, that sees the rhetorical comedy in Chaucer's *Troilus*, that reads rightly the back- and front-stage heroism of Shakespeare's *Henriad*.

We might carry this matter of historical accuracy one step further. Consider the most famous oration ever composed, Cicero's *First Oration against Catiline*. Who can forget "O tempora! O mores!," or all the guff that goes with it, the hot air about that famous Ciceronian consulship praised, as Seneca said, *non sine causa sed sine fine*. Yet, as an historical document, what is its domain? It is a document, an event. It was delivered. But delivered by one acutely aware of his place in history, aware that he was making history. His artifice is sincerity itself, the desire to act the role he has earned. His real motive? To play Cicero and thus to establish Cicero's reality. Further, this role is to be played by a speech which defines the situation and places it in time— and thus is itself an act of historical analysis—and also one which imposes that definition on *patres conscripti*, so that Cicero can then be the Cicero Cicero wants to be remembered as having been. (The strategy worked, we owe it to him to remark. He has been remembered as he wished to be. Sallust left a different account of Cicero's role than Cicero left himself, but who do we remember as the "real Cicero"?) All this is *secundum litteram*, *what happened*. No objective narrative can get even close to an accurate mimesis of it. The decorum of rhetoric, a well-known history of narrative tells us, is antihistorical and antimimetic. Here—almost everywhere—such a statement is but a half-truth. We can see here too the weaknesses of a simpleminded front-stage/back-stage debunking. "Reality" must come from both stages taken in all their complex relationships. Division into objective event and fictional coloration simply makes no sense.

Cicero's immense self-consciousness suggests a response to the charge that the speeches depict a shallow characterization, black-and-white motive. As we try to understand that huge and exuberant Ciceronian egotism, we come again and again to a motive essentially neither selfish nor patriotic but simply dramatic. Isn't this the lesson rhetorical literature as a whole teaches? Kenneth Burke has supplied a phrase for such a motive—"pure persuasion," the actor's attitude toward his audience. In a dramatistic, rhetorical world view, the dramatic motive—pure pleasure in impersonation—forms the groundwork of all "respectable" motives. Acting establishes the self. Sterne certainly thought so, and his mentor Hamlet moves us profoundly just because he sees this, penetrates to the essentially dramatic nature of human motive. If this is not the heart of his mystery, that he knows he would rather unpack his heart with words than pack off Claudius with a bare bodkin, then Eliot is right that the play lacks an objective correlative. Contemporary fiction seems preoccupied with motiveless malignity for just this reason—it sees motive as amoral, as wholly aesthetic. Rhetorical narrative does better. It offers an imitation of dynamic motive, of the flight into and out of the histrionic center. Compared to this critique of motive, the profundities of the psychological or of the "new" French novel seem a little, well, shallow. Each sees only half of the self. For realistic fiction, the self is assumed to be central, whole, as real as everything else; for the nonrealist, dramatic only. Neither will see the other half.

We touch here the center of a nominalist view of rhetoric, a new definition of persuasion. One thinks of it as changing the opponent's mind. This is hard to do; this is the philosopher's way. Far easier—here sophist and Madison Avenue are one—to change his self. To redefine him so that he will do what you like spontaneously, hypnotically, by desire. Psychoanalysis does much the same thing, R. D. Laing's analysis of schizophrenia as bad domestic drama being perhaps the clearest case of this. Offer the patient another frame. Cast him in another play.

Consider, as an example of this strategy, what is generally thought the most outrageous rhetorical chromo bequeathed to us by classical antiquity, Gorgias's oration over the Athenian dead:

> For what was missing from these men of what ought to be present in men? And what was present of what ought not to be present? Could I say what I want, I would want to say what is necessary, escaping divine retribution and fleeing human envy.

For these men possessed divinely-inspired *arete* but human mortality; many times preferring the gentle equitable to the remorseless righteous, and correctness of reasons to strictness of law, judging this the most divine and most commonly shared usage: as to what is needed and when, both to speak and to keep silent, both to act ⟨and to let pass⟩; and two things in particular training of what it is necessary to train, intellect ⟨and bodily strength⟩, the former by deliberating, the latter by performing; attending upon the unjustly unfortunate, punishers of the unjustly fortunate, stubborn for the advantageous, good-tempered for the fitting, with sensibility of mind putting a stop to mindlessness ⟨of bodily strength⟩, violent against the violent, orderly toward the orderly, causing no fear in those who cause no fear, terrifying in terrifying situations. [*Epitaphios*][4]

H. J. Rose (in *A Handbook of Greek Literature*) apologizes for the compulsive σχήματα by saying that, though stale to us, these patterns were fresh to the Athenians. Well, not after the second line. And, of course, not at all. Gorgias they knew. Unless they were naive to silliness, what pleased them? How did Gorgias work upon them?

We are mightily offended. In the face of death we fancy a lugubrious sincerity. Who wants to be sung to his final rest by a flight of *homoioteleuta*? But Gorgias knew the guard of honor was for the living. And he could not pretend the dead were not dead. He did not have our sentimental options. How might he console us? He could not change the event. How might he change our way of looking at it? Well, we have to have the sentiments. But they change nothing. How might he truly persuade us to do the only thing one can do about the dead, to forget them? He sets out a game and invites us to play. Name the tropes as they go by. Catch an antithesis by the tail. The more contrived the language, the more allegorical the style becomes—the more it serves its purpose. The meaning is not weakened by the style but rein-

4. The Greek text can be found in Hermann Diels, *Fragmente der Vorsokratiker*, 8th ed., ed. Walther Kranz (Berlin, 1956), 2, s.v. "Gorgias," A1. The translation tries to reflect the word-formations of the original.

forced. For it is the style which metamorphoses the grief into pleasure, makes us forget grief in the tremendous pleasure of expressing it.

Gorgias's subject becomes finally man's tremendous resources of verbal pleasure, his endless ability to metamorphose one emotion into another by means of the word. Thus what is imitated is the process by which man can interpose words between himself and death, make of death a pleasure and finally—his self transformed—*enjoy* it. Gorgias deliberately makes the ostensible contrast between style and subject as great as possible just to show us what he is doing. He wants to show us a new version of ourselves, man in the process of accommodating. himself to death. Gorgias illustrates this technique of rhetorical narrative most brilliantly, but Cicero seems to have used it, too, in his now lost *Consolatio* for Tullia, and it is parodied in *Tristram Shandy*. There Sterne constructs in the scene of Bobby's death a similar self-consoling rhetoric and forces us to acknowledge what he is doing by referring to the *Consolatio*.

We might represent this mixed pattern thus:

$$\underline{\text{narrative}}\boxed{\text{speech}}\underline{\text{narrative}}$$

that is, as an alternation of narrative and speech, dramatic action and speech, translucent and opaque style, teller naive and teller self-conscious; or, more largely, the serious world and the rhetorical in oscillation. This middle state is flanked by two unstable extremes. About serious, mimetic, organic form nothing further needs to be said here. But its theoretical opposite requires comment. For rhetorical man, like his serious counterpart, possesses a characteristic literary form. Open, obliging, for the occasion, it neither begins nor ends. It plays games with both beginning and ending, with narrative expectation. Sterne's *Tristram Shandy* constitutes the type of rhetorical literary form, as Sterne's ancestors, Burton, Rabelais, Lucian, Apuleius, Ovid, had defined it. Again, conventional generic distinctions tell us little. The rhetorical documents are the ones everyone has trouble classifying. They seem to war on the stable .orientations literary genres enshrine. They think narrative coherence a sham, not because it is unreal but because we impose it on the world without acknowledgment. They seek to make us self-conscious about the imposition, about literary form at all points. Their narratives are always posing; their style aims always for effect. They keep faith with their own pleasure, not with a reality somewhere "out there." They play games with literary form. Literary form, in fact, constitutes both their subject and object, theme and reality. Like realistic fiction, they constitute a theoretical extreme, not an historical beginning, and like such fiction, they tend to bounce back toward the center. Like realistic fiction, rhetorical "narrative" is straightforwardly and consistently mimetic—but of an obverse reality, rhetorical not serious.

Much critical confusion could have been avoided had these two characteristic forms been allowed each its own manner of proceeding. Literary history in the last two hundred years has delighted in applying serious, realistic coordinates either to the center, where they half fit, or to rhetorical forms, where they don't fit at all. The critical history of *Tristram Shandy* provides one instance of misapplied coordinates, *Gargantua and Pantagruel* another, Ovid's *Metamorphoses* a third. A formal matrix might help.

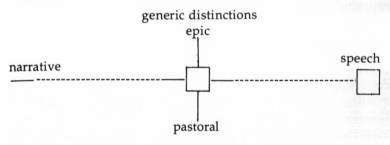

On such a matrix we can plot the difference between the *Aeneid* and the *Metamorphoses* without agonizing over whether Ovid really wrote epic. The matrix supplies a neutral ground for, to borrow a phrase from Richards, "arranging our techniques for arranging." On such a ground, we need no longer talk of rhetoric's malign influence on Western literature, no longer reinterpret two millennia of literary eloquence in terms of a formal strategy which represents a theoretical extreme, a necessary extreme to be sure, but one which has never prevailed long. The

central and preponderant strategy in Western literature has been
stylistic contrast, the —□— pattern in some form or another.
After bouncing between extremes, there seems an inevitable,
though as yet uncharted, return to the richer central —□—
pattern. This pattern involves the reader in a characteristic way.
He is not asked for simple suspension of disbelief, willingness to
identify a single fictional reality with reality itself. Nor is he told,
as the rhetorical documents tell him, that many realities make
none. He is asked to consider more than one reality but not an
infinity of them. It is not a pose which invites poise. It is inten-
tionally hard to sustain. The Jamesian world is easier and so,
paradoxically, is Sterne's or Rabelais's rhetorical one. The —□—
pattern does not establish a precedence—logical or temporal—
for either mode of apprehension; it sees them as stages of a
ceaseless oscillation. Such an oscillation suggests both when
they arose and how. They arose together as the Western psyche
cohered, and they represent its fundamental modes of ap-
prehending the world.

There seem to be two characteristic modes of Western literature, then, narrative and speech or serious and rhetorical, and
two ranges of motive, one serious and purposive and the other
dramatic and playful. The more one ponders these parallel
dichotomies, the more clear it becomes that we really need two
poetics to make sense of them. Aristotle's *Poetics*, we can
perhaps now see, is essentially a serious poetic. Its view of the
self, and of referent reality, is—not surprisingly—Platonic. A
referent reality stands beyond words—at whatever remove—
and a central self (what else does tragedy exist to affirm?) forms
part of it. Thus Aristotle concentrates his mind on *how* literature
is related to such a reality, on the nature of mimesis. It is no
exaggeration to say that from Aristotle's *Poetics* to Auerbach's
Mimesis, the focus has remained the same, on the nature of
imitation. Our sketch of the rhetorical ideal suggests that this
exclusive focus is incomplete. What of the reality imitated? Posit
a rhetorical, rather than a serious, reality, and mimesis is reversed 180 degrees. If reality is rhetorical, dramatic, then "serious" literature is no longer serious, realistic literature no longer

realistic. Lewis Carroll becomes a realist, George Eliot a surreal abstractionist.

A comprehensive poetic must be as complex as the Western self, and in the same way. It must be equipped to deal with these two fundamentally different realities, and to deal with them as they really occur, in a bewildering pattern of alternation which invites inappropriate coordinates. Often the misapplication seems willful, even ludic. But once we get the coordinates straight, a great many critical confusions come clear. We stop trying to judge Sterne by Fielding, Rabelais by Froissart, Ovid by Virgil. We cease to apply serious generic terms like *comedy* and *tragedy* to works not themselves serious and hence not built on the referential central self both comedy and tragedy premise. Such a double poetic might perhaps solve some traditional conundrums of literary theory. It could acknowledge, for example, that literature both is and is not autonomous vis-à-vis "real" life. It all depends on which reality is consulted. If we posit a serious reality as referential, then literature is clearly autonomous. Its identities are all roles, its realities all dramas. Its relation to life is by way of pseudostatements. But if reality is rhetorical? Is not literature here truly isomorphic, real in exactly the same way as life? Same self and same society? Not mimesis but enactment?

Any truly comprehensive critical theory will have to plot a continuum of reality from rhetorical to serious, parallel with its mimetic continuum from literal to formal imitation. The confusion that has ensued because it has failed to do so is nicely illustrated by the basic inconsistency of formalist criticism generally. The formalist argues that literature is autonomous, but he bases his argument on its formal properties, its literariness, on that part of literature which is *not* autonomous. He wants to use rhetorical coordinates without acknowledging them, without admitting a rhetorical reality as alternate to the serious one.

And if critical theory in the West has, until now, been only half complete, the same thing can be said for the Western theory of history. The rhetorical view of life excludes neutral statement by nature. Perhaps this accounts for the bad press *homo rhetoricus* has gotten from scholars searching for historical reality *wie es eigentlich gewesen*. For rhetorical man, there is no such thing as a fact, or a text, as it actually happened. To perceive is to color with intention, conceive as self-satisfying pleasure. Rhetorical man thus implicitly attacks the existence of the world "scientific" historians want to study. The rhetorical ideal thus forces on us a double conception of historical event. Serious history, of whatever persuasion, is based on a recreation of motive. Collingwood seems in this respect wholly correct. Whether we consider political motive, economic, religious, hardly matters. To chronicle purposive behavior we recreate purpose. Motive, purposive behavior, is the causality of history. But what if human behavior is not purposive to begin with? How then? What if we posit as referential the rhetorical, playful range of motive? It is not simply the history of literature which must be rewritten but the literature of history. We need a new literary history, that is, in two senses—a new history of literature and a new conception of history as essentially literary, as animated by dramatic motive, play instead of purpose. And again, fully serious history will combine both conceptions of event: purposive and playful.

III

We will also need a new theory of style. Of all the unexamined premises rhetoric took over from serious philosophy, clarity has perplexed the most. Since Aristotle it has figured as a central goal for verbal expression. Theorists, without giving the matter special thought, seem to have considered clarity a property of the text. Yet clarity describes many styles and audiences. Used to describe a particular verbal configuration, clarity cannot mean anything at all. Style's central term is hollow. It simply points to success. The most intellectual, conceptual, scientific virtue of style turns out to be entirely emotional. If everyone is happy, clarity has arrived. The definition of clarity participates fully in the circular argument for normative style. Since a style reveals the clarity against which it is measured, you can speak finally only of your own satisfaction, either as writer or audience. A serious premise turns out to be rhetorical.

The problem of clarity becomes the problem of analyzing each individual victory for the ingredients which have satisfied those concerned. These ingredients are not hard to generalize. They are, however, neither particularly intellectual, philosophical, or moral, nor are they specially flattering to man as a tireless clear communicator. Custom plays the biggest role. Pull a sociologist from his desk and sit him down to Dryden, the usual Bureau of Prose Standards yardstick of limpid clarity, and he will stumble. Feed him sociologese and all is light. So with all of us. Clarity is at least partly, and often predominantly, a temporal phenomenon, a problem of period. One century's brightness becomes murk for the next. Clarity no more permits objective standards than custom itself.

Of course we like some alien styles more than others, and some styles transcend their time completely. Clarity does not lie entirely in the eye of the beholder. It lies in formal properties, too, and these suggest a second general and neglected criterion, pleasurability, a style's success in tapping sources of formal pleasure irrelevant to content. Samuel Johnson has not been alone in rearranging the world into more agreeable antitheses. We constantly work things over into a more pleasurable form, one more ideally reflective of how we see the world—often, as in Johnson's case, in strong blacks and whites—and then bestow on our comfort the flattering name of clarity. We might, in this regard, salvage the frequent insistence that writing be done in a fit of absence of mind, as naturally as breathing. Perhaps thus we tap most efficiently the subconscious resources of formal pleasure that galvanize clarity. If language does not photograph things but, as Delacroix insisted, constitutes them, then it fits with what we know of perception psychology to see formal pleasure as playing a central role. Not clarity, then, but formal hunger may determine the shape of symbolic expression. It is generally assumed that language originally tried to be clear and only later degenerated into self-pleasing rituals. Why not the other way round—pleasure first?

Clarity comprehends a third element beyond familiarity and pleasure, ludic scoring. Clarity must not show off. But serious prejudice aside, clarity contains enormous show-off zest. Clarity signifies, after all, an immense act of exclusion, of restraint. It is an affair of timing, potentially—like brevity—of wit. Clarity, no one points out, always means daring simplification and much trickery. Dryden, the great model of clarity, is full of both. No designs on you, eye on the object, he ends up with your assent. Clarity gets back in combativeness the pleasure it sacrifices in renouncing ornament. Sanctimonious moralizing about style again gets things backwards. The honest style is self-conscious, proclaims its designs on you. Rhetorical style seems less miraculous because it does not hide the amplifying powers of language, it waves them in our faces. The real deceiver is the plain stylist who pretends to put all his cards on the table. Clarity, then, is a cheat, an illusion. To rhetorical man at least, the world *is* not clear, it is *made* clear. The clear stylist does it with a conjuring trick. For this trick we return thanks. We are reassured. The world is made like our minds. We don't want to reflect, consider that it may be an illusion. This weakens the gesture, the feeling of isomorphic comfort. So, if we have it not, we assume a naivete that will not sustain close investigation.

The very act of writing (or of prepared speaking), we might reflect, is dishonest. Why is reading fun? It condenses and transfers power. It takes much longer to write than to read. From this discrepancy grows the primary pleasure of written communication. The reader gets, in a rush, what has taken the author ten times as long to create. We feel a tremendous transfer of power, an infusion of *virtù*. This rush of power carries no necessary charge of honesty, virtue, or truth. It rather resembles, in fact, the sublime style's putative *modus operandi*.

The serious conception of verbal composition depends on a naive, one-time model which proves equally deceptive. Buffon, in his celebrated inaugural "Discourse," expresses this simplification as well as anyone:

> Pour bien écrire, il faut donc posséder pleinement son sujet,
> il faut y réfléchir assez pour voir clairement l'ordre de ses
> pensées, & en former une suite, un chaîne continue, dont
> chaque point représente une idée; & lorsqu'on aura pris la
> plume, il faudra la conduire successivement sur ce premier

trait, sans lui permettre de s'en écarter, sans l'appuyer trop inégalement. . . . C'est en cela que consiste la sévérité du style, c'est aussi ce qui en fera l'unité & ce qui en réglera la rapidité, & cela seul aussi suffira pour le rendre précis & simple, égal & clair.[5]

To write well, you must possess your subject fully, reflect upon it sufficiently to see clearly the order of your thoughts, to put them in a continuous order of which each point represents a single idea. And once you have taken up your pen, it must follow from point to point without wandering or dwelling overlong on a single point. . . . It is this that makes a style rigorous, lends it unity, paces it—and this alone will render it exact and simple, balanced and clear.

Who writes this way? What of every writer's dependence on the suggestive powers of language? None of us knows what he thinks till he sees what he writes. We surrender ourselves to language, and not once but over and over, we oscillate between language and concept, from draft to draft. We shuttle continually between a nominalist universe and a realistic one. To think that, the world once clearly seen through some clairvoyance, we then try to fix it in language, burlesques the process of composition by restricting it to a single cycle. We make a reality, polish, remake, keeping faith to something alternately "out there" and in our minds. Clarity at its best embodies continual movement.

Fanciers of clarity through the ages never remark its dependence on previous circumstance, on context. It shines by contrast, thrills by variety. I mean something more than primal context, the big, buzzing confusion. I mean shared thought and feeling. When Leonidas posted the Thermopylae order-of-the-day, "Breakfast here; supper in Hades," his gemlike clarity depended on an overpowering unstated context. The aphorism cannot sum up this context for us unless we share and pass through it. It cannot define reality its way until it has been defined another way. And the alternation repeats. Clarity, like the creative oscillation which engenders it, forms part of a proc-

5. *Oeuvres Philosophiques de Buffon*, p. 502.

ess. Alberic of Monte Cassino illustrates, albeit unwittingly,
both stages of the alternation in offering some elegant variations
on "Have you eaten?":

> Percepitne hodierna die tuus debitum cottidianum exactor?
> exquisitor uidelicet uenit? uel persoluistine debitum cot-
> tidianum exactori? uel suntne incentra gutturis temperie
> delinita uel ab ubertate sufficienti extincta? id est *comedisti
> an non*?[6]

And the whole cycle stands revealed in a bawdy routine which
The Committee, a San Francisco comedy troupe, used to put on.
It was called "The Date" and consisted of two parts. The first
pantomimed the process of an old-fashioned formal date: knock
on door, corsage, formula greetings and smile, holding door of
car, cheerful conversation within, car door again, all up to formal
shake-hands good-by. In the second part, the young man, having said farewell, comes back, knocks again, and when the
surprised young lady answers, asks, "Ya wanna screw?" The
first half works in an opaque, a rhetorical style, the second as
briefly as clarity could demand. Reality needs them both, needs
both languages. Neither can say what the other says. The wit of
the second depends on the preparation of the first. All clarity
works this way. When it ceases to work against something, it
ceases to be fun. The life forsakes it; the long slide into jargon
begins. (Thus we see, on a small scale, the same kind of alternation that forms, on a larger scale, the structural principle of
Western narrative.) Clarity needs the opaque styles to be itself.
Without them, we may mistake clarity for reality. When we do
this, we cease to see, and so to understand, clarity at all.

The great rhetorical stylists understood this home truth. Indeed, it was precisely their refusal to identify reality with clarity
which has made posterity misunderstand them. Some, Rabelais
and Sterne, mocked clarity outright. Others, Ovid, Chaucer,
Castiglione, Shakespeare, took pot shots in passing. But all insisted on calling attention to their tricks. They had to be honest,

---

6. De Dictamine, in *Briefsteller und Formelbücher des eilften bis vierzehnten
Jahrhunderts*, ed. Ludwig Rockinger (Munich, 1863; rpt. New York, 1961), 1:42.

warn us of the verbal deception at the heart of things, design
narrative structures to illustrate the same truth, remind us that
whatever order we see, we have at one stage or another imposed,
that man is imposing as well as imposed upon.

Familiarity, then, pleasure, stylistic contrast, and authority
can measure clarity, lend the term substance. And a substantive
clarity can no longer banish style, banish language, in its name.
The more you try to pump clarity empty of attitude, the more
attitude floods in. The more objective you try to be, the more
intuitive you become. The styles of clarity are rich and full, not
inane and jejune. They stand a rich, full opposite to the rhetorical styles. Clarity never ceases to imply what it has banished,
what in culture at large Ortega called "la presencia de lo au-
sente."

The usual high-middle-low stylistic division cannot
adequately describe either a rhetorical style or a style based on
normative clarity. The three-fold division, whether figured as
three discrete stages or as a continuum, leaves out the observer
and leaves out time. It is predicated, that is, on a naive observer.
To anatomize reflective intelligence requires that we build in
continuous interaction between self and environment. Precisely
this needs to be done for the traditional three-fold division of
style. We might first expand it into a continuum, with the high
and low styles stretched yet further into theoretical extremes.
The spectrum runs from referential to emotional language, from
mathematics to infantile babble.

> —babble
> —religious chant
> —Henry James
>
> —neutral reportage
>
> —Hemingway
> —telegraphese
> —geometry

Yet nothing on this modernized three-level spectrum can reflect a rhetorical attitude. It can chart only serious attitudes
toward the world. It could never reveal that Hemingway is as

self-conscious and as allegorical a stylist as James; that we are to notice each style *as a style*. The spectrum makes no provision for a self-regarding style. Here rhetorical theory has never isolated the natural premises of its own world view. It has never included the observer in a dynamic way. The reason is clear. From the beginning, from Aristotle (*Rhetoric* 1404B), style was not supposed to show. This was the great desideratum at any level. "Excess" meant any style which showed. The nonsense perpetuated by this leftover serious prejudice would be hard to assess. We can begin to dispel it by admitting stylistic self-consciousness into the community of human thinking and feeling. There is nothing intrinsically good or bad about it. To build it into the accepted stylistic scheme, we must have a matrix like this:

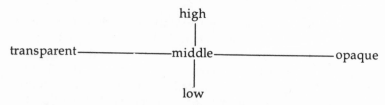

The horizontal axis seeks to plot not configurations of language but our attitude toward them, our stylistic self-consciousness, how much we notice style as style. Tacitus's imploding syntax, though very different from the low styles parodied in the *Cena Trimalchionis*, much resembles them in the degree to which it asks to be noticed *as a style*. The horizontal axis provides a place to plot this likeness. This axis does not vary independently of the vertical axis. It changes it at every point. So in the "Will" sonnets of Shakespeare: the five-way puns, schemes, surface decorations from a naive, show-off sonneteer become tropes, true wit, from Shakespeare the self-conscious manipulator of language. "Excess" regarded as self-conscious play is no longer excess. The ways of triggering such self-consciousness will preoccupy us throughout this book. Historical context becomes significant. How sophisticated was the audience? Within the rhetorical documents various release mechanisms recur—devices of repetition, of structure, direct self-reflexive comment (E. K.'s remarking "a prety Epanorthosis . . . and withall a Paronomasia" in *The Shepheard's Calender*), dramatic juxtaposition, confessed parody (as in 2.4 of *I Henry IV*), plays within plays, dramatic and linguistic. Indeed, controlling stylistic self-consciousness becomes the main formal problem the rhetorical stylist faces.

The additional axis solves many problems. We can describe a style in unmoralistic terms. "Excess," "decadence," all the left-over moralizings can be discarded. No style can *be* "excessive" in this matrix. If a writer wishes to draw attention to words as words, for whatever reason, he is free to. Such a matrix does not prohibit value judgments, but it slows them down and clears them up. It precludes judging by an irrelevant norm. We are free to remember times and places, notice different attributes. We no longer need judge Lyly by Dryden. The whole range of verbal style need no longer be judged by standards of denotative clarity which describe only a small part of it. The expanded matrix eliminates normative criticism as an initial stylistic judgment.

Vices of language, then, need no longer concern a student of style. To the degree that a style ceases to illuminate its subject, the style will become its own subject. You can talk intelligently or stupidly about language, of course, coherently or not. It is a rhetorical commonplace that every virtue can turn into a vice: *ne quid nimis*. But it works the other way, too. Every vice can become a virtue. We might argue that imposture becomes sincerity. The rhetorical stylist has no central self to be true to. In the Arnoldian, highly serious sense of self, he boasts no self at all. At his center lurks a truly Ciceronian vacuity. He feels at home in his roles and to live must play them. When he poses, he *is* being himself. The more artistic his performance, the more authentically representative it is. Rhetorical man is an actor and insincerity is the actor's mode of being. The wider his range of impersonations, the fuller his self. The more smoothly he can manage a sudden role-change, the more genuine the effect, and the effort. Thus when Ovid adopts, in the *Amores*, first one role then, in the poem following, a diametrically opposed one, or when Shakespeare changes pose from one sonnet to the next, they move *toward*

faithful representation, not away from it. They just keep faith
with a different reality. Arnoldian "sincerity" offers not a stylistic judgment, a judgment of taste, but a philosophic judgment. A
different kind of self is demanded. Terminology runs to moralizing because the matter matters. Reality stands at stake.
Might we not think such self-consciousness more "sincere"
than the evaporated, disembodied authorial presence? Can't it
tip us off that the writer is going deep, deep enough to doubt the
substance of his own identity as well as ours? Such posing
challenges those who think identity, authorial or otherwise, far
more substantial than it is. We can learn noble sentiments,
Quintilian reminds us (1.2.30), by speaking nobly. Can't self-
consciousness be seen as an attempt, potentially at least, to *create*
a self? Expression sustains the self. Self-conscious posturing
attempts to keep faith with dramatic reality. So does language
which reminds us it is language, reminds us that we see only by
means of language. Such language does not fool us, invite us to
fool ourselves, into accepting a wordless, symbol-less world.
Again the two views of life: from serious premises, all rhetorical
language is suspect; from a rhetorical point of view, transparent
language seems dishonest, false to the world.

No topic has more exercised rhetorical theorists than decorum.
A comprehensive matrix renders this debate otiose. Appro-
priateness in prose style is inevitable, inescapable. Our job is to
imagine the reality for which such a style would be appropriate.
When we call a style inappropriate, we mean that we don't like
the reality it creates, that we find that reality incoherent or
jejune. Fair enough. But we should recognize the disagreement
as with reality, not style.

If a discussion of rhetoric has meant mostly a discussion of
style, discussion of style has meant mostly a discussion of ornament and its rules. This discussion seldom fails to evoke in the
beginning student a nomenclatural wonder, bewilderment at
rhetoric's fondness for overschematized cataloging. The cataloging seems often to run on for its own sake, levitate into bureauc-
racy, become a self-pleasing machine. But the same phenomenon haunts serious inquiry. Do away with the jargons and what
is left of metaphysics? What Rube Goldberg machines have *not*

worked under the banner of binary oppositions? Philosophy is complicated because, as with rhetoric, it is more enjoyable that way. Behind the controversial *controversiae* skulks a humble truth: people often debate largely for the pleasure it gives them. Artificial debates are more sincere than "real" ones.

An opaque Kantian philosophical vocabulary stands truer to the nature of man than plain speech. Profundity is as enjoyable as conflict; if people cannot get enough in real life, they will seek it somewhere else. If to profundity they can add the pleasures of dramatic impersonation, as mock-debates do in one way and philosophical jargons in another—how tell the philosopher if not by his big words?—so much the better. So with rhetoric's complex rules. It does not matter what they are, so long as they are detailed, self-contradictory, unclear in application—and so infinitely discussable. If we define *academic* to mean discussable rather than significant—and the history of scholarship leaves us little choice—we can pin down rhetorical ornament's unpopularity more precisely. It is academic and honestly so. It thus constantly threatens academic inquiry with comic exposure. Curiously enough, rhetoric's ornament-deliberations have always proceeded on serious premises, assuming a naive speaker and listener engaged in one-time encounter. If we dispense with the serious premise, some interesting things happen.

Rhetoric has usually been depicted as a woman, especially an overdressed one—the harlot rhetoric. We might begin liverishly by developing the comparison. Students of rhetoric cannot have had much direct experience with harlots. Harlots do not paint to improve nature. They paint to invite a certain attitude. The cosmetics, since they are not referential, cannot be excessive. Their excess is their meaning—until, at least, all womankind follows suit. Likewise their dress. It is not calculated to improve their figures—it usually distorts them—but to invite a particular sort of attention. Cosmetics and dress, then, in this puritanical comparison of the philosophers, are allegorical, not referential. So is verbal style.

As Morse Peckham has pointed out,[7] printing poetry in verse

7. *Man's Rage for Chaos*, p. 204.

works the same way. The typographical convention invites certain attitudes toward what is said and discourages others. It invites us to look at words, not through them, to allow ourselves an extraordinary verbal pleasure. Gorgias aimed to trigger the same release mechanisms by his resolute balance and antithesis, the oral-culture analogue of printed verse. The convention of printing poetry line-by-line is thus an "ornament" just like isocolon. It evokes a certain kind of attention. Since all grades of attention can be requested, it follows that no essential dividing line separates prose and poetry.

The cosmetic analogy of the philosophers proves more illuminating than insulting. Personify the high style and the low, woman dolled up and woman made plain. Both are inviting us to assume certain attitudes. Eye makeup says, look at my eyes: I consider them sexually provocative and invite you to attach the same value to them. So with any detail of dress; it calls attention to, envaluates, an element of structure. It does not try to look natural, look unseen. If it really escaped notice (*summa ars celavit artem*), why bother? It wouldn't work. Like a verbal style, it must be seen as such in order to function as an analogue. Nor can plain Jane escape. In a fallen, cosmetic world, she is asking *not* to be considered, wants to be overlooked—or perhaps to claim attention by contrast. She is as rhetorical as her made-up sister, proclaims as loudly an attitude. Thus the whole range of ornament, from zero to 100, is equally rhetorical, equally deep or equally superficial. The kinds of attitudes invited vary widely; the nature of the invitation, symbolic rather than substantial, very little.

Ornament, in a way then, seems more honest than plainness. It does not affect a naturalness in the nature of things unattainable. Ornaments are free forms, not immediately bound up with the subject, and thus more likely to tell you what is on the artist's psyche, if not on his mind, than the bound forms, the forms that are immediately expressive of subject. Think of Sterne's games with the physical appearance of a book, his blank and black pages, changes in type face, and so on. The Victorian saw only the shameless gesture, but the rhetorical point of view shows a mocking attempt to be honest, to declare the impostures implicit in a codex format. Was he not warning against just that codex, that "realistic" acceptance of book as coterminous with reality, upon which the Victorian novel was to be founded? Here again we come upon rhetorical sincerity, the insistence that we become maximally self-conscious about the artifice which rules us. The way to naturalness lies through artifice, not around it. "How little," Wölfflin reminds us, "style is determined by observations of nature alone, . . . it is always decorative principles . . . to which the last decision is assigned."[8]

It may perhaps be fruitful to view style as a self-corrective circuit. A movement toward either extreme on the spectrum generates a counterpressure back toward the middle. A totally serious, referential use of language never lasts long. It becomes stylized, turns playful. Bureaucratic jargons start out as purely denotative, strictly business, but end up as games of euphemism, of obfuscation, of plain verbal nonsense—"buzz words" which can be glued together in any combination. And the same process is happening to advertising. Language cannot last long without returning to its rich resoures of play. The clarity in whose name it becomes purely purposive itself depends, as we have seen, on language's fund of pleasure. The very process of composition generates an oscillation between play and purpose. But at the same time a movement toward the opposite extreme, toward pure verbal play, activates our resources for making meaning, our impulses for purpose. We try to "make sense of" nonsense. The more absent the sense, the more we supply it. As Freud said, no one can talk nonsense for long. He will start talking about himself, pouring himself into the Rorschach inkblot.

A strong force seems to operate, keeping us in the rich, mixed middle ground of the stylistic spectrum. And a similar force seems to operate with human motive. When we become purely purposive, we become pathological, "take ourselves too seriously," as folk wisdom properly puts it. We ascribe to ourselves too durable and preexistent a self and think our "reality" the only

8. Heinrich Wölfflin, *Principles of Art History*, trans. M. D. Hottinger, p. 51.

one there is. In such moods, we need a comic counterpressure, and thus change roles, go away on a trip, move in a different society. We relieve ourselves of the burden of that superserious self. And, conversely, when we have too long been all things to all men, played at life, we feel the need for commitment. Some people remain at either end of the spectrum, of course—zealots and triflers. But Western society has generally thought both extremes sociopathic.

It seems otiose to ask whether the stylistic circuit came first or the self circuit. Surely they grew up together, synergistically. Together, they embody the self-corrective force of self-consciousness. Without role playing, we would never grow up; we never finally grow up unless, when we need to, we can stop role playing. The self needs periodic reminders that it is part of a society, takes its existence from it, and that it has its own identity as well, can stand apart. Verbal style both engenders this self-corrective oscillation and expresses it. Rhetorical literary works, as we shall see, often seem finally therapeutic, aiming to heal. Their therapy lives just here, in this necessary process of self-correction.

It may even be possible, if we carry the argument a stage further, to see the function of literature as part of such a cybernetic scheme, an attempt to keep man in the rich central confusion of the mixed self. The value terms of the New Criticism—*tension, paradox, irony*—all seem apropos here. They refer to just the mixed middle, a self by turns central and social, a language first transparent and then opaque. *Paradox* and *tension* are terms that point to pain, the pain of a self guiding and sustaining itself. They applaud literature when it is doing its job best, keeping the two kinds of self in fruitful collision. When it veers toward pure concept on the one hand, or pure play on the other, it impoverishes man rather than enriches him, and is subject to self-corrective guidance. We start to play with the concepts or conceptualize the play. The narrative-speech-narrative pattern I have just commented on embodies the same attempt at fruitful collision, self-corrective oscillation.

IV

You cannot read Renaissance literature for long without noticing everywhere a delight in words, an infatuation with rhetoric, a stylistic explosion. When you come to the learned commentary on this literature, however, you soon surprise a serious anomaly. On every hand you will be admonished to deplore just this delight, regret just this adolescent infatuation. The age, you are told, took a long time to outgrow its stylistic adolescence; so long, in most cases, that by maturity the Renaissance was over. You are, in a manner of speaking, invited to deny the age itself. If you push your investigations back further, you find that the Middle Ages were, in a different way, as infatuated with rhetoric as the Renaissance. Yet there too rhetoric must be deplored. If, sufficiently bemused, you revert to classical antiquity, again the same anomaly, writ yet larger.

C. S. Lewis has confronted the issue with more self-awareness than most:

> Rhetoric is the greatest barrier between us and our ancestors. If the Middle Ages had erred in their devotion to that art, the *renascentia*, far from curing, confirmed the error. . . . Nearly all our older poetry was written and read by men to whom the distinction between poetry and rhetoric, in its modern form, would have been meaningless. The "beauties" which they chiefly regarded in every composition were those which we either dislike or simply do not notice. This change of taste makes an invisible wall between us and them. Probably all our literary histories, certainly that on which I am engaged, are vitiated by our lack of sympathy on this point. If ever the passion for formal rhetoric returns, the whole story will have to be rewritten and many judgements may be reversed.[9]

9. *English Literature in the Sixteenth Century*, p. 61.

The great barrier amounts, for Lewis, to a matter of historical taste. But it was also a barrier between some of our ancestors and others: a typical, as well as an historical, discontinuity; less a difference of taste, we can now see, than of world view, a difference of cosmology, not cosmetics. When Lewis confesses that he—and we—have lost the taste for rhetoric, he really confesses that he has lost his taste for half of Western literature and half of Western man—a curious confession for a man who has argued so eloquently against, to borrow his own title, *The Abolition of Man*. In Lewis's case, it is easy to see why. A religious dogmatist and a delayed Victorian, he recoiled instinctively against the whole idea of rhetorical man. The rhetorical man dealt with many orientations, not one; many selves, not the high-minded heroic soul, the Victorian manliness Lewis sought everywhere in literature's best and greatest. He could not openly dismiss this rhetorical half of man. It would seem too dogmatic—*he* would be abolishing man—so he dismissed it under the rubric of changing taste. We have not that excuse. The whole story does indeed need to be rewritten. For Western literature, and especially the Renaissance, has been not simply misunderstood, but methodically misunderstood. This has usually been managed by applying serious coordinates to rhetorical texts, but it also works by reversing the misapplication.

The task of the critic, as of the cultural or literary historian, is not to choose sides and then ignore the other half. Nor is it to try, however tempted, to adjudicate the dispute, decide who is right and *then* simplify. He need join neither the Chamber of Commerce nor an Eastern religion. His job is rather to describe the conflict accurately, to insist on criteria condign to each side. Such criteria, such coordinates, more readily come to hand for serious reality than for the rhetorical view, but neither side is, in principle, more difficult to understand. The history of Western literature must be rewritten as precisely the symbiotic relationship of the two theories of knowledge, theories of style, ways to construct reality—rewritten as the quarrel between the central self and the social self, between society as drama and society as highly serious, one-time sublimity. We must, that is, rehearse again the quarrel between philosophy and rhetoric. And this time around, we must do more than use philosophy to debunk rhetoric, as the scientific world view has done. This debunking ends in that thinning of reality's texture, that ontological discomfort, those tremors of nonexistence, so familiar to us now as science's last best gift to a grateful mankind. But unhappy consequences threaten also in the opposite procedure, the language- and game-centered debunking of natural philosophy, the attack on any certain connection between man and the appearances he dwells among. We surprise again the centrality of literary study. Seeing Western literature correctly depends on controlling these two contradictory theories of knowledge, of self, of style. But we must invert this, too. Upon seeing Western literature aright depends our ability to hold together the two different ways of knowing which *together* make us human.

2

The Fundamental Strategies:
Plato and Ovid

The two dominant conceptions of reality, serious and rhetorical, found, in antiquity, their respective champions in Plato and Ovid. Both authors were to have a preponderant influence on later times and especially on the Renaissance. Plato, in defending the central, serious self, naturally adopted a central figure to embody it—the Platonic Socrates. And he naturally brought the inevitably yoked issues of self and style to a climax in a central work, the *Symposium*. Ovid, of course, did neither. His central figure was conspicuous by its absence; his theme was that he could envisage no hero greater than his diffuse authorial self. Nor did he focus the self and its stylistic implications in a single great work. His treatment of this cluster is, again naturally enough, as diffuse and social as his self.

The issues as posed by both great poets are typical and fundamental. Serious reality and the central self must finally make the kind of stylistic decisions Plato makes in the *Symposium*. The rhetorical stylist will inevitably, like Shakespeare, reincarnate Ovid. It may thus clarify the theoretical opposition I am trying to develop to look briefly at both fundamental positions. For all serious poets finally, like Plato, posit a referential mystic center and all rhetorical stylists try, like Ovid, to avoid one.

I

Finding the center of the *Symposium* is not easy. Plato has hedged it round with defenses. We hear the report of a report of an evening long ago, not the whole story but an imperfect recollection of an imperfect recollection (οὔτε πάνυ ὁ 'Αριστόδημος ἐμέμνητο οὔτ' αὖ ἐγὼ ἃ ἐκεῖνος ἔλεγε πάντα [178A]:[1] Aristodemus did not remember everything, nor I everything he told me). Prefatory·machinery introduces the dialogue; more prefatory machinery starts up the speech-making contest. And several speeches, rhetorical and agonistic, precede a Socratic centerpiece which claims to be neither. Our way in is controlled, the context of sublimity artfully contrived. But we finally get there, we come face to face with beauty itself; not a mere representation but "the thing itself, unique of itself, existing alone by itself, always." This crucial phrase is striking: ἀλλὰ αὐτὸ καθ' αὑτὸ μεθ' αὑτοῦ μονοειδὲς ἀεὶ ὄν (211B). We have navigated a ritual purification of rhetorical excess, dutifully laughed at Erixymachus's pedantry, Aristophanes' exuberant fancy, Agathon's euphuism. Now we are to get reality. But we don't get reality. We get polyptoton: αὐτὸ . . . αὐτὸ . . . αὐτοῦ. We get assorted vowel music. With the following phrase (τὰ δὲ ἄλλα πάντα καλὰ ἐκείνου μετέχοντα τρόπον τινὰ τοιοῦτον) we come face to face not with reality but with ploce, homoioteleuton, and assonance. If we glance at the phrase just before that carrying reality itself, we confront again compulsive ploce, alliteration, homoioteleuton: οἶον ἐν ζῴῳ ἢ ἐν γῇ ἢ ἐν οὐρανῷ ἢ ἔν τῳ ἄλλῳ. The centerpiece phrase comes heralded by a long series of neither/nors; forms of οὐδέ or οὔτε occur fourteen times in seven lines, with appropriate repetitive patterns accompanying: οὔτε γιγνόμενον οὔτε ἀπολλύμενον is followed by οὔτε αὐξανόμενον οὔτε φθῖνον, yielding both a pair of pairs and a chiasmus. Then a series of Gorgianic antitheses:

οὐ τῇ μὲν καλόν, τῇ δὲ αἰσχρόν
οὐδὲ τοτὲ μέν, τοτὲ δὲ οὔ
οὐδὲ πρὸς μὲν τὸ καλόν, πρὸς δὲ τὸ αἰσχρόν
οὐδ' ἔνθα μὲν καλόν, ἔνθα δὲ αἰσχρόν
ὡς τισὶ μὲν ὂν καλόν, τισὶ δὲ αἰσχρόν

Then an equally gorgeous anaphoric gradatio:

1. *The Symposium of Plato*, ed. R. G. Bury, 2d ed. (Cambridge, 1932). All subsequent quotations are from this edition.

οὐδ' αὖ φαντασθήσεται αὐτῷ τὸ καλὸν οἷον πρόσωπόν τι
οὐδὲ χεῖρες
οὐδὲ ἄλλο οὐδὲν ὧν σῶμα μετέχει
οὐδέ τις λόγος
οὐδέ τις ἐπιστήμη
οὐδέ που ὄν ἐν ἑτέρῳ τινί

And then reality itself as it really is.

Can this be Socrates, elsewhere hammer of the rhetors? Is sauce for the sophist sublimity for the philosopher? From Agathon, A. E. Taylor remarks, "we get only 'words, words, words.' " Yet Agathon, in all his glory, was not arrayed like one of these. The *Symposium* thus poses in a specially awkward way the problem of mystical language. The soaring mystic forever falls back into the lap of ornament. He can soar beyond language only if we agree beforehand to overlook his language. His chronic problem, as a poet, is to fabricate a structure which will encourage this act of oblivion. Stylistic self-consciousness for him means disaster. He must avoid it at all costs. Otherwise, God will seem to have studied under Gorgias. Like every other mystic, Plato must express transcendent truth with untranscendent words. He must create a context which does not notice words as words.

Now the odd thing about the *Symposium* is that it does just the opposite. It calls our attention to the verbal surface in every way Plato can think of. The occasion is an oratorical contest. We are to relish each speech not as philosophers but as rhetorical connoisseurs. The aim is victory not wisdom. Such an attitude grows in our minds over a series of speeches. Socrates exacerbates it, out-sophists the Sophists. We must consider him as both oratorical contestant and soaring mystic. An atmosphere of scoring pervades the dialogue. The conversation occurs the evening after Agathon's victory in the tragedy competition. It is itself a private victory celebration, a verbal game celebrating victory in another verbal game. The guests decide to play at speechifying because they are all too hung-over for agonistic drinking. They will drink not seriously but only πρὸς ἡδονήν, as much as they want. The speech bout is clearly billed as even less serious than the drinking bout they cannot handle. In the larger context of the framing tale, Apollodorus's unnamed friend asks particularly to hear not about love but the speeches about love (περὶ τῶν ἐρωτικῶν λόγων τίνες ἦσαν [172B]). Socrates himself complains because his late speaking turn makes his task harder. He so ironizes about the eloquence of others that we cannot overlook his own. The occation too is not simply a rhetorical contest but a contest in the most rhetorical of rhetorical devices, the most gratuitous of oratorical occasions, the encomium, the speech of praise. Editors disagree about which speeches parody what, but parody obviously hovers in the air. The speeches exemplify or parody a broad range of Athenian speaking styles. We look at them first as oratory, only secondarily for meaning. Stylistic contrast and variety seem to have been the main criteria for deciding which speeches were worthy to be remembered, ἀξιομνημόνευτον. The contrast of Aristophanes' plain style with Agathon's ornate one suggests the stylistic juxtaposition characteristic of the rhetorical *florilegium*, not of a philosophical treatise. Even the jokes seem related to words as such, to a self-conscious speaking voice. The hiccoughs—let us hasten to allegorize in yet a new way Aristophanes' much-debated spasm—supply the only truly spontaneous, sincere vocal gestures in the *Symposium*.

We are constantly asked, in such a contest, to separate what is said from how, speaker from speech. Are these habits simply switched off when we come to Socrates and the serious part of the *Symposium*? It can't be done. Not even Plato could do it. To see the comedy of Phaedrus's speech, or Agathon's, we must observe the stylistic surface. But such rhetorical coordinates are fatal when we come to Socrates' heavy troping. To laugh at Aristophanes' allegory, we must cultivate the allegorical habit of mind, come to think Aristophanes' original-double-man myth comic because so outrageously convenient, so preposterously an after-the-fact explanation as to cast the allegorical habit in doubt. But what, then, when we meet the outrageous contrivance of

Diotima's "ladder," that handy escalator so nicely devised to carry us from the flesh we would flee to the αὐτὸ καθ' αὑτὸ we seek? And the narrative context further compromises Socrates' position. The person who tells the whole story is Apollodorus, a pupil of Socrates so admiring that his nickname is "fanatic" (ταύτην τὴν ἐπωνυμίαν ἔλαβες τὸ μανικὸς καλεῖσθαι [173D]). Thus the whole dialogue may be radically biased testimony. Further, as Plato strives to tell us, it is rehearsed testimony. He has told it to Glaucon only the day before. He is "not unrehearsed" (οὐκ ἀμελετήτως [173C]). Again, a rhetorical qualification. Worse, yet more rhetorical, he talks for pleasure, loves to talk on philosophical topics, as he confesses immediately after this. The *Symposium*, thus, is retold by someone speaking for propaganda and for pleasure. And Plato deliberately establishes this characterization, although thematically it does not again figure in the dialogue.

Does not this context undermine Socrates' own pose? He palms off, after all, the hoariest double-chestnut in rhetoric's history. He will be plain and he will be brief. Like Polonius? In the *Euthydemus* (303–04), Socrates admonishes his audience that rhetorical trickery ought to be practiced only before an audience of connoisseurs. Can he himself be doing this in the *Symposium*? Agathon had concluded with a naked avowal that he spoke neither wholly seriously nor wholly in jest: Οὗτος, ἔφη, ὁ παρ' ἐμοῦ λόγος, ὦ Φαῖδρε, τῷ θεῷ ἀνακείσθω, τὰ μὲν παιδιᾶς, τὰ δὲ σπουδῆς μετρίας, καθ' ὅσον ἐγώ δύναμαι, μετέχων (197E). Such a spirit suffuses the *Symposium* from the undermined beginning seriousness to the allegorical vignette at the end, Socrates flanked by tragic and comic poet. No one has ever really allowed for self-parody on Agathon's part, admitted that *his* excess might be ironic. Yet he tells us so himself. The logic of Plato's form urges us to extend the same courtesy to Socrates. When we do so, it is not only his mask that seems a Silenus box but the whole *Symposium*.

Yet if Socrates' oration is not the center, what is? Alcibiades' praise of Socrates? But this oration is yet more suspect, Alcibiades being the Prince of Rhetorical Coordinates. And Alcibiades does not even pretend to judicious comment. He is a rejected lover, an apostate disciple, an allegorical Bacchus. He does not overlook Socrates the disputant, calls him in fact ὑβριστής, a bully. He likens him famously to a Silenus figure, ugly outside but stuffed with rare unguent within. And he makes a disquieting charge: Socrates has spent his life pretending, ironizing, *playing with* people rather than being straight with them (εἰρωνευόμενος δὲ καὶ παίζων πάντα τὸν βίον πρὸς τοὺς ἀνθρώπους διατελεῖ [216E]). Even with Socrates himself, there is no telling when he is serious. What, then, of Socrates' allegory of Love as the child of Penury and Contrivance? How serious is this? The third movement of the dialogue, the Alcibiades interruption, leaves us then just where the first movement had—in the midst of rhetorical coordinates. The seriousness of Socrates' report of Diotima's sublime utterances about love is qualified, squeezed, from both sides.

Faced with such a rhetorical-serious-rhetorical structure, how do we decide what premises to invoke and when? Why did Plato create a literary form which seems to work against his serious purpose? Why build an altar to essential beauty, and to the essential self needed to find it, on such alien ground? The *Symposium* is generally accepted as Plato's greatest *literary* creation, but the primary thing to emerge from the *Symposium* as literature is this extraordinarily uncertain tone.

We can choose to credit Socrates' indirect report, of course. But if we do, it will not be because the literary structure of the *Symposium* lends his words extraordinary authority. It will be because it is Socrates who says them. This is Plato's point and he has made it obviously. Socrates is exalted by a mystic seizure on the way to the party. He speaks, enraptured, of Eros. Alcibiades describes his long mystic seizure at Potidea. And Socrates is a genuine mystic. He testifies to the power of his δαίμων by how he lives, by absolute self-control. Even alcohol cannot affect him. And so the logical and structural necessity for Alcibiades' interruption and encomium. Seriousness comes to be certified by the character of Socrates. In the *Symposium* Plato becomes a be-

haviorist. Words cannot be trusted. We must look to deeds to
certify the only real truth, mystic illumination. The center is left
out—argument. No rational connection stretches between man
and God. Only spirits intervene, especially the greatest of these,
Eros. Again, Socrates is explicit: θεὸς δὲ ἀνθρώπῳ οὐ μίγνυται
(203A). God does not deal directly with man. It is not rhetoric and
philosophy which contend in the _Symposium_ but rhetoric and
religion. Cognition has been omitted from the _Symposium_:
rhetoric, ineffable illumination, and nothing in between.

This dialogue, then, enshrines the Platonic opposites in extreme form. Follow the universal admonishment to read the
Symposium as literature and we find it a careful imitation of the
rhetorical ideal of life. Our only way out of this circle of play lies
in religious commitment to Socrates. Socrates has often figured
as a generalized humanist savior, but the divine sponsorship in
the _Symposium_ is exact. Socrates represents, for Plato, an embodiment of essence, the only way out of a hopeless relativism in the
society surrounding him. Only a maximum stylistic self-
consciousness could put the weight of the dialogue where Plato
wanted it, on Socrates, on the nature of his self. The arguments,
Socrates' or anyone else's, do not constitute the serious center.
Plato was wont to say in his old age that his writing had never
adequately represented the substance of his thinking. Thinking
needed to be embodied, felt. That skepticism shines clearly in
the _Symposium_. The real center, the felt experience, was there,
embodied but beyond words. Let the rhetoricians have the
words then. The more carefully we read the _Symposium_ as literature, the more strongly we feel Plato's own contempt for literature, for the written word, his own as well as everyone else's.

So extreme a strategy prompts a general reflection on Plato's
dialectic, here so prominent by its absence: its absence doesn't
make much difference. The truth is known if not expressible. No
dialectic will really _lead us_ there. Dialectic can only, like the
famous ladder of love, offer a highly unsatisfactory model of how
someone, a very great someone, did get there. Yes, and like the
ladder, dialectic is a cosmetic, a scheme not a trope, finally a

rhetorical model. The *Symposium*'s omission of a cognitive center backlights the ornamental quality of Platonic dialectic generally. The dialectic does not prove a conclusion. It illustrates it. Socrates is thus the great master of rhetorical, sophistic dialectic. Perhaps this is why Aristophanes attacks him as such in *The Clouds*. Plato would not have been troubled by the old charge that he was rigging his dialogues. He would have admitted it cheerfully. Why not? The world was not being constituted but reconstituted, illustrated in a hopelessly inferior medium. What was obnoxious about the Sophists was not that their arguments were ornamental, but that the Sophists thought they were not; they pretended to constitute rather than reconstitute the world.

Plato has thus chosen a very original form in which to present his encomium of Socrates. He makes the possibility of human seriousness depend on Socrates, on accepting him as a referential type of self, as divinely inspired. Only the extraordinary force of Socrates' personality, his lived presence, can lead us out of the magic circle of rhetoric which surrounds him in the *Symposium*. It is not Socrates' arguments—the famous ladder—that persuade us but the man himself. His arguments can only imitate, and very imperfectly, what he has felt and what his presence communicates. The ladder is not irrelevant but it is only illustrative. If we are not willing to accept the authority of Socrates, then we are thrown back on rhetoric, on the tonal cacophony the *Symposium* creates.

Plato set out to show what Socrates' teaching meant, how much was at stake. This is what a serious, as distinct from a rhetorical, encomium had to do. To show what a serious encomium involved, Plato chose a form which used the standard rhetorical encomia but transcended them. The *Symposium* thus possesses a perfect thematic unity. By juxtaposing what Plato considered a true encomium with false ones, it exposed the real nature of an encomium, the encomium, as he would doubtless have put it, as in itself it really is. Plato thus makes his form perfectly answerable to his purpose. It is here, I think, and not in love and its ladder, that we must find Plato's artistic triumph.

The encomium of Socrates is made to seem so important by making the only alternative to Socrates the model represented by all those other encomia.

The *Symposium*, then, does not convince us of its serious premises. It simply insists on them. If we refuse to accept them, Socrates will become just another orator. I don't think Plato would have been bothered by this criticism. *Anything* written down in words would run the same risk, Plato would have argued. Indeed, it was just this risk he was writing about. All language needed an external sanctioning authority and such an authority would not be suggested by language but must be imposed upon it. You could not mount the ladder unless you wanted to leave language behind.

The ladder's checkered history now comes into focus. If you insist on remaining within language, deny Socrates' mystical credentials, then the ladder will seem, as it has seemed to many, a preposterous rhetorical trick. If you are willing to accept serious premises, then the ladder provides a convenient illustration of a movement that lies beyond proof.

Plato has devised in the *Symposium* a literary form which illustrates the final serious, philosophic failure of any literary form. He has thus put us, as literary critics, in a classic double bind. The more we object, the more we prove him right, the more we have confirmed the necessity for Platonic mystic seriousness. I've said that the rhetorical context prevents us from choosing serious coordinates. Now we can see that this is just Plato's point. In Platonic terms, we cannot decide on a seriousness. It must decide on us, visit us as a δαίμων. Nor can we call the form a failure because it insists that its seriousness is the only possible kind. That is what the form was invented to do. It is indeed an artistic masterpiece and one can see why it has been so cherished by Platonists. It poses the choice between rhetorical and serious reality in archetypical terms. And it seems to prove that Platonic seriousness is the only kind.

We cannot, then, fault the *Symposium* as a work of art. It is a brilliant success. It insists on being read within its own terms. And it is also, as we have seen, a brilliant work of rhetoric. It uses language to maximum effect at the same time that it repudiates it with maximum effect. That Plato could contrive such an artistic and such a rhetorical victory at the same time still seems, across the gulf which separates us, the most dazzling and extraordinary of verbal accomplishments.

All of this, however, comes at a cost, or at least at a risk. Plato insists that style be certified from outside and for this a Redeemer is required. What if your Redeemer is repellent? As Socrates, from a rhetorical point of view, certainly is.

No one, to my knowledge, has discussed the Platonic Socrates as fictional archetype, Serious Man, but this is clearly his role. In the *Theaetatus* Socrates argues that the lawyers and orators have shrewd and worldly minds, but meanly unimaginative ones. They can neither think deeply nor soar. The philosopher's soul, on the other hand, free, deep, and rich, can do both. But does Socrates actually illustrate this comparison? Is he a large-minded man? From the rhetorical point of view, Socrates shows signs of not really knowing himself. Has he ever asked himself, a rhetorical critic might inquire, why he so enjoys disputation? Why he has to single out the Sophists as the primary enemy? What is so attractive about binary oppositions? About universals? Why he always forces his discussion in terms of them? Has he reflected on the continual self-flattery of his gadfly role? Socrates is, in his way, as vain as Alcibiades. Virtue too has its vanities, though he seems not to have realized it. Has he ever reflected, in his scorn for the rhetorician as a professional flatterer, that the philosophic conception of man flatters us yet more? That his fame might be based on just this flattery? That philosophical debate might be as self-pleasing, as ornamental, as sophistic debate? One looks in vain for that unrelenting down-to-the-ground self-examination that overcomes the really introspective man.

Socrates never looks beyond his own coordinates. He can speak only one language. Every humanist from Plato's day to our own has praised Socrates for trying to know himself. It is legitimate to ask whether his self was especially worth knowing. Isn't it really the testy, impatient, intolerant self of the religious zealot? It is no charity to the historical Socrates to accept Plato's allegorical portrait of him as what one might call ἄνθρωπος σπουδαῖος, Serious Man. So full of self-importance and self-satisfaction (if he knows nothing, at least he is the only person in Athens who *knows* he knows nothing), so willing to preach to others the error of their ways, is this man, whose whole life plays variations on "Why the world should be more like me," the perfect teacher? Is he indeed the model for Western man?

A man can posture on the gallows. The dramatic power of Plato's portrayal of Socrates' martyrdom in the *Apology* and the *Crito* has so formed later imagination as to make Socrates, as Erasmus called him, the humanist saint. His death stands at the center of seriousness, verifies the central self by a tragic death. But even Socrates did not present his death in this way. He was choosing, he argued, to remain loyal to the role he had chosen to play in Athens. One sees running all through the *Apology* the dramatic sanction of identity. But this rhetorical sanction at the center of his Athenian life Socrates could never see. Neither could Plato. Had he seen it, he could not have contended with the Sophists as he did. He would have realized he was partly, as we all are partly, one of them. Socrates would have recognized, had he truly known himself, the rhetorical ingredient in all human behavior, would have seen his truth as only half the human truth, half the human self. As it is he did not found humanism, a knowledge of the self, but only half of it.

The arguments are not serious, but the arguments—if we have not participated in the mystic illumination—are all we have. It has been long debated whither they tend but the direction is clear. They all suggest how the self constitutes and preserves itself. Freud was right to think himself Platonic about Eros. It was erotic force, whatever that was, which realized the self. The arguments in the *Symposium*, taken as arguments, strike us by their glacial narcissism, their obsessive inversion. The homosexuality theme, however vexing to the commentators, is no historical accident. Plato made much of it because it so fitted his concept of love. If by heterosexual love we mean throwing ourselves open to difference, not a line in the *Symposium* shows that Plato really knew what this meant. Behind the arguments lurks that monstrous Platonic egotism, that compulsive ontological insecurity. Love must integrate the self, confront and melt into essence. Plato shunned heterosexual love for the same reason he fled politics. Both were rhetorical, chancy, always changing, developing outward or collapsing altogether; process not essence, verb not noun.[2] In the *Symposium* we touch the central failure of Plato's concept of man. Plato gives away too much. He recognizes only a sublime self but condemns himself to talk of it in rhetorical terms, and in rhetorical terms the sublime self is highly vulnerable. What is left out is play, just the spontaneity and difference that Plato cannot tolerate.

The form of the *Symposium* suggests a seriousness higher than one-time sublimity, a long way around (μακρότερα περίοδος), a movement *through* an unstable, surrounding social self to a richer oscillation of the self between process and essence, but Plato declines the invitation. He gives too much away to rhetoric, takes his stand on the central self, on the figure of Socrates. Neither as philosopher nor personality can Socrates stand the pressure. Plato's idol has stood so long as Martyr-of-the-Central-Self that it seems blasphemous to consider him dispassionately. One is quarreling with a fundamental Western ideality. His attraction to posterity has been enormous, and for the same reason that he fascinated Plato and Alcibiades. He stood as central self incarnate, utterly his own man. He allayed ontological fear. He proved, by his life, that one could live entirely by one's own rules. The problem is endemic to Plato's writings, not just characteristic of the *Symposium*. Plato's final reference point is always the Acts of Socrates, his personality and what it represented. His final failure is the failure of "seriousness itself."

Thus Plato's quarrel with rhetorical style leads to the center of his concern—the problem of the self. His disagreement with the

2. "The really important grammatical achievement of Plato was the definite segregation of the noun and what we must call 'the verb' (ὄνομα and ῥῆμα). Others, for example Protagoras, had begun this, but to the best of our knowledge it was first made explicitly by Plato." R. H. Robins, *Ancient and Mediaeval Grammatical Theory in Europe*, p. 17.

Sophists was not a matter of taste but a matter of self. His failure to understand the stylistic surface insured that his philosophy could attain only a limited seriousness, that it remained, in a fundamental way, superficial. Man has a "motive," an urge, just to be alive, to reenact his own existence, and thus bolster, intensify it. It is this urge, this eloquence of behavior, that the rhetorical styles come to express and to allegorize. It is this urge which Plato and Platonists take pains to deny. They suspect—though they rarely see how—that it is deeply subversive of their own kind of seriousness. They thus condemn themselves to a mistaken and introverted defense of the realized self.

The self must be embodied just as thought must find the body of words. Plato denied both embodiments. But it is from them that love comes; there is no path around them. Thus Plato's conception of love remained fundamentally narcissistic. To really love another, one must face the profoundly disorienting properties of language, of human society, and learn to enself and thus control them. This facing-down of dissolution constitutes the artist's task par excellence and so Plato fears the artists. The artist faces the problem Plato would define out of existence. But it will not go away. When Socrates builds his ladder and climbs it he is not solving the problem the *Symposium* sets us. He is running away from it. To face it requires more intelligence as well as more courage than Plato's Socrates could muster. For a sufficiency of both we must turn to Socrates' opposite number, to the prophet of the surface, to that most unlikely philosopher, P. Ovidius Naso.

II

If seriousness can acknowledge Socrates as its saint, the rhetorical ideal may claim Ovid as its martyr. He suffered as an exile in Tomis, and in modern commentaries he has suffered yet more. He wrote too much and was too fond of what he wrote, showed sensibility but no principles, no sincerity, no heart. His universe was superficial, his religious sense undeveloped, his grasp of abstract thought shaky at best.

And, of course, he failed to be Virgil, betrayed continually "an utter lack of sympathy with the 'serious' or 'earnest' Augustanism that was so classically expressed in the *Aeneid* and in the great odes of Horace."[3]

If such a serious view fails to account for Ovid's poetry, it fails with equal method and determination to explain his reputation and influence. More even than Spenser, Ovid was the poet's poet. Shakespeare's favorite, the delight of Spenser and Milton, Ovid casts an immense shadow over Chaucer and the Middle Ages as well. In visual art before the Romantic revival he seems omnipresent. Misreading of Ovid is both indicative and predicative, immensely so. The same questions of seriousness have been asked of Andreas the Chaplain, of Chaucer and the Gawain poet, of the *Romance of the Rose*, of Castiglione and Rabelais, of the early, especially the nondramatic, Shakespeare. Misconstruction of structure and tone in the *Metamorphoses* parallels that of *The Faerie Queene* and, differently, of Sidney's two *Arcadias*. Neither the Middle Ages nor the Renaissance worshipped Ovid by accident. Their efforts to imitate his spirit did not constitute one long chronicle of misapprehension. To understand him correctly means more than to engender again the real alternative to Virgil. It means redeeming the whole Ovidian *nachleben*, the rhetorical tradition in the West.

Ovid felt, from the beginning of his poetic life, the pressure to write an epic. He also felt a strong pressure to express his own reality, his own sense of human identity and human society. He felt, correctly, that his own reality contradicted directly that of Augustan Rome. All his great work deals, in one way or another, with this clash. In the *Ars* and the *Amores* he tried, using love as metaphor for the private life, to work out the implications of his rhetorical view. That is why those poems are so didactic. In the *Metamorphoses* he sought to commemorate a Rome far less serious than Augustus's official version, yet a Rome, as he felt, no less Roman.

Ovid's strategy in both the love poetry and in the *Metamor-*

---

3. Brooks Otis, *Ovid as an Epic Poet*, 2d ed., p. xiii.

phoses stands opposite to Plato's. Plato sought an externally
sanctioned center beyond language; Ovid writes poems that
have holes in the middle. He denies any sanctions his poetry
itself has not created. In the love poetry it is the difference
between the pressures of a serious world and the behavior of a
dramatic one which constitutes the gap. In the *Metamorphoses*, it
is the gulf separating primitive, mythical Rome from the Rome of
Virgilian propaganda.

In the *Ars Amatoria* Ovid poses as a teacher, a poet of statement. Take this for the moment at face value. What does he
teach? He begins by insisting that he speaks from experience.
Love does not happen by accident. It must be sought. Search is
counseled in colonnade, law court, theatre, arena, banquet. Each
is thought a stage-set for pursuit. There is no end to such,
"numero cedet harena meo." Any scene serves as stage for the
private drama you choose to enact there. The only necessary
assumption is that all women are willing, or, if not willing, at
least enjoy being asked. Corrupt the maid first. She can set the
stage, choose a propitious time. Try to win her without a gift
("primo sine munere iungi"). Learn the arts of rhetoric to this
end. Ignore no attentive gesture but don't act the fop. Make sure
your behavior allegorizes attention to her, not to you. This
Praeceptor Amoris stresses what we call transactional analysis,
phatic communication, the psychopathology of everyday life. He
insists that every gesture, every look, can be rhetorical ("saepe
tacens uocem uerbaque uultus habet" [1.574]).[4] The range of
purposive human behavior stretches far wider than we usually
acknowledge.

So all behavior must be stage-managed. Drinking should be
moderate, better still feigned, song and dance essayed only if
you know how. Above all, play the lover ("est tibi agendus
amans imitandaque uulnera uerbis" [1.611]). Here the main
Ovidian tactic first surfaces: Begin with illusion. Reality will
dependably follow. Contrive external circumstance. Begin by

4. All quotations from *Amores* and *Ars Amatoria* are from the Oxford Classical
Text, ed. E. J. Kenney (Oxford, 1961).

allegorizing your own behavior. It is the *situation* which convinces. Arrange the external coordinates carefully and to your liking. The reality you desire will be established by them. They are not superficial embellishments. They are everything. Ovid recommends what Plato seems most to have feared; by enacting a passion you come to feel it. A generalization lurks behind this practical advice, had Ovid chosen to drag it forth: Does the tactic amount to a strategy? Is this how emotion begins?

Ovid continues with variations on the "Promise her anything but give her attention" theme, and in the midst of these betrays how deeply he is committed to the primacy of illusion. Don't hesitate, teacher says, to swear falsely by the gods: "per Styga Iunoni falsum iurare solebat / Iuppiter" (1.635–36). And then follows a line that does not follow: "expedit esse deos et, ut expedit, esse putemus." If the gods are needed to swear falsely by, well then, let them exist. The gods, too, become creatures of dramatic necessity. The first book ends with a disavowal of rigid rules. The ability to construct reality, though it may be taught at the beginning, is finally a skill, a talent, a principle of dynamic balance amidst change: "mille animos excipe mille modis."

The second book tells how to keep the lady. Cultivate the mind, for the body does not last. Cultivate the arts of indulgence. Yet Ovid here recommends no world beyond appearance. Arts of the mind, like those of the body, are dedicated to sustaining a posed agreeability, encapsulating the woman in a bubble of "Yes": "arguet: arguito; quicquid probat illa, probato; / quod dicet, dicas; quod negat illa, neges" (2.199–200). We all yearn for *agreeable* illusion. And the *discipulus* has now gone further into the poem. He knows that if he can impersonate agreeability well enough, he will spontaneously *feel* agreeable. Notice how Ovid, with his famous superficial puerility of syntax, has created a syntactic model of the reflectivity he seeks to describe. Agreement is identity and the polyptoton ("arguet: arguito") shows it.

Ovid forever exhorts his pupils to put aside *pudor* and get on with it: "discedite, segnes." The exhortation conceals a home truth. When the lover learns to don the mask that pleases his mistress most, and then becomes the mask, he has dissolved his self. Ovid has offered a rhetorical parallel to sublimity, dissolution of self into the beloved. Again, a generalization lurks in the wings. In the world of the *Ars*, self and purpose seem to vary not concomitantly, as we usually think—character is destiny—but inversely. The more we want to do something, the more we must relinquish the self that wants it. The wanting self becomes an actor.

The lesson continues with a caution against nontactical absences. Love, defined by situation, cannot long outlive it. The present must be perpetually sustained by reenactment. Such a view allows no past or future. All efforts go toward dramatizing the present. The lesson, then, ponders the nature of space and time. Thus you can love two people at once: "nec mea uos uni donat censura puellae; / di melius!" (2.387–88). No hypocrisy is involved. Situation determines self: different situation, different self. The advice following counsels a theatrical presentation of self which again denies spontaneity at every point: "quis credat? discunt etiam ridere puellae" (3.281). For the woman, the scene is coterminous with reality; "quod latet, ignotum est" (3.397).

The poem closes with advice on decorous positions for sexual intercourse and on how to fake the most sacred spontaneity of all, sexual climax. Here special care is needed to avoid being caught faking though, for "arcanas pars habet ista notas" (3.804). The body then imposes a reality if the mind cannot? Hardly. If she has sustained the illusion up to now, played the part well enough, spontaneity takes care of itself.

The *Ars* read in so schoolmasterly a way is not the poem Ovid wrote, but it is part of it and the part we must see first. It provides a clear exposition of rhetorical reality. Critics have often called love, for Ovid, only a pretext. When they think it a pretext for showing off, they are only partly right. Of course he was a show-off. Such posing was endemic to the rhetorical view, it created identity. But beyond this self-conscious cleverness, which runs through everything Ovid wrote, the poem offers a straightforward exposition of love *sub specie rhetoricae*. Love stands central to the serious view of life, the central self. By insisting *arte regendus Amor* (1.4), Ovid makes of it from the beginning—from the decision to write an *Ars* on Love (or Loving)—a metaphor to illustrate the rhetorical self. The "outrageousness" of the poem comes from the straightforward didacticism in a poem which neglects to offer the premises of the lesson. Instead, it offers, in a manner repetitive and heavy-handed, the premises of the serious world, the epic world of Augustan *gravitas*. The poem's didacticism remains consistent with itself. It constitutes an accurate, useful tactical field manual. Its vices, its catalog repetitiousness, its chatty cheek, come from the field manual as well. There is nothing cynical about the world depicted, taken within its own rhetorical coordinates. But Ovid chose to place this metaphorical exposition of rhetorical reality in a serious context, and it is the relation of the two worlds which reveals what kind of game—of *lusus*—Ovid has constructed.

We must begin with the personae Ovid chooses to don. He is a teacher, lawgiver and learned counsel of love; he is a στρατηγός, a general of love; and he is its poet. He thus takes upon himself, unsystematically and at pleasure, all the serious careers Rome offered. Teacher, lawyer, and general by virtue of the imagery, he makes more—hilariously too much—of his role as poet of love. He opens the poem with a heroic invocation on the epic scale: "Si quis in hoc artem populo non nouit amandi, / hoc legat et lecto carmine doctus amet. / arte citae ueloque rates remoque mouentur, / arte leues currus: arte regendus Amor." He begins by posing as poet, then by indirection becomes a sea captain, then the charioteer of Achilles and the helmsman of the Argo ("Tiphys et Automedon dicar Amoris ego"), a neo-Achilles, a teacher, a martyr testifying to love's power by wounds as well as poetry, *not* a pupil of Apollo, a pupil of experience, a priest of secret lovemaking, and finally a charioteer again. Ovid's practical persona, like Pandarus's in Chaucer's *Troilus*, seems unhealthily close to pander pure and simple. A characteristic Ovidian split, it works to the poem's purpose. On the one hand, Ovid plays heroic Virgilian *vates*; on the other, a more fundamental role, poet as fabricator of a pleasant reality.

The same split emerges repeatedly in the poem as the poet emphatically recalls himself from the minutiae of love (poet as

pander) to his heroic enterprise (poet as epic singer and—
almost—epic hero). The poet pitches heroic celebration of himself yet higher at the end of book two. Doctor, Lawyer, Warrior
Chief, the poet can stand comparison with them all. But as a
lover! "Tantus amator ego"! He then, modestly enough, asks a
similar celebration of his abilities as poet, as vates: "me uatem
celebrate, uiri, mihi dicite laudes. . . ." At which point, the
Virgilian pose of heroic, Homeric imitator is being given a joyful
ride. And the same meiostic pattern recurs again in book three.
First the comparison with military leadership, with legal counsel, with the rhetorician's political career, and with plain old
money, then the plunge to bold bawdry. A poet's gifts rival those
of men like these! Outdo them. A poet by nature knows more of
love, and can—celestial inspiration his specialty—immortalize
it. By now Ovid's obsession stands clear: his social role. Ovid
gazes at the profound discontinuity between serious and rhetorical views of life. He sees that the kind of poet he is differs
fundamentally from the kind of person a lawyer or general pro-
fesses to be. He lives entirely within his craft, lacks a certain
identity outside it. He cannot think his talent negligible, yet it is
denied any social role. The poet's persona seems, then, an attempt at identification. If it is a public display of personality, it
also reenacts a public search for a personality, for an anti-
Virgilian *vates*.

What Ovid's persona does in little, the *Ars* does in large: it
brings the traditional attributes of Roman greatness to the service of love. Ovid inverts the Roman world. *Gravitas* now serves
Amor.

The attack falls often on the city of Rome. Rome becomes a vast
stage-set for amorous plots. "Et fora conueniunt (quis credere
possit?) amori." (1.79) Here, as so often, Ovid's conception of
Rome seems too Augustan for comfort. The Emperor thought it a
stage-set too, but not for love. After dwelling on the female
variety Rome offers, for example (in book one), and pointing out
how the mock naval battles enriched the foreign selection, Ovid
breaks off abruptly to praise Caesar's conquest: "ecce, parat
Caesar, domito quod defuit orbi, / addere" (1.177–78). He con-

tinues in this vein fourscore lines. The transition from the previous passage scarcely exists and we are left to make the connection: Caesar's world conquests are undertaken further to swell the already rich Roman supply of women. The Roman virtues fare equally ill. Look, for example, at the passage in book two urging a claim for the older woman:

> utilis, o iuuenes, aut haec aut serior aetas:
> iste feret segetes, iste serendus ager.
> dum uires annique sinunt, tolerate labores:
> iam ueniet tacito curua senecta pede.
> aut mare remigiis aut uomere findite terras
> aus fera belligeras addite in arma manus
> aut latus et uires operamque adferte puellis:
> hoc quoque militia est, hoc quoque quaerit opes.
>
> [2.667–74]

Into the service of love comes Roman reverence for the soil, for old age, for naval, agricultural, military service. All parallel that greater service to—The Older Woman. Nor does Ovid stop with Rome and Roman virtues. The cosmos is ransacked. Consider the wonderful digression on the creation in 2.467 ff. The problem is lovers' quarrels, the only solution, lovemaking swift and sure: "quae modo pugnarunt, iungunt sua rostra columbae, / quarum blanditias uerbaque murmur habet" (2.465–66). Then, with no introduction whatever, Ovid cuts to a cameo presentation of the creation: "prima fuit rerum confusa sine ordine moles / unaque erat facies sidera, terra, fretum; / mox caelum impositum terris, humus aequore cincta est, / inque suas partes cessit inane chaos" (2.467–70). This explosion of high style runs on a bit, then the birth of sexual intercourse is narrated (Venus attending), then a catalog of how each beast easily finds its mate. It is all as if, halfway through a magazine love story, we suddenly confronted Genesis 1.

There are a great many more such belittling comparisons, but the principle is clear, a studied alternation of rhetorical *ars* and serious allusion. What kind of reality does this oscillating structure as a whole create?

Not orthodox high comedy. The Roman inability to write high comedy has been often remarked. Satire, yes. Ovid unmasks the rhetorical ingredient in serious behavior, and debunks it. Such unmasking may constitute, in fact, satire's standard operating procedure. But both comedy and satire require a referent self Ovid neglects to supply. Its absence stands at the center of the *Ars*. Ovid's serious self, with its windy posturing, seems absurd enough, but so does the sophisticated rhetorical self, the butterfly machiavel. Ovid knows this and plays upon it. He never fills in the hole in the middle or suggests how it might be done, how a complex self might be constituted.

The only element common to both is Ovid's deplorable, superficial, excessive, glib show-off style. It *is* true that without his style Ovid would be nothing. The *Ars*'s two parts are held together by poetic virtuosity. The same couplet can compass the high style and the low. For the *Ars* was intended, we must remember, to be a showcase of Ovid's talents. He makes a point of playing every note on the organ, mimicking every effect. The couplet was indeed, as L. P. Wilkinson has remarked, Ovid's criticism of life. It represented an allegory of control. The two worlds could be held together by a virtuoso act of style. Such a style had to be opaque, hold us at a distance, prevent entrance into either orchestration unreservedly. The rhetorical lover plays acknowledged slave to his desires—how heavily Ovid stresses the slavery convention of earlier Latin love poetry—and the serious world unacknowledged slave to its high-minded desires. The poem's only real freedom is a delight in style, in the art of control for its own sake, an act of pure display. Take a typical and much-traduced Ovidian line, the one Ovid thought his best and his friends the worst: "Daedalus, ut clausit conceptum crimine matris / semibouemque uirum semiuirumque bouem" (2.23–24). One can argue a kind of decorum here. Ovid is talking about a creature who is half-and-half, and so constructs a visual, verbal model of half-and-halfness. But this does not "fit" the verbal play into the context, render it transparent. Far from it. The line embodies the theme of verbal cleverness which runs through the hollow middle of the poem. Verbal cleverness, Ovid thought, finally would save us. It keeps us at a distance—so we can admire. Yet, because it is a game, it draws us in—so we can win. It allows us to live in a self-conscious, rhetorical reality. Ovid did indeed pick the crucial line.

The *Ars* stands halfway to Ovid's final form for the long poem and the major statement. It shares many motifs, of course, with the *Amores*. The *Amores*, too, was a self-advertisement. It, too, sought for sincerity, putting all its rhetorical cards on the table, offering a showcase of conflicting poses. And there too the great subject is repudiated: "magna datur merces: heroum clara ualete / nomina: non apta est gratia uestra mihi" (2.1.35–36). He defends, there too, his own career as poet against the *Livor edax* which reproaches him for not pursuing the soldier's life, the lawyer's, or the politician's. And there, too, the result of this well-dramatized struggle is to make the status of love poetry and the love poet the subject of the poem.

Ovid depicts, in both poems, a sentimental love. Not sublimely so, but sentimental in the sense of "feeling for the sake of feeling." To call Ovid's love manufactured, artificial—no real Corinna—is to see but not to see. The artificiality of love, its gratuitous creation and re-creation by the lovers, is just Ovid's point. The sustenance of the self demands gratuitous artifice. So the self-interference rituals must always be reconstructed, as in 2.19. Ovid's love poetry often urges that objects be put in his way so the game may continue. So the *Remedia*. So book three of the *Ars*. We need the interference, the recalcitrant circumstance, to strike the poses on which the self depends. Secret love is no love, says Ovid. The statement less vulgarizes serious reality than denies it. As in the Elizabethan love sonnet, love is most faithful when most public; most sincere, true to the real self, when most changeable.

In the *Amores* and the *Ars*, Ovid felt his way toward an ultimate sincerity, an ultimate faithfulness to his own genius. Eagerly, almost frantically, he strives to remain true to his own reality. That it was not Roman reality Ovid never ceased to regret and, in weak moments, apologize for. (And to the end of his life; e.g., *Ex Ponto* 3.3.31 ff. and *Tristia* (4.10.17 ff.)

Anthropological understanding of myth began when scholars
ceased to force scientific coordinates on it, stopped trying to
"make sense of it" and let it make its own kind of sense. Ovid's
Metamorphoses could not be plainer about the kind of invitation
it extends. A poem about changes, it insists on dynamic rhetorical premises, not static serious ones. Identity is, by nature in this
poem, as fluid as the other categories of life. The underlying
assumption here is unity of life, not aristocratic domination of
one species by another, Virgilian triumph of master spirit and
master race. Ernst Cassirer poses the issue:

> The real substratum of myth is not a substratum of thought
> but of feeling. . . . Its view of life is a synthetic, not an
> analytical one. Life is not divided into classes and subclass-
> es. It is felt as an unbroken continuous whole which does not
> admit of any clean-cut and trenchant distinctions. The limits
> between the different spheres are not insurmountable bar-
> riers; they are fluent and fluctuating. . . . Nothing has a
> definite, invariable, static shape. By a sudden metamor-
> phosis everything may be turned into everything.[5]

Thus the *Metamorphoses* cannot have a plot, in the conventional
sense, because plot depends on a consistent identity myth does
not allow. Mythic thought is situational. Identity bends to situation and not vice versa. We move from situation to situation in
no logical way. Situations swim up as in a dream. The vexed
problem of transitions in the *Metamorphoses* evaporates in such
an atmosphere. Chance analogy or no connection at all connect
the scenes of the *Metamorphoses*. "Convincing" transitions depend on a conception of fixed identity the poem takes pains to
deny.

Comprehension in the *Metamorphoses* is not scientific but
"participated." We do not observe the object as detached, separate from us. It is part of us. We may soon, in such a world, "be"
it. The mythic world is suffused with feeling. As Cassirer argues,
"All objects are benignant or malignant, friendly or inimical,

5. *An Essay on Man*, p. 81.

familiar or uncanny, alluring and fascinating or repellent and threatening." Such a world makes space and time depend on perceiver not perceived. We swim in an immense present hedged round with dangers. What a terrifying world the *Metamorphoses* is, anger and violence everywhere. It is a taboo culture where, like Actaeon, we always inadvertently offend. There is no sense of justice in such a world because there is no sense, not because there is no justice. And because it cannot fall back on an antecedent logical structure, such a world cannot afford to stop being perceived. So Ovid's poem must be a *carmen perpetuum*, a poem which embodies this necessity to go on, blurs its book breaks by run-over stories. The point is not to hierarchize—there are no hierarchies here, and no perspectives either—but just to keep going.

The *Metamorphoses*, then, is a mythic mythology. (Deciding to compile a compendium of myth need not imply creating a mythical mythology. Compare the *Metamorphoses* with Apollodorus's *Library*. Mythic reality was Ovid's deliberate choice.) Medea can emblemize its stunning combination of sex, violence, beauty, magic, eloquence, and caprice. If the elegies lack spontaneity, the *Metamorphoses* more than compensates. It is often a dark and dangerous world, but it is not consistently even that. It is magnificent poetry—in poetic re-creation of mythic reality Ovid's only rival is Spenser—but Ovid's world, by itself, doesn't mean anything. It is just there. Unlike Spenser, Ovid does not invite us to allegorize or philosophize myth, make sense of it. We do so spontaneously, as Ovid knew. Allegorizing bridges behavior and explanation. But Ovid makes us aware that this level of meaning comes from us not from the poem. We hasten to make meaning: the Narcissus story seems immediately to allegorize a dangerous genesis of the self; the moment of metamorphosis as the moment of most intense wishing clearly allegorizes the poetic imagination and its transformational possibilities. One could write a history of Western literature as just this kind of allegorizing. Ovid does not. He leaves his form open, aleatory, waiting to be realized. Thus he stresses our own contribution. Ovid, in our time, would have been a very anthropological poet, if not a poetical anthropologist. He was all his life curious about the surface of behavior. He has been ticked off as an antiquary, but the open allegory of the *Metamorphoses* proves otherwise. To understand the mythic world view, you must participate in it, help sustain it, rather than generalize about it.

Why did Ovid choose to construct such a world? What does he make with it? A recent overdue critical reaction to neo-Victorian disparagement has considered the *Metamorphoses* as mock-epic. But the great mock-epics are short. When they get longer, as in *Orlando Furioso, Gargantua and Pantagruel, Don Quixote,* and *Tristram Shandy,* they outgrow mock-heroism. Mock-epic uses serious coordinates. When it grows longer it tends, as here, to be about those coordinates. Thus the *Metamorphoses* comes less to attack seriousness, though it does do this, than to expose and reflect on serious assumptions by juxtaposing them with the mindless world of myth. Mock-heroic elements, once admitted, seem to pop up everywhere: domestic gods, absurd heroes like Polyphemus, ridiculously inappropriate Virgilian echo, parody-founding of Rome. But Ovid has challenged epic seriousness on a deeper level. Mock-heroic mocks excess. The challenge here is not to epic excess but to the possibility of epic.

The mock-heroism functions as perpetual reminder of the epic context and expectation Ovid plays off against, but it has no life of its own. It was not that Ovid was a bad plotter. The rhetorical view denies that plot is possible. It was not that Ovid "had no taste for heroes and, certainly, no capacity for creating them," as Brooks Otis charges. He did not believe in heroes, or the self they were based on. He was not bad at transitions; he *wanted* to lose the reader. He was not incapable of tracing a coherent genealogy for Rome; he did not believe in the Virgilian conception of history upon which such descent was based. He was not too dense to master a suitable repertoire of Augustan philosophical clichés; he denied the theory of knowledge from which they grew. Too skeptical to think the whole truth contained in a single myth, he thought the epic genre a fraud, an obvious pretense that the world makes more sense than it does.

Dido can be left behind because Virgil accepts Rome as an

external sanction, the source of all legitimating explanations. There is no external sanction in Ovid's poem. Ovid, by his refusal to supply one, points to the circularity of the Virgilian argument, and of any nonreflective epic. The epic seeks to legitimize power, refound a state. But to do so, it accepts as its basic orientation, its fundamental reality, what it seeks to prove. It must end with the status quo duly celebrated. The conclusion justifies the plot which is supposed to justify it. Ovid's own mythic form points to this fundamental illogicality. No mock-heroism can bring off such an attack. Ovid ends up writing about the genre he is writing in. And as in the *Ars*, he worries about the poet's role. Virgil thought of himself as Hercules. Ovid thinks himself a virtuoso juggler. He dramatizes his own pleasure in form. Like the sonneteer who must make yet another sonnet, he must bring forth yet another narrative on the theme of metamorphosis. And if you don't dramatize your own creative pleasure, you may mistake your creation for reality itself. Ovid saw the fraud implicit in any act of writing and wanted to declare it. What strikes us is the force of Ovid's sincerity. Formal pleasure represents a fundamental ingredient in any reconstruction of the past. If it is not declared, the poet is not truly engaged. He has become a propagandist.

Ovid's strategy in the *Metamorphoses* seems plain. He builds a mythic reality and then plays sophisticated games with it. Some are mock-heroic, but there are others. He constructs a tour de force of tone and effect in Latin poetry. He can be seriously philosophic, as in the closing Pythagoreanism. Metempsychosis, after all, fits the mythic view well enough since from that view it first emerged. The poem is a compendium of stylistic effect, of scenes, rhetorical occasions; it absorbs this climactic one effortlessly. Ovid is also compiling a mythology, an Augustan master plot for his poetic posterity. Anything can fit between creation at one end and Roman Now at the other. Critics have missed a self-justifying master plan. There are plenty of them, too many to keep track of. The great game is to juggle them. As always, the poet "has at heart our getting lost." Some coordinates of the *Metamorphoses* are clearly nonliterary. Not only a scholarly compendium of myth, it tries to write a genuine history of Augustan Rome. It is an act of anthropological reconstitution, an act of literary criticism, a discussion of genre and an allegory of style. Latinists will continue to find it encrusted with recollections, often for no seeming reason, of earlier poetry. It is Ovid's *apologia pro vita sua*. The moral is clear. *Nothing* has only one meaning, context, justification. When all the world is made to converge on and yield up a single entity—people, place, or city—watch out. The Virgilian epic, Ovid thought, preserved a simplistic, single, naive conception, a world view the West could no longer accept. The *Aeneid* did so not least in its generic purity, in succeeding so well at being both Roman and epic. The *Metamorphoses* is no single genre. Its open form, in all its complexity, constitutes generic counterstatement. We can see now why, though the coordinates of serious epic do not apply to mythic reality, Ovid so sedulously introduced them. They apply to Rome and of Rome, finally, he writes.

There is nothing fortuitous about the strategy (the sum of the structures) of the *Metamorphoses*: base of mythic reality, overlap of sophisticated game—and nothing in the middle. Ovid made his poem this way because *that is the way he saw Rome*. He saw not Augustan seriousness but Augustan sophistication. Beneath it, he saw the mythic world of superstition Rome had also inherited. The subject of the *Metamorphoses* is the mythic inheritance of Rome and the Roman attitude toward it. It is a compendium of attitudes, possible responses, a future as well as a past. Ovid might have put the argument this way: "Rome was not founded. The very idea of foundation, so basic to the *Aeneid*, and the city, conveys a false conception of how cultures grow. Civic nature no more than human nature comes into being this way. Values cannot be taken from one culture and bestowed on another so easily as Roman rapacity thinks. You cannot borrow values. You must live, incarnate, them. We are celebrating a Greek idea of city, and a Greek idea of self, but we are no longer living them." Thus the very need for an authenticating myth, Augustus's need for a theatrical reality to make his Rome seem real, itself bespeaks a crisis. The simplicity of naive Roman virtue no longer sufficed. It made you, for one thing, a dupe of Augustus, who sought to re-create naive Roman virtue as a tool of propaganda. Yet the only alternatives to naive *gravitas* were frivolity and immorality. Both, plus the advertising-slogan *gravitas*, were the air Ovid grew up breathing. Is it according too much to think that he looked about him and had eyes to see?

The *Metamorphoses* denies the possibility of any easy, fundamental legitimations, any one-time beginnings or endings. The violence of man's nature will not permit it. You cannot leave Dido behind. She will not oblige by sacrificing the private life, the life of the feelings, to the greater glory of Rome. She will curse you, come after you. Accommodate the life of feeling or you will end up with daughters and granddaughters like Augustus's two Julias. Ovid, then, points to the central Roman weakness, to the lack of a full and balanced interiority, of a rich self. All Ovid's poetry before the exile explores this split, this gap in the center, in one way or the other. It was his obsessive great subject and he embraced it all his poetic life.

Rome had come of age, but Ovid did not want it to adopt the philosophy of governance new and more complex times, a role as world leader, seemed to demand. More rhetoric and less *gravitas* were needed. Augustus was moving the wrong way. A boundary of self-consciousness had to be crossed, certainly, but there were honest and devious, poetic and propagandistic, ways to cross it. Ovid wanted to be honest and Augustus did not. No wonder Augustus banished him. Ovid was caught peeking not into the younger Julia's boudoir but into her grandfather's heart. Augustus was, in his own way, just. Ovid paid a political penalty for a political crime.

Perhaps Ovid was a thinker after all. What shines through his poetry is the desperate sincerity and brilliant penetration of his social vision. Virgil patriotically wrote a eulogistic myth for Rome. Ovid saw the Rome that needed mythologizing. He need not have apologized for the kind of person he was, and we need not apologize for him. Had he not been as he was, he could not have seen what he saw, given us, as he did, the most authentic portrait we have of Augustan Rome and the problems it left to an admiring world.

I have tried to sketch a rhetorical explanation of the *Metamorphoses*. It is adequate, I think, but not complete. What of that hole in the middle? Is there no central principle in the poem? Does anything persist in this poem of endlessly changing tones, motifs, spoofs, and reassertions? *Only the style*. And if we accept this as an allegory for stylistic control, we can begin to see a center forming. It is defined by the stylistic surface. The greatest Ovidian fault, his faultless style, proves to be his greatest triumph, the poem's controlling reference-point. It is style as the endless debunker, and rebunker, of human values which provides the human center of Ovidian reality, Ovidian seriousness. If we are not in direct touch with reality, we do touch language, and with it realities can be examined, discarded, created. With language, much can be done. Ovid, until the exile at least, seems a cheerful man. Surely it came from the confidence, the instinctive psychological certainty, that only a total control of language can bestow. And it was that control which prompted the European poets of the next millennium and a half to return to Ovid for their idea of what poetry meant, what language was for.

3

Games and High Seriousness: Chaucer

With the greatest of Ovid's medieval admirers, Geoffrey Chaucer, confusion of rhetorical with serious premises has again been a central problem. The fundamental issue was first focused, of course, by Matthew Arnold:

> And yet Chaucer is not one of the great classics. His poetry transcends and effaces, easily and without effort, all the romance-poetry of Catholic Christendom; it transcends and effaces all the English poetry contemporary with it, it transcends and effaces all the English poetry subsequent to it down to the age of Elizabeth. . . . And yet, I say, Chaucer is not one of the great classics. He has not their accent. . . . However we may account for its absence, something is wanting, then, to the poetry of Chaucer, which poetry must have before it can be placed in the glorious class of the best. And there is no doubt what that something is. It is the σπουδαιότης, the high and excellent seriousness, which Aristotle assigns as one of the grand virtues of poetry. ["The Study of Poetry," *Essays in Criticism*, 2d series]

I do not say this classification should stand, but with rhetorical and serious reality carefully distinguished, we can at least recognize that Arnold was pointing to a real, isolatable element in Chaucer's poetry. Character, not subject, was Chaucer's handicap. This Arnold was the first to see. We observe Chaucer seizing potentially serious subjects left and right—the matter of Troy, the chivalric confrontation of *The Knight's Tale*, even the pilgrimage—and then using them as vehicles for analysis of human character. His conception of human character consistently prevented him from treating the "high" elements of his potentially "high" subjects—the battles for Troy, the spiritual aspects of the pilgrimage—nearly so fully as the low or private aspects. Even in the midst of the tournament in *The Knight's Tale*, which Chaucer does treat *in extenso*, our main interest is likely to be in character: which knight deserves Emelye more? If literature is really to recapture the high seriousness of religion, then it must put the same intense ethical stress on the individual moral being—on soul, on character—which religion has traditionally placed on it. Character must be a fixed entity. Final, homogeneous, responsible, it is the building block of an ethics of temptation. To Chaucer, however, character was a variable and imperfect, not a final, entity. This attitude toward character, toward what constitutes human identity, and not simply Chaucer's decision to write comedy, was Arnold's real target. Chaucer, Arnold saw, conceived the self in rhetorical rather than serious terms.

Chaucer's conception of society was equally rhetorical. He saw it consistently as a game. A pilgrimage becomes a game of tale telling. A famous love story becomes a self-conscious game of courtly love, a dramatic creation presented as such. Chaucer characteristically chose to imitate a reality frankly rhetorical, a poet-poem-audience triad. The Canterbury pilgrims are not just pilgrims. Each is a poet, each tale a poem performed for the audience of the other pilgrims. Pandarus's job in the *Troilus* is to get each lover to perform properly for the other, while he plays audience as well as stage manager and director. The self imitated is characteristically the performing self, just as Chaucer's own characteristic pose (the lonely scholar, the dreamer, the shy but appreciative pilgrim, the sorrowful reteller of another's tale) is observer, audience of one.

The Chaucerian framing apparatus always creates just the dramatic, rhetorical reality that prohibits serious, single-level experience. Chaucer's final reality is always a context, and his words for context, in this sense, usually come from the group of tropes and schemes which cluster around the concept of "game." I do not know whether, in sheer numbers, Chaucer uses *game*, *play*, and *jape* more than other English poets whose works have been concordanced, but these words appear frequently. And we are dealing, I think, with a subconscious set of mind rather than a definite, self-conscious pattern. Chaucer was predisposed to view the world *sub specie ludi*. Games embody precisely the kind of ambivalent, rhetorical attitude toward seriousness which we find in Chaucer's poetry. They are set apart from life, related only symbolically, detached. They have, as literature does, a special set of rules within which their meaning is created, their life lived. Games, again like poetry, can compel the most intense concentration, can be as serious as anything which serious life affords, and yet run no danger of being confused with it. They offer to the spectator a distinctive combination of delight in the process, in following out the pattern (this, I think, is what Arnold meant when he praised Chaucer's technique, his craftsmanship, and the smoothness of his verse), with strong anxiety about the outcome. The reality of the game is serious, like everyday life, in its concern for the goal or result of behavior, and yet constantly teeters on the edge of the essentially frivolous—the joy of an elaborate series of acts which follow a carefully preordained pattern simply for the fun of it.

What Arnold suspected when he said that Chaucer lacked high seriousness was that life seemed to Chaucer more often than not a series of different games, none of them ultimately real or serious. And even more damaging in Arnold's eyes, one suspects, was the concomitant suspicion that to Chaucer literature was still more of a game than life. This is not to say that Chaucer gave full attention to neither one; within their own different sets of rules each was of the most absorbing interest. Each, and both together, offered the most intense delights one could experience. But the only ultimately serious concern to Chaucer, in the sense in which Arnold used the word, was death itself and what lay behind it. One can restate this two ways, each with its own connotations. Chaucer, by background and temperament, did not take life seriously; he had seen so many styles of life that he found it hard to accredit as serious any single one. Or Chaucer was, surface evidence to the contrary, the most religious of the great English poets.

The Canterbury Tales is not simply a collection of tales organized to present a "God's plenty" panorama of fourteenth-century England, but a series of tales told, in the form of a game, to while away the time on a familiar journey. The pilgrims as sightseers are the least curious on earth, surely. They are not interested in their "real" experience on the way to Canterbury but in their rhetorical adventure in tale telling. Their journey is, to be sure, a serious one, a pilgrimage. But Harry Bailly imposes on it the pastime context of a game. Each pilgrim becomes both poet and player, pilgrim and contestant. The pilgrims constantly move, that is, from a serious to a rhetorical range of motive and back. And so must we. Their tales are for us alternately serious poems and rhetorical ploys. This ambivalence is not, we might note, of the same kind as the comic-serious juxtaposition of *The Knight's Tale* with *The Miller's Tale*, for example, though obviously it will often overlap it.

Chaucer undertakes, then, to show us the way we are to read *The Canterbury Tales*. He has chosen to superpose a rhetorical reality on a serious one and invites us to alternate from one to the other. Here, it seems to me, lies the real center of the famed Chaucerian tolerance. It is not that, either as man or as poet, he seems to have suffered fools especially gladly. It is just that he can hold both rhetorical and serious judgments in his mind at once. Ethically, the Pardoner gets bad marks; rhetorically, good ones. No tolerance is involved, if by that we mean forgiveness. Forgiveness is as serious as goodness or sin. Chaucer's "tolerance" comes from recognizing a wholly different, nonserious range of motive and giving it its due.

Indeed, in *The Canterbury Tales* it is given more than its due. The game context weighs more heavily than the pilgrimage context. Harry Bailly keeps things firmly in the game sphere and salvation looms less immediately than the prize dinner. It is not a comic atmosphere he fosters but a rhetorical one. The tales can be comic or tragic but they must remain tales and they must remain weapons, for the dinner and against boredom.

The interstices of the *Tales* are filled with remarks by Harry Bailly which aim to preserve the overall matrix of a game. He says after the Knight has finished his tale: "For trewely the game

is wel bigonne" (*Miller's Prologue*, l. 3117).[1] Later, in exhorting
the Clerk, he emphasizes the distance the pilgrims as audience
stand from the game: "Telle us som myrie tale, by youre fey! /
For what man that is entred in a pley, / He nedes moot unto the
pley assente" (*Clerk's Prologue*, ll. 9–11). The shifts between
seriousness and game are pointed up in his exchange with gentle
Roger the Cook: " 'But yet I pray thee, be nat wroth for game; / A
man may seye ful sooth in game and pley.' / 'Thou seist ful
sooth,' quod Roger, 'by my fey!' " (*Cook's Prologue*, ll. 4354–56).
The precise meaning here is important: a man may tell the truth,
even in the context of a game. He does not say that games can
turn into serious conflicts. They never do in the *Tales*. The context of game is preserved.

This necessity for unbroken context may tell us something
about the Host's motivation in humiliating the Pardoner. As
long as the Pardoner is telling the pilgrims about his con game
within the established and controlled framework of a set of
flyting tales, no one is offended. Only when he steps over the
barrier between game and life, when he tries to put the game to
work here and now, does the Host use what he must know is the
ultimate weapon against the Pardoner. The Host's exact words
are significant: "I wol no lenger pleye / With thee, ne with noon
oother angry man" (*Pardoner's Tale*, ll. 958–59). The game implies
a certain detachment, an agreement of the pilgrims to assume a
harmony even if they have it not. The Pardoner, in his zeal to
turn a profit, and to pull off a self-confessed fraud, breaks the
game sphere and throws Harry Bailly off balance. So the angry,
serious reply.

The Host does succeed in preserving a decorum consonant
with his somewhat rough-and-ready sense of the socially fitting.
He makes sure the Knight gets the shortest straw, he defers to the
Prioress, he jests with the Monk. We should not forget, though,
that his sense of decorum overlays a well-developed fondness for
games of all sorts. His natural sphere of life is the play sphere,

1. *The Works of Geoffrey Chaucer*, ed. F. N. Robinson, 2d ed. (Boston, 1957). All
subsequent quotations are from this text.

and he is practiced in keeping high spirits in order without dampening them. The seriousness-in-jest excuse he uses to the Cook, he also presses into service in cajoling the "gentles." "Ryde forth, myn owene lord, brek nat oure game" (*Monk's Prologue*, l. 1927), and a few lines later, "But be nat wrooth, my lord," he says to the Monk, "though that I pleye. / Ful ofte in game a sooth I have herd seye!" (ll. 1963–64). Harry Bailly is one of the very few harmonizing forces in a poem filled with pilgrims who have little use for one another. If he cannot make them friends, he at least keeps them from each other's throats. Characteristically, he does this by insisting that they are, after all, playing a game. And though he vows repeatedly that a game can be the vehicle for serious wisdom, he holds that in the last analysis it must still be a game. The matrix must be preserved. Society must remain a game. Harmony depends on it.

Into the matrix Chaucer fits a series of tales which are themselves very like a series of autonomous games. Each has its rules and the rules create a universe of possible meanings and exclude all other possible universes of meanings. Now all games can look silly to those not involved in them, as do all different styles of life, and this is repeatedly Chaucer's point. Surely the search for a "meaning" in *The Knight's Tale*, for example, has suggested this observation again and again. Two alternative games, love and war, are held up for examination. Each illuminates the follies endemic to the other. Theseus, the old warrior who has left love behind, can now laugh at it. He has not yet learned to laugh at war, at ceremonious conflict (though *we* learn to, in *The Miller's Tale*).

In *The Knight's Tale*, Theseus does not speak for the thoughtful reader when he, with the great good humor natural to princes, sardonically comments upon Palamon and Arcite, ankle-deep in blood: "Now looketh, is nat that an heigh folye? / Who may been a fool, but if he love?" (ll. 1798–99). The question Chaucer poses is this: Which attitude toward life is more foolish, Theseus's or the lovers'? Neither one is foolish, he would indicate, given the rules of the particular game in question. To assess character we must look at context. We shall mistake entirely the nature of

Chaucer's seriousness if we assume that his moral judgment precluded tolerance of "courtly love," diffuse and vague a game though it may at times have been. Chaucer did not look at a game, be it habit, genre, life-style or whatever, and first ask, "Is it right or wrong?" This is not his habitual orchestration of conflict. He consistently asks a question leading in precisely the opposite direction: What kind of life does such a pattern lead to? He did answer this question in *The Knight's Tale*—and the moral implied is unmistakable. Whoever better plays the game, bitterness and frustration for somebody will follow. (Which of the heroes better deserves Emelye seems, for this reason, an irrelevant question.) Chaucer is passing an analytic, not an ethical, verdict on the pattern of emulative strife in terms of which Palamon and Arcite choose to pursue the woman of their dreams. The game they play, as Chaucer clearly saw, is zero-sum. That is what is wrong with it. (In a zero-sum game the interests of the two combatants vary inversely; the sum of their two interests is always zero.) One should not, however, generalize this verdict on *The Knight's Tale* too far. Judgment has not been passed on the vanity of human endeavor *in toto*. All games are not zero-sum. The *Troilus* shows this perfectly—while showing also that non–zero-sum games can be fully as painful. But this one happens to be such. The evil of it is that it permits no harmonious solution.

Perhaps the point made about *The Knight's Tale* will become clearer if an analogous one is offered to explain another dominant segment of the *Tales*—*The Wife of Bath's Prologue and Tale*. What to make of Alisoun has always been the question of questions. The answer has been in terms of sex. When she confesses, "For myn entente is nat but for to pleye" (l. 192), we should, I think, understand her to mean, as is very often the case in *The Canterbury Tales*, sexual play. This oldest of games is her game. But it has been increasingly apparent to recent students of Chaucer that her real game is not sex but rhetoric. Logomachy is her vocation; sexual enjoyment a cherished avocation. We do not admire her for the undiscriminating gusto which has brought her to five husbands. It is her skill and versatility as disputant which kindles our (and to an even greater extent, the medieval audience's) interest. When she looks back over her past with such spirit ("But, Lord Crist! whan that it remembreth me . . ."), we admire her not so much for the life she has led as for the "gameness" with which she has led it. When she takes on the masters of the game of rhetoric, the clerks, and beats them, she elicits the admiration due to skill in almost any activity.

Surely this fondness for rhetorical contest drains some of the acrimony from the Wife's struggle with the clerks; the virulence which characterized the antifeminist tradition was, much like the vitriol Sir Thomas More affected in religious disputation, a matter of convention. Here, as in *The Knight's Tale*, the game, not the result, is most important. Perhaps too much has been made of the Wife as the whole race of Eve taking vengeance on a biased conception of womankind. The sovereignty which she earns by hard work she gives away, after all, at the end of her tale, and partly, at least, for the same reason that she had gained it— rhetorical victory. As for doctrine, the *demande* expectation prevails. The debate will be endless; the paradox is permanent; but what fun to argue it all over. The fundamental rewards which love offered in *The Knight's Tale* were not those of lust itself but of the ritualization of lust. So the Wife, though no one would belittle her enjoyment of the opposite sex, enjoys the struggle with the opposite sex still more. She glories in the histrionics of her situation. She enjoys the game because it is a game. This enjoyment is perhaps a surer clue to her longevity in love than her perdurable physical toughness. She will flirt, we know, at eighty.

The Miller's Tale places this primacy of ritual enjoyment beyond reasonable doubt. Granted that Nicholas wants to seduce Alisoun, as the tale presents their encounter getting there is half the fun. A similar purpose animates the tournament in *The Knight's Tale*. Conflict is resolved by ritualizing it, making it more, and more widely, enjoyable. The two tales, as has been often pointed out, are ironically juxtaposed. This juxtaposition fits nicely into our thesis; two kinds of games are compared. One ritual doubtless comments on the other, but in each case ritual is important. What one does seems less important, and less satisfying, than how one does it.

It is *The Clerk's Tale*, though, that most nicely illustrates Chaucer's rhetorical center of gravity. Consider the tale's position in the larger matrix of the *Tales*. It is told by a clerk who is party to a dispute about marriage. The Clerk also stands in a special relationship to the Wife—the concluding stanza of the tale proper alludes to her directly. He must tell a tale that responds to hers, if it does not precisely "quite" it; he must tell a tale which a clerk might decorously tell; he wants, we may reasonably infer, to tell a tale which will demonstrate his wit as formidable and hence earn him a place in the company which his shy demeanor cannot; finally, he reveals in the envoy a desire to demonstrate a manly *savoir faire* most uncharacteristic of the usual quiet clerk. The tale he tells satisfies all these sometimes mutually exclusive demands; here lies its success. That the tale presents an extremely illogical doctrine is regrettable but rhetorically irrelevant. The Clerk can hardly care about this illogicality. The tale has been fully expressive of his purposes. He asks no more. The tale is designed to be many things to many men; it has dramatic significance but no single meaning. Its meaning is the uses to which he puts it, its function in the game. Such an autotelic justification from a good Aristotelian like the Clerk should hardly surprise us.

The Clerk's Tale picks up, first of all, the Wife's gage of challenge, thrown down most obviously when she describes how she treated her clerk, Jankyn. If the Wife is a compendium of all the nightmares a celibate clergy might have about woman, Griselda collects all the elements of their fondest dreams. She is a perfectly inverted image of the Wife: submissively rather than aggressively sexual; well-mannered, not vulgar; patient, not hot-tempered; wholly loyal, not roving of eye; inexpensive to maintain; obedient. Griselda becomes, in fact, the pattern-perfect wife of the *Ménagier de Paris*. Had the two tellers no connection whatever, she would still stand as a rebuke to the Wife, an opposite literary ideal come alive. But the rebuke wears

a clerical gown of mild agreement and sad confirmation. The
Wife jeers that no clerk ever speaks well of women; Griselda
proves her wrong. The meek Clerk refuses to reply in kind;
instead, he offers the other cheek by praising the sex which has
attacked him and by casting aspersions on his own. The Wife
starts out to tell of the woe that is in marriage for woman but
changes this defensive stance to an offensive one by telling of the
hell which marriage can become if husband does not obey wife.
The Clerk again refuses to attack; he tells a story which obligingly
fulfills the Wife's original intention, to demonstrate the woe that
is in marriage for women, even—nay, especially—for the best of
all possible women. The Wife has been roundly rebuked, but so
disarmingly that she cannot reply.

    The Clerk's Tale, read another way, damns the Wife still
further. For Griselda may be the best of women, but she is still a
monster. The Clerk might respond by pleading that he could
hardly carry his idealization of womankind any further. If she
still turns out to be reprehensible, well, the vice of the sex must
be ineradicable. Pushing female virtue to such an extreme does
not, of course, really indicate the Clerk's zeal for fairness. It is a
rhetorical trick. Again as a good Aristotelian, he knows that
virtue is a mean between two extremes. By letting the two extremes fight to a morally repugnant standstill, he implicitly advances his own system of ethics. Thus he expresses his own
opinion under the mask of excessive justice to his opponent.

    The Clerk's Tale appears, as it should, wholly orthodox. It
conveys an unmistakable moral lesson to the pious. The Clerk, as
a religious, should garner praise for his worthy tale as well as for
charitable behavior to the Wife. Both are beyond reproach—
precisely as he intended. And yet he has managed to express his
own attitude toward both the Wife and the orthodox lesson of
obedience his tale teaches. He remains, though, vulnerable to
criticism; he is an ineffectual ivory-tower dreamer teaching a
hopelessly ideal virtue. Not at all, he replies, in assuming still
another attitude toward the story he has told: "This storie is
seyd, nat for that wyves sholde / Folwen Grisilde as in
humylitee, / For it were inportable, though they wolde" (ll.

1142–44). Everyone should just be constant in adversity. He is not naively idealistic, not pushing goodness beyond the limits of common sense and good taste. No, he seems to say, just do the best you can, ladies, and bear up under adversity. This counsel would certainly be acceptable to the company—they had already heard a ponderous version from the Knight, and were to hear a bitter one from the Merchant. The scholar thus becomes a realist, not isolated in the rough-and-tumble of the Canterbury pilgrims, but one of them.

He shows himself willing to go even one step further, and play the role of a sophisticated man of the world: "But o word, lordynges, herkneth er I go: / It were ful hard to fynde now-a-dayes / In al a toun Grisildis thre or two" (ll. 1163–65). There really is no danger from excessively ideal women while the Wife and her sect still dominate the world. Here, at the verge of outright sarcasm he reverses himself completely and affirms that the Wife has really been right all the time. Yes, ladies, he seems to say, I know—even though I am only a clerk—how the world wags. Thus knowledgeable-man-of-the-world emerges as the last pose and the final defense. The Wife's analysis of the marriage predicament is correct. But the Clerk never admits that it is right, for it is correct only because women are like the Wife. Thus the joking admission of defeat is really no admission at all, but rather a final back-of-the-hand at his rhetorical opponent.

All the pilgrims could hardly have seen through all the Clerk's stratagems, taken all his meanings. But enough accepted the different lessons to establish him in the eyes of the group as a clever fellow who for a clerk showed unusual common sense. To the reader, the Clerk reveals himself as a master rhetorician and disputant, a gamesman par excellence. He has satisfied everyone, enhanced his own position, and said precisely what he thought. Only consistency had to be sacrificed. Every listener is offered good arguments for whatever attitude he chooses to take toward it. There are obvious morals for obvious people like Harry Bailly; there are sophistries for those trained to ferret them out. What is Chaucer's, in contradistinction to the Clerk's, final attitude? He doesn't assume one. He offers only a marvelous instance of the clerkly mind at work in its favorite game, rhetorical disputation.

What I have been trying to say about *The Canterbury Tales* as a whole is this. Implicit in the matrix of the *Tales*, in the game on the way to Canterbury, and in Geoffrey Chaucer's detached role within this game, is a characteristic attitude toward human behavior—the rhetorical attitude. We see a gallery of portraits remarkable for their self-consciousness as much as for their diversity. They are all, to one extent or another, trying to play a part, to establish an identity in this particular situation. Chaucer assesses both the morality of the pose adopted and the skill used in adopting it. He is not fooled into taking pose for fundamental identity. Or, to put it another way, he was reluctant to hold the person fully responsible for the pose the circumstances force upon him. He saw too clearly the histrionic element in all human behavior.

If "master of the game" is an apt title for the Host of the *Tales*, it is still more fitting for the "host" of the *Troilus*—Pandarus. Even more than Harry Bailly, he makes things move. The game for which he knows all the rules is, of course, courtly love. In the *Tales* Chaucer is fond of postulating a set of rules and a pair of protagonists and then seeing what would happen. In the *Troilus* he does this, and then makes clear that, without the leaven of Pandarus, nothing at all would happen. The confrontation, potentially, is stillborn. *Troilus and Criseyde* can hardly be styled a glorification of the courtly code. Love triumphs over the code rather than working through it. The code would have been in the poem for those of Chaucer's audience who wished to find it—and it alone—there. But for a reader prepared to receive the poem in its fullness, Pandarus's presence radically compromises the elaborate game of love by setting out to play a new and different game. This, the traditional role of the pander, he manages to intertwine with courtly love throughout the poem. At every point, in other words, the aristocratic game of conflict must be helped along by the bourgeois one of pleasure.

Pandarus, when he forces from Troilus the blushing admission that his love is known to Pandarus, exclaims, "A ha! . . .

here bygynneth game" (1.868). When he comes bearing Troilus's letter, he jokingly says to Criseyde, "Loke alwey that ye fynde / Game in myn hood" (2.1109–10). In the third book he confesses to Troilus his uneasiness at pandering: "For the have I bigonne a gamen pleye, / Which that I nevere do shal eft for other, / Although he were a thousand fold my brother" (ll. 250–52). Troilus himself, just before he faints at Criseyde's bedside, exclaims (not altogether truthfully), "God woot that of this game, / Whan al is wist, than am I nought to blame" (3.1084–85). Her reply, when he comes to his senses, continues the metaphor: "Is this a mannes game? / What, Troilus, wol ye do thus for shame?" (l. 1126–27). She repeats it just before they part: "O herte deere, / The game, ywys, so ferforth now is gon, / That first shal Phebus fallen fro his spere, / . . . Er Troilus out of Criseydes herte" (3.1493–95, 1498). Finally, in book five Troilus replies to Pandarus's reproaches for his sorrow: "I am no thyng to blame, / Syn I have lost the cause of al my game" (ll. 419–20).

Why does Chaucer do this? Why does he continually endanger his serious conclusion by Pandarus's levity? But is it really his serious conclusion that he is endangering, or only our own response to it? Pandarus is in the poem to introduce a countervailing game. With two games going at once, Chaucer must have reasoned, the reader will not enter into either in the wrong spirit. The wrong spirit would here be final commitment to one or the other, rather than final detachment from both. No one, surely, can understand the poem who does not see that it is a comedy fully as much as a tragedy, but it is the game concept that holds the two together.

Troilus and Criseyde unites the games of war, love, and rhetoric, but the last is finally the most important. The poem is rhetorical not only in its use of the flowers of rhetoric, but in its fundamental attitude toward language. Language, in this poem, almost always conceals an ulterior motive. Here again, the conflict between aristocrat and bourgeois pertains. The courtly rhetoric does not work; it does not get Criseyde to Troilus's bed. The bourgeois rhetoric, the rhetorical game of colloquialisms, the rhetoric of the marketplace, does succeed. Thus the puzzling presence of Pandarus at the consummation scene fits completely. It offers two wry observations on the game of courtly love. First, that since the game of love is ritualistic, it demands, not merely tolerates, an audience. Pandarus's presence, in other words, is necessary for the lovers' full enjoyment of one another. Second, that Pandarus, the bourgeois "fixer," the diligent craftsman in human behavior, should by right be allowed to see his handiwork—the fully developed courtly product. Pandarus has as much right to witness the consummation as Lenin had to view the revolution. Again, love triumphs over the code and not through it. For love in this sense is a bourgeois, not an aristocratic, phenomenon which has managed to overcome the elaborate set of aristocratic rules standing between it and consummation, between it and physical pleasure.

If Pandarus stands, then, like the Host in *The Canterbury Tales*, as the controller of games, and hence as the giver of pleasure, where do we place Troilus? He is, according to John Speirs (*Chaucer the Maker*), "the least Chaucerian of the trio." This is a very perceptive remark. Whether a tragic prototype of final commitment to love and life or a silly milksop, Troilus will always be internally consistent. This unwonted straightforwardness prompts Speirs's remark. If we are puzzled by Troilus, he does not, at all events, puzzle us in the same way Criseyde does. His love for her is beyond question, his bravery beyond doubt. For the role of courtly hero, he is a perfect fit. He *is* the role he plays, the central, serious self he embodies. He never sees, around its edges, a series of other roles which, given time and place, he might play. He remains the same Troilus wherever he goes, whatever he does.

The pattern which the three principal characters of the poem trace now stands clear. Troilus has, as few of Chaucer's creations have, a homogeneous identity independent, once it has been formed, of his environment. Love can affect him, yes, but not govern him. There are acts—the important acts, as the poem proves—which not even tortured love can force him to do. Pandarus is more pliable. He can play many roles, but is fooled by none. He has risen above his social environment enough to try to control it but not so much as to renounce its values. His ends are his own but his means determined by society. Criseyde stands at the opposite extreme to Troilus. The essence of her character is that she lets others define it for her. Who is the "real" Criseyde? Surely the troublesome assumption is that there is only one. There will be, Chaucer tells us with infinite regret, as many Criseydes as there are situations in which she finds herself. "Slyding of corage" is not really the crucial set of her behavior. Rather, we should look at the overall pattern of her life. She has had to learn to adapt. She is afraid to stand out from the crowd. Vanity compels her to refrain from hiding, if not to display, her beauty, but otherwise she wants continually to blend into her background. This desire she obeys as resolutely as Troilus obeys the dictates of *trouthe*. She is as true to herself—if we know what we mean by self—as Troilus is.

The tragedy of *Troilus and Criseyde* is not that Troilus loses Criseyde (he ends up in the eighth sphere, after all); and it is not that there are women like Criseyde around to deceive honest men; no, the tragedy emerges when we put the two lovers together, and find a world where such widely disparate attitudes toward the role one plays can coexist, where rhetorical and serious reality live side by side. The tragedy of the poem is fundamentally a social rather than an individual tragedy, then; it emerges from a consideration of the characters as types. Society, Chaucer tells us, can create such different types as these three and put them together. When it does, there will be inevitable anguish, inevitable waste. Such waste is built into the way society creates us. The conflict of rhetorical and serious identity is fundamental to the way we become what we are.

Troilus and Criseyde is, then, neither Aristotelian nor medieval tragedy. Both these types, and their Shakespearean variant, are tragic types of individual assertion. They are created by a society as forms of social control. "If you step out of line," they say, "here is what will happen." They aim, finally, at conformity. This is less obviously true of the Aristotelian type than the medieval, but still true of both. The tragedy Chaucer offers in *Troilus and Criseyde* pictures an inevitable waste of human spirit wholly within the social context. Troilus is no rebel. He has no illegitimate ambitions. He searches, finally, like Criseyde and like Pandarus, for pleasure. And yet his suffering is saved from pathos, because it is universalized. He reenacts a universal pageant of waste and shame. Chaucer has written, not a tragedy of a human person, but the tragedy of human personality.

To talk of "forgiving" Criseyde, then, is to apply serious coordinates to a rhetorical character. The Middle Ages, oddly enough, would have been less likely to make this mistake than the twentieth century. To insist on a rhetorical identity for Criseyde corrects an anachronism. For the Middle Ages, human character was first and foremost typical and social. A character would behave as the situation called for. Identity was to a large extent determined by the game one played. One's alternatives in a particular game, or series of probability calculations, are offered by the game, not by the player. All that is asked for from the player is a goal, and hence a willingness to play. The game will do the rest. This is a simplified synecdoche for human behavior but not fundamentally erroneous. We have seen, in *The Canterbury Tales*, that approaches to the poem through context—that is, through situations of conflict—are more promising than approaches through character analysis traditionally conceived. For situations of conflict generate a rhetorical concept of character.

The main battle over *The Canterbury Tales* has been, I suppose, between those who look upon the *Tales* as drawn primarily from life and those who find them drawn from literature. The metaphor of game combines the two. If we look upon life as a series of overlapping games, and ourselves as players shifting from one to the other as required, we can see that Chaucer, equipped with the same perception, could synthesize his patterns, his games, as the *Tales* certainly are, equally well from life as from art. The boundary between the two was continually blurred.

We can, perhaps, make a contribution to the solution of a second hoary paradox. Are Chaucer's characters "realistic" or frankly allegorical? Neither. They work very hard, as we do, at being the types society demands that they be. They are "real" in the sense that Chaucer has created, self-consciously, a series of characters most of whom are themselves self-consciously attempting to be "types" of one kind or another. Their attempt is organized and their goal is set by whatever game Chaucer chooses to engage them in.

Chaucer is not, then, a poet of high seriousness. Arnold was right. For high seriousness (and the serious tragedy which *Troilus and Criseyde* is not) requires a conception of human character as single, solid, substantial, and important. And the harder Chaucer looked at human behavior (and he was, after Shakespeare, the most profound student of society, and especially of social structure, which any literature offers us), the harder it became for him to sustain that conception of character which a philosophy of high seriousness requires. Human personality was the very opposite of single, solid, or substantial. It emerged from the social situation as a fragile growth which, like Troilus's Criseyde, withered as soon as the supporting social context was removed. Oncé a poet has become acutely aware of the *poseur* in all of us, indeed that often we are little else, it is difficult for him to be other than a rhetorical poet. For a medieval poet blessed with such awareness high seriousness was not difficult: it was impossible. The rhetorical vision would inevitably marry the religious vision. Nothing beneath heaven is really serious. And, the poet sees, even the most serious of sufferings look droll from another angle. From the heavenly perspective, from the eighth sphere, we are doubtless all fools. But we don't really need the heavenly perspective; the conclusion can come as easily from a plurality of earthly viewpoints. This plurality Chaucer's detachment gave him. He could generalize from suffering because he could generalize from strife. Both, he might say, are endemic to life, to the way human personality is created and sustained. And because he saw beyond personality to the way it was formed—because he saw society as a game and us as players—he could not hold human personality with ultimate seriousness. Suffering, too, was but an interim reality; high seriousness too limited an attitude toward human life—not, finally, serious enough.

4

The Ovidian Shakespeare:
Venus and Adonis *and* Lucrece

Shakespeare's two narrative poems, *Venus and Adonis* and *Lucrece*, are both masterpieces in the old sense of the word—pieces made by an artist to prove he is a master. The masterpiece, as a genre, emerges more naturally from the rhetorical view of life than from the serious. Self-conscious display and scoring carry no stigma there, nor does a self-consciously rhetorical style. And the poem as private gesture toward a particular place and time, rhetorical as well as poetical act, occurs there as a matter of course. It makes symbiotic sense that both Shakespeare's masterpiece gestures are poems *about* rhetorical identity and the strategies of rhetorical style. Lucrece's selfish, and Venus's flamboyant, eloquence finds a parallel in the poet's. Shakespeare thus offers a paradigm of stylistic sincerity, knows and confesses what he is doing, whereas Lucrece does not. Shakespeare often describes and exemplifies at the same time; he writes about the form he writes in. So with *Venus and Adonis* and *Lucrece:* poems about the rhetoric of display, about the motives of eloquence. If we ask *what* Shakespeare displays, we must answer, human motive as essentially dramatic and feeling as largely social, realized in public enactment. In both *Venus and Adonis* and *Lucrece* Shakespeare is the opposite of frivolous. A didact just like Ovid. Both poems are poems of statement. In addition to identity and eloquence, Shakespeare seems in both to be trying to sort out sexuality's relation to metaphor. He wants to close the circle, show that if passion often appropriates the feudal metaphors, they in turn can play under the mask of passion. Perhaps he concludes that passion is by nature—by the need for metaphor—doomed to narcissism, that a psychic superstructure will always preponderate over the passion it is metaphor's business to create. *Venus and Adonis* and *Lucrece* show, then, Shakespeare coming to terms with the moral implications of being a dramatist. If, as William James said in *The Principles of Psychology*, as often as not we grow angry because we strike and not vice versa, the playwright is in on the genesis of morality at least half the time. It is a theme to which Shakespeare repeatedly returned.

The fundamental relationship of *Venus and Adonis* and *Lucrece* lies in their concern with motive. The beginning premise of *Venus and Adonis* is comic and rhetorical, that of *Lucrece* tragic and serious; they both arrive at the same rhetorical conception of identity and motive. Taken together they argue, like Socrates at the end of the *Symposium*, that the same poet can write both tragedy and comedy. Perhaps this submerged aphorism forms part of Shakespeare's advertisement for himself.

I

Venus and Adonis did for Shakespeare what he asked of it. It made his name as a genteel Ovidian. Whether it does for us what he wanted remains less certain. For what Shakespeare wished above all to demonstrate was his mastery of the Ovidian tone, the complex, self-conscious attitude toward literary rhetoric, and it is just here that *Venus and Adonis* tends to blur for us. Its highly polished rhetorical surface has embarrassed and confused Shakespeareans ever since the poem resurfaced at the end of the eighteenth century. "As we read on," C. S. Lewis tells us in *English Literature in the Sixteenth Century*, "we become more and more doubtful how the work ought to be taken." Take the rhetoric seriously and we confront an overcooked eroticism which has offended as much as it has titillated. Viewing the rhetoric rhetorically yields ironic comedy. The serious and the rhetorical reader confront different kinds of rhetoric and rhetorical expectation, one might almost say different poems.

I would like to suggest a third poem, a poem about the relation of the two patterns of expectation and their attitudes toward language. Shakespeare deliberately, and intricately, juxtaposes the two. Adonis argues for virtue but symbolizes death; Venus speaks the lines of literary temptress but symbolizes life, hope, the future. Their relation is composed not of a single antithesis but of two conflicting ones, one dramatic, the other ethical. Shakespeare superposes these two contradictory antitheses to call attention to a large Ovidian gap in the middle. Venus's argument proceeds on a physical, explicitly sexual basis; Adonis's case is as conceptual, moral, and philosophical as Venus's is physical. The poem observes man's comic inability to connect the two spheres. It needs a Pandarus. No one speaks for common sense. Ordinary affection is unrepresented. The antithetical structure succeeds here very well. We are invited to posit a complex middle ground ourselves, to make common sense out of sex, out of a role-reversal where the woman exhibits voracious male appetite unavailingly to a feminine cold male. Shakespeare so exalts both imaginative love and unimaginative virtue that neither can touch the other.

Venus and Adonis represent not only antithetical rhetorics but antithetical attitudes toward rhetoric as well. Unlike Venus, Adonis does not let poetry fool him, does not fool himself, but he cannot understand poetry either. Beauty is blind to beauty. Venus can create her golden world, serve as genetrix of eloquence, but she pays a price for her sight just as Adonis does for his blindness. She can be carried away by her own feeling, by her own passion, just because she can express it, to herself and to others, so well. Again our attention is drawn to the middle ground between the antitheses. A reader is required whose involvement with language is sophisticated but not blinding. Adonis's distance must somehow marry Venus's eloquence. A steady self-consciousness about language must be preserved. We must always look at the stylistic surface before we look through it. At stake are moral as well as aesthetic concerns, for our moral judgment in the poem is at the outset a rhetorical one. As in all true tragicomedy, we must become expert in a rhetorical universe before we can enter a moral one. The poem is obviously about sex. The poem is, not so obviously, about the rhetoric of sex, about the symbolic structures we build on sex. If sex is a moral problem, to get at it we must first traverse a rhetorical problem. To get at the feeling, we must traverse the language which both expresses and creates it.

And the language almost always stands at odds with plot, characterization, or both. The faddish sexual role-reversal in the poem creates its comedy largely by disenfranchising its Petrarchan rhetoric. Venus, Dame Rhetoric, plays an eloquent Petrarchan aggressor such as the world has seldom seen:

> Were I hard-favored, foul, or wrinkled old,
> Ill-nurtured, crooked, churlish, harsh in voice,
> O'erworn, despisèd, rheumatic, and cold,
> Thick-sighted, barren, lean and lacking juice
>   Then mightst thou pause, for then I were not for thee;
>   But having no defects, why dost abhor me?
>
> [ll. 133–38][1]

Against such exhortation, Adonis can offer, after a long opening silence, only a maidenly "Fie, no more of love! / The sun doth burn my face—I must remove." Now such role-reversal creates spontaneous humor and spontaneous self-consciousness about language, from the sheer incongruity of the thing. Poets can triumph over this handicap—witness Camilla or perhaps Britomart—but these reversals portray woman in man's role. It proves much harder the other way round. Male chastity has always been something of a joke, never more, one would think, than at the court of Elizabeth.

Venus's behavior calls her language into question in yet another way. Her *carpe diem* arguments and their lush orchestration fit her, as Protean temptress, perfectly. Yet they fit not at all the strapping, energetic virago who snatches Adonis from his horse and effortlessly pins him to the ground. Nor the predatory Venus established by the imagery, the "empty eagle, sharp by

---

1. Ed. Richard Wilbur, in *William Shakespeare: The Complete Works,* gen. ed. Alfred Harbage, Pelican text revised (Baltimore, 1969). All subsequent quotations of Shakespeare's poems and plays in this book are from the Pelican edition; hereafter only specific editors' names will be cited.

fast" (l. 55). Decorum and indecorum are mixed in equal parts. Male aggressiveness is given to the female, but she keeps the rhetoric of temptation. Adonis retains the rhetoric of virtue, but is awarded the characterization of blushing maiden. When Venus propositions him with a favorite double entendre (" 'Fondling,' she saith, 'since I have hemmed thee here / Within the circuit of this ivory pale, / I'll be a park, and thou shalt be my deer' " [ll. 229–31]), Adonis "smiles as in disdain," his maiden ears are too tender, and the dimples which come hard upon his smirk more maidenly still. To Venus's eagle, he plays a divedapper who "being looked on, ducks as quickly in" (ll. 86–87). When he blushes, it is the "maiden burning of his cheeks" (l. 50) Venus must quench with her tears. Shakespeare plays with our pattern of expectation: right lines, right characters, wrong sexes.

The indecorum intensifies, the rhetoric becomes yet more opaque, when Shakespeare superposes a maternal relationship on Venus and Adonis. Venus as dramatic character reminded C. S. Lewis uncomfortably of the big, blowzy women who kissed him too moistly when he was a child. His sense of literary association was, as always, acute. Venus is bigger than Adonis, stronger, older, treats him as a child—her child. She plucks him from his horse, pushes him to the ground and, by locking "her lily fingers one in one," she keeps him in the desired position. Adonis is young, callow, by his own admission "green," easily upset, afraid of love: "Lest the deceiving harmony should run / Into the quiet closure of my breast; / And then my little heart were quite undone" (ll. 781–83). Deep into the love hunt, Adonis, in a series of reductive metaphors, metamorphoses from prey to favorite child:

> Hot, faint, and weary with her hard embracing,
> Like a wild bird being tamed with too much handling,
> Or as the fleet-foot roe that's tired with chasing,
> Or like the froward infant stilled with dandling,
>   He now obeys and now no more resisteth. . . .
>   [ll. 559–63]

He is dependent, managed, childlike. Venus, playing anxious mother, rushes to find him at the real hunt, "like a milch doe whose swelling dugs do ache / Hasting to feed her fawn hid in some brake" (ll. 875–76).

Venus, in the imagery, becomes a mythic, not a dramatic, character, Venus Genetrix. Her body is the bawdy old earth itself, the park for an Adonis, with its sweet bottom grass, rising hillocks, and brakes obscure. She is the cause, as the embodiment, of infinite desire. Adonis moves mythward too but, from Venus's point of view, plays Narcissus as much as Adonis:

> Is thine own heart to thine own face affected?
> Can thy right hand seize love upon thy left?
> Then woo thyself, be of thyself rejected;
> Steal thine own freedom, and complain on theft.
> Narcissus so himself himself forsook.
> And died to kiss his shadow in the brook.
> [ll. 157–62]

As myth normally has it, Adonis must cooperate with Venus to fructify the world. Shakespeare, by making him balk, dislocates our mythic expectation as well.

Both Venus and Adonis play still another role—disputants. Venus does not rape Adonis; she argues with him. Adonis, unable to flee, argues back. The arguments of each do, and do not, fit their characters. Venus, as pagan goddess, can legitimately advance the doctrine of increase which she, like the first seventeen sonnets, preaches: "Torches are made to light, jewels to wear, / Dainties to taste, fresh beauty for the use" (ll. 163–64). So Venus should speak. But what about the virago aggressor? For her, this is merely a gambit, a rhetorical stratagem, a reach of the poet in all lovers. When it seems to fail, she tries taunting Adonis (ll. 211–16) with his cold asexuality. And after that comes the last of female rhetorical gestures, heartbreaking sobs. After a while she returns to her idle overhandled theme ("So in thyself thyself art made away"), and Adonis is right to rebuke her, "O strange excuse, / When reason is the bawd to lust's abuse!" (ll. 791–92). Yet he is hardly the man (if that is the word) to advance it. As Narcissus, he might argue thus with fitness. But for the naive boy in need of guidance, for the minnow and green plum ("Before I know myself, seek not to know me. / No fisher but the ungrown fry forbears. / The mellow plum doth fall, the green sticks fast, / Or being early plucked is sour to taste" [ll. 525–28]), such moralizing sounds like shallow, copybook wisdom. Listen to the parrotlike tone of his catechism:

> Love comforteth like sunshine after rain,
> But Lust's effect is tempest after sun.
> Love's gentle spring doth always fresh remain;
> Lust's winter comes ere summer half be done.
> Love surfeits not, Lust like a glutton dies;
> Love is all truth, Lust full of forgèd lies.
>
> [ll. 799–804]

Exactly so. His rhetoric is shallow too, "The text is old, the orator too green." He wants only to get back to the hunt. The argument of each fits his and her mythic characters (Narcissus and Venus). For their dramatic characters, each argument is equally insincere, equally irrelevant.

Dramatic characterization, then, is only part of the story. Both Venus and Adonis have a mythic character too, and a rhetoric queasily in between. The whole character of each encloses a paradoxical, inconsistent, comic combination of all three. Shakespeare has imitated man acting, man talking, man talking about acting, man's acting as being largely talk ("Your treatise makes me like you worse and worse" [l. 774]). The rhetoric of the poem has been dramatized, made part of the story, Venus a Venus Genetrix of words. Adonis is short not only on deeds, but on words. When Venus explodes with surprise at a sudden burst of speech from the hero, we share her feelings: " 'What! canst thou talk?' quoth she. 'Hast thou a tongue?' " (l. 427). So much of the poem's action is talk that the two blend in our minds, we confuse resolute action with volubility. To talk well is to be alive, to see, hear, feel. To all of these, serious, inarticulate Adonis is insensitive. Venus really creates with her own praise the Adonis who can represent beauty. She creates herself with her own praise. She creates the significance of Adonis's death by her descriptive sorrow. She creates everything. Her eloquence dominates the poem. Only she can give meaning, not only to her desire for Adonis, but to his for the boar. Her poetic powers in the poem stand as synecdoche for her fructifying powers in the world.

Coleridge, in chapter fifteen of the *Biographia,* emphasizes Shakespeare's detachment from his poem, "the utter aloofness of the poet's own feelings." But Shakespeare's voice in the poem, the narrator, portrays not so much aloofness as neutrality, a position amidships the bathos and pathos, a careful trimming. Look at the first stanza in the poem:

> Even as the sun with purple-colored face
> Had ta'en his last leave of the weeping morn,
> Rose-cheeked Adonis hied him to the chase.
> Hunting he loved, but love he laughed to scorn.
>   Sick-thoughted Venus makes amain unto him
>   And like a bold-faced suitor 'gins to woo him.

The first two lines belong to the neutral ground of the poem's action; the next two (especially in the simpering chiasmus of line four) to the adolescent Adonis; the last two, to the cosmic Venus. The narrator gives everyone his due, keeps his distance, lets the reader sort the indecorums out. The smooth stylistic surface forms part of this distancing strategy. It is brilliant. It reflects. We see in it the premises we bring to it.

The narrator makes of his own cleverness a defense. He does not, as mask for Shakespeare, speak straightforwardly any more than Venus and Adonis. To preoccupy ourselves with "Shakespeare's" feelings, to apply the litmus paper of sincerity, we must examine the whole poem, the interaction of the three rhetorics comprising it. Adonis has his point of view. Venus hers, which contradicts it. We may think hers the more comprehensive, or his. What does the narrator think of Venus and Adonis? The careful centrality of his diction makes it impossible to tell.

> Forced to content, but never to obey,
> Panting he lies and breatheth in her face.
> She feedeth on the steam as on a prey
> And calls it heavenly moisture, air of grace,
>   Wishing her cheeks were gardens full of flowers,
>   So they were dewed with such distilling showers.
>   [ll. 61–66]

The narrator calls the scene as he sees it. Adonis pants and breathes in Venus's face and she makes of it heavenly moisture, air of grace. He shows no signs of noticing that after the second line we notice a change in tone. He is deaf to tone though he faithfully reports it; he can mirror but he cannot comprehend. What does the narrator think of Venus and Adonis? He does not think at all.

What do we think of him? He possesses a rich poetic power but no judgment to go with it. To him Shakespeare has lent his pen but not his mind. Such a divorce, perfect though it is for a satire of love and love's language, has caused serious misunderstanding. The narrator's view has been thought Shakespeare's. *Venus and Adonis* is a complex rhetorical structure to which sincerity supplies the wrong entry. The complaints about insincerity show the need to discriminate the three rhetorics of the poem, describe what each does, and specify their relationship. The narrator is Ovidian indeed. He springs surprises on us in the couplet. He condenses within the line by chiasmus, ploce, polyptoton. He models sense in syntax. He describes both Venus and Adonis with the tone appropriate to each. Thus a constantly shifting decorum is preserved. Shakespeare sees all three characters and beyond, arranges the comic juxtapositions, remains— like Ovid—completely in control. Far from being infatuated with rhetoric, he fashions a mature satire in which it becomes a principal target.

The poem's comedy tempts us to deny it any seriousness whatever, to blunt its pathos, render it a perfect trifle, Shakespeare's comedy of language. But the comedy does not explain or explain away the pathos of Adonis's death. If Shakespeare had in mind straightforward romantic comedy, why choose such a story as that of Venus and Adonis? And, having chosen it, why expatiate upon the "trembling ecstasy" Venus undergoes before and during the boar hunt? Why, instead of romantic comedy's redemption of love, offer his story as exemplum for the future horrors of love? Still more, why couch those horrors in cosmic terms? "For he being dead, with him is beauty slain, / And, beauty dead, black chaos comes again" (ll. 1019–20). If tone guides us in the poem, tone here has changed. Why include such pathos only to cancel it?

The poem is usually read as an allegory of lust (Venus) and love (Adonis). But the rhetoric of Adonis is as compromised as that of Venus, and his characterization a banner beneath which virtue could not fight, at least not for long. Serious ethical allegory just does not work. Yet the arguments of both Venus and Adonis may be serious for us if not for them. Each uses arguments as rhetorical stratagems, but must we not still consider them as arguments? The plain sense of the story as exemplum supports Venus. She argues, pleads, sighs, and groans that Adonis's brand of virtue is suicidal, narcissistic. However virtuous, it can end only in death. It does. The boar makes love to Adonis in the role of maidenly chastity he had chosen.

> 'Tis true, 'tis true! thus was Adonis slain:
> He ran upon the boar with his sharp spear,
> Who did not whet his teeth at him again,
> But by a kiss thought to persuade him there;
>   And nuzzling in his flank, the loving swine
>   Sheathed unaware the tusk in his soft groin.
>
>   [ll. 1111–16]

This is Venus talking, of course. She imagines how she might have done the thing, had role-reversal really taken place. But he does get killed. Narcissism is punished. Such narrative logic reverses the moralizing rhetoric. Venus seems sympathetic, Adonis callow, their arguments unfelt gambits. But we are also meant to weigh the arguments of each as arguments, meant to award Adonis conventional wisdom, Venus only plain license. We are also meant to follow a narrative logic which proves conventional wisdom disastrous.

What, then, of Venus's prophecy? It follows neither the old, un-Shakespearean myth, in which Adonis must be slain that the earth may bloom, nor the new Shakespearean version, which makes him Narcissus. Because Adonis is dead, Venus argues, love shall be accursed:

> Since thou art dead, lo, here I prophesy
> Sorrow on love hereafter shall attend.
>
> . . . .
>
> It shall be fickle, false, and full of fraud,
> Bud and be blasted in a breathing while.
>
> . . . .
>
> It shall be raging mad and silly mild,
> Make the young old, the old become a child.
>
> [ll. 1135–36, 1141–42, 1151–52]

But this describes the love affair we have already seen! So Venus
herself found fate's last best joke when she fell for Adonis. The
"prophecy" stands ridiculously at odds with the narrative. What
she maintains that Adonis's death has caused—the sweet-and-
sour dish of love—she had already felt while Adonis lived, felt
because Adonis was what he was. Adonis alive caused precisely
what, she tells us, his death is going to bring on.

The allegory of Adonis's death seems clear. He is punished for
an empty heart. The allegory of what follows his death is equally
clear. Venus embodies love pagan and innocent. Adonis is not
tempted by her at all. He has fallen before the poem begins.
Self-love, in such a pagan context, resembles original sin. It is
simply there. We do not see Satan falling. We see him fallen.
(That Adonis presses the rhetoric of virtue into service hardly
surprises us; it is fallen man's favorite weapon.) After the poem
has reenacted this fall, this rencontre between spontaneous,
natural affection and narcissistic, suicidal self-containment, we
see what is to follow. But "to follow" means what has happened
in the poem, too, since Shakespeare cannot imitate the change
from innocence to self-love any more than Milton can imitate
Satan falling. After one such love affair there is no course for
Venus but to make her way back home through the empty sky.
There is no place for her here. But why does she say love is
accursed *because* Adonis has died? No reading of the poem
seems to make sense of this. If Adonis is beauty he has not
deserved to die. And beauty need not die with him, unless it is a
cold and self-sufficient beauty (in which case we are back to the

allegory just sketched). And that beauty need not *always* be cold, Venus herself, warm and beautiful, proves.

Venus speaks possessed by love. She says the right thing but for the wrong reason. Rhetoric stands once more at odds with plot. Venus deceives herself. We are wrenched back again to the literal level of the poem. Venus is in love, and when her love is taken from her, there is nothing left for her. But this is not true for us; Adonis was not to us what he was to her. Beauty is not dead for us. Our perspective remains detached. Venus's tragedy is not shared, not cosmic. Thus we participate in the serious allegory of the poem, but not as Venus does. We stand at a distance. For Venus, the boar has stolen the beauty of the universe. For us, self-love has perished but love and beauty have not. That we cannot adopt either Venus's perspective or Adonis's does not mean that we cannot have one of our own.

We return to the problem of kind, what type of tragicomedy *Venus and Adonis* is, what kind of seriousness it may be said to possess. Chaucer, at the end of the *Troilus,* can make Troilus laugh because the proud, final individuality of man which makes tragedy possible seemed to him not final at all. The basis of human individuality was first social and dramatic, then, in a single and final leap, divine. *Venus and Adonis* puts these two selves together in one poem, makes their confrontation the over-arching allegory of the poem. Adonis embodies the central self tragedy demands. Venus, in urging him to "be prodigal," urges him to be not simply another person but another kind of person. "So in thyself thyself art made away." The maxim gathers in upon itself just as Adonis does. The exhortation to use up the essence of himself, to lend the world his light, really pleads that true individuality is social, that to gain one's individuality one must lose it. Venus plays the antitype, the comic role-player whose identity changes from context to context. She has—is she not the Goddess of Love?—as many selves as there are lines to speak, roles to play. In the way Adonis requires it, she can never be serious. She would, like Criseyde, have to change her self, become another *kind* of character. So would the poem, if it were to profess seriousness. By its insistent role-reversal, it refuses to do so; it remains within rhetorical coordinates. It teaches seriously, but what it teaches is the suicidal incompleteness of seriousness, of the tragic Adonis-like self. It questions, too, the honesty of un–self-conscious language, the neutral style of ethical instruction. The poem possesses, then, the peculiar serious/ rhetorical ambivalence toward character and language characteristic of Chaucer's poetry and Ovid's. If we are tempted to call *Venus and Adonis* a tragicomedy, it is because Shakespeare's poem invites us to flesh out this generic neuter with an older and deeper ambivalence.

II

The Rape of Lucrece seems the "graver labor" promised Southampton in the dedication to *Venus and Adonis*. It appeared a year later (1594) at any rate, and no one has ever questioned its gravity. The two poems ask to be grouped together: Shakespeare's only narratives, his only "dedicated" polite poems, both seen through the press with care, both Ovidian *epyllia*, show-off diploma pieces short on action but long on speeches, intensely rhetorical in their verbal polish, both dealing with sexual passion and beauty in compulsively antithetical ways, both preoccupied with two central figures, unified in time (one takes a day, the second a night), both gestures of social courtship toward an aristocratic patron, both products—if really written during the plague years—of the only leisure Shakespeare was to know until retirement, and both directed to an aristocratic audience habituated to such leisure. In some respects they seem complementary; one a mythical subject and one historical; woman as sexual aggressor (mock-rape) in one and man (real rape) in the other. But finally more important are the antithetical tones of the two. The problem *Venus and Adonis* presents is how take it, in what spirit to read. There is nothing like this in *Lucrece*; no bawdy punning, no sex, a pitilessly serious tone, plenty of moral platitudes. The question here is why the world master of double plotting pitched his tent on such solemn ground. As in the earlier poem, nothing happens except the focal incidents. Preparing for these and following them comes a great deal of heavy speechifying about motive. It seems logical to conclude that *Lucrece* explores the motives for these two ultimately serious acts. Let us assume as a premise: a poem about serious motive, also a poetic and rhetorical masterpiece, however cloying to the modern palate. Manifestly an act of courtship, *Lucrece* may also preface the plays somehow. What does it say about motive? What magisterial poetic powers does it demonstrate? What gesture of courtship does it embody? And what, if any, relation does it bear to the plays to follow? Or toward its Ovidian twin sister?

The prose argument, which represents a reasonable conflation of Ovid's version with Livy's, does not reflect the Shakespearean version it prefaces. This has puzzled commentators into obelizing it as non-Shakespearean or at least betraying Shakespeare's impatience with detail. But neither *Venus and Adonis* nor *Lucrece* betrays signs of haste. Just the opposite. Maybe the discrepancies form part of the poem, an intended juxtaposition between the received version of the story and the version Shakespeare chooses to tell. The prose argument does not skimp the poem's argument. It is, if anything, fuller. But a page of argument and eighteen hundred lines of poem; does this not indicate a Shakespeare less interested in event than in motivation for event, in exploding an historical moment for analytic purposes? The first difference between argument and poem concerns Tarquin's motive. The story has him falling for Lucrece when he and his messmates post home to check on their wives and he *sees* her. "Forma placet," Ovid tells us, "niueusque color flauique capilli" (*Fasti* 2.763). Livy adds her chastity as an attraction ("cum forma tum spectata castitas incitat" [1.57]), a detail Shakespeare borrows for the poem but not for the argument. But in Shakespeare's pamphlet "without beginning," as the dedication calls it, Tarquin falls in love from report only. The husbands' quick trip home is left out. Not beauty but *envy* stimulates Tarquin to ultimate rashness. The poem's opening strategy drives the point home. The first stanza surprises Tarquin in full cry: "From the besiegèd Ardea all in post, / Borne by the trustless wings of false

desire, / Lust-breathèd Tarquin leaves the Roman host. . . ."
Having set a rapist malignity thus loose on the world, the narrator in the second stanza starts guessing at what motivates him:
"Haply that name of 'chaste' unhap'ly set / This bateless edge on
his keen appetite. . . ." Livy's secondary motive becomes primary. Collatine had, most unwisely in our moralizing narrator's
eye, been bragging about his good fortune, "the possession of
his beauteous mate." Tarquin, that is, does not fall in love. He
comes to envy a possession. The narrator asks, "What needeth
then apologies be made / To set forth that which is so singular?"
(ll. 31–32). Not so otiose a question as it seems. We come to learn
that in this poem unpublished things don't exist. But here the
question interrogates the prose argument. What kind of man
bets on his wife's virtue, makes a public trial of it? In one of the
abrupt discontinuities this poem depends on, the narrator goes
on to answer, not this question, but the previous one, Tarquin's
motive: "Perchance his boast of Lucrece' sov'reignty / Suggested
this proud issue of a king; / For by our ears our hearts oft tainted
be" (ll. 36–38). The OED first listing for "sov'reignty" as
"Supremacy or pre-eminence in respect of excellence or efficacy"
is for 1340, and the last 1610. This slightly antique sense calls
attention to itself. Tarquin is stimulated, we are asked to specu-
late, by an entirely symbolic, indeed *ludic,* motivation. He wants
to rape Lucrece *because* she is preeminent in virtuous woman-
hood. Debauching here must be the essence of rape. The narrator
hastens from this sick motive to one slightly less despicable:
"Perchance that envy of so rich a thing / Braving compare, dis-
dainfully did sting / His high-pitched thoughts" (ll. 39–41).
Envy and jealousy of rank, if less vile, are still bloodless motives,
entirely symbolic. They have nothing to do with sex. They are
the best the narrator can do, however, since Shakespeare has so
pointedly removed the obvious motive—sight of the beloved.
The narrator, as third guess, just gives up: "But some untimely
thought did instigate / His all too timeless speed, if none of
those" (ll. 43–44). When Tarquin arrives at Collatium, we might
expect a little flesh-and-blood feeling. Not at all. An allegorical
background is described:

But Beauty, in that white entitulèd,
From Venus' doves doth challenge that fair field.
Then Virtue claims from Beauty Beauty's red,
Which Virtue gave the Golden Age to gild
Their silver cheeks, and called it then their shield,
    Teaching them thus to use it in the fight,
    When shame assailed, the red should fence the white.
                                                    [ll. 57–63]

The sense is deliberately hard to follow. We must stop and puzzle it out: red and white, when he looks at her, change to gold and silver. Red and white stand halfway between flesh tone and symbolic value, and his gaze moves them entirely into symbol. The next stanza admits to the poem's surface what we had already privately acknowledged (another habit of this poem). Tarquin sees in Lucrece's face a *heraldic crest:* "This heraldry in Lucrece' face was seen, / Argued by Beauty's red and Virtue's white" (ll. 64–65). If this poem were really about passion, we should be by now knee-deep in feudal metaphor, Lucrece's face lit up like an allegorical light show:

This silent war of lilies and of roses
Which Tarquin viewed in her fair face's field,
In their pure ranks his traitor eye encloses;
Where, lest between them both it should be killed,
The coward captive vanquishèd doth yield
    To those two armies that would let him go
    Rather than triumph in so false a foe.
                                                    [ll. 71–77]

Again the sense is hard to follow, the imagery not. Tarquin sees the same complex of motives the narrator had just guessed at. We don't see Lucrece at all. We see her beauty and virtue translated into their feudal equivalents. We see a mind which thinks in heraldic pageants. Tarquin's "lust" has nothing to do with sex and, finally, nothing to do with Lucrece. It is entirely narcissistic, made up wholly of self, and this self is built up of clustered feudal images, images so frequent in the first half of the poem as to seem less excessive than obsessive.

While Tarquin lies thinking on the great treasure yet to gain,
the narrator treats us to a digression on greed and envy less
relevant to sexual passion even than Tarquin's revolving
thought.

> Those that much covet are with gain so fond
> That what they have not, that which they possess,
> They scatter and unloose it from their bond,
> And so, by hoping more, they have but less;
> Or, gaining more, the profit of excess
>   Is but to surfeit, and such griefs sustain
>   That they prove bankrout in this poor rich gain.
>
> The aim of all is but to nurse the life
> With honor, wealth, and ease in waning age;
> And in this aim there is such thwarting strife
> That one for all, or all for one we gage:
> As life for honor in fell battle's rage;
>   Honor for wealth; and oft that wealth doth cost
>   The death of all, and all together lost;
>
> So that in vent'ring ill we leave to be
> The things we are for that which we expect;
> And this ambitious foul infirmity,
> In having much, torments us with defect
> Of that we have: so then we do neglect
>   The thing we have; and, all for want of wit,
>   Make something nothing by augmenting it.
>
> [ll. 134–54]

The meditation bears less on the vanity of human wishes than on
the ironies of possession. It is not that we fail but that success,
and the striving for it, destroy the self. "We leave to be / The
things we are." Not the things we *have* but the things we *are*. The
something we make nothing is our *self*. We spend our youth
preparing for a waning age of honor, wealth, and ease which will
be spent looking back on a youth spent looking forward to the
time when we will look back. Honor, wealth, and ease add up to a
definition of aristocratic *otium*, and Shakespeare points out the

inevitable internal contradictions such a definition contains. But what has this to do with Tarquin?

> Such hazard now must doting Tarquin make,
> Pawning his honor to obtain his lust;
> And for himself himself he must forsake.
> Then where is truth, if there be no self-trust?
> When shall he think to find a stranger just
>   When he himself himself confounds, betrays
>   To sland'rous tongues and wretched hateful days?
>   [ll. 155–61]

The connection is a self which splits apart like those favorite lines in *Venus and Adonis* and *Lucrece* and the sonnets which divide in half, "And for himself himself he must forsake." His "honor," however, *is* his "lust." The poem's imagery has worked hard to conflate honor, wealth, and ease. Thus Tarquin's motive is at the same time narcissistic and self-dividing, suicidal. The final culprit is "want of wit," our naive slavery to symbols and the words which carry them. By this point in the poem Tarquin has come to be a study of symbolic motive. Shakespeare has inquired into the most serious motive and found it the most rhetorical. Tarquin cannot see outside his own universe of feudal metaphors. He betrays his imprisonment fittingly enough in a pre-rape apostrophe to the torch which will light him to Lucrece's chamber:

> Fair torch, burn out thy light, and lend it not
> To darken her whose light excelleth thine;
> And die, unhallowed thoughts, before you blot
> With your uncleanness that which is divine.
> Offer pure incense to so pure a shrine.
>   Let fair humanity abhor the deed
>   That spots and stains love's modest snow-white weed.
>
> O shame to knighthood and to shining arms!
> O foul dishonor to my household's grave!
> O impious act including all foul harms!
> A martial man to be soft fancy's slave!
> True valor still a true respect should have;

> Then my digression is so vile, so base,
> That it will live engraven in my face.
>
> Yea, though I die, the scandal will survive
> And be an eyesore in my golden coat.
> Some loathsome dash the herald will contrive
> To cipher me how fondly I did dote;
> That my posterity, shamed with the note,
>   Shall curse my bones, and hold it for no sin
>   To wish that I their father had not been.
>
> [ll. 190–210]

He must inflate Lucrece into a saint so as to add resonance to his desire. His regrets, of course, have nothing to do with the rape or with Lucrece. They focus on *him*, his chivalric, martial, feudal identity, past, present, and future. His impious act, symbolic of all motive, including all foul harms, is "to be soft fancy's slave." It means one thing to him. He thinks he is in love with Lucrece. It means something else to us. He is a slave to fancy indeed, to metaphor, to the golden coat of arms on which he is ciphered, to symbolic motive.

Shakespeare has denied Tarquin the motive that fiction—and life—usually awards, sight of the lady, to concentrate not simply on another motive but another kind of motive, a motiveless malignity which turns out to be the self-generating malignancy of the imagination. Tarquin has *no* "real" motive for the rape, no hunger for revenge ("Had Collatinus killed my son or sire"), and both friendship and kinship urge against it ("But as he is my kinsman, my dear friend"). He stands to lose everything, to gain only "a dream, a breath, a froth of fleeting joy." An imagery of treasons, leagues, and maps accompanies him to Lucrece's chamber and what he sees when he arrives is, again, not Lucrece but a miasma of feudal value-symbols, worlds unconquered, himself a foul usurper, Lucrece first a rich statue (ll. 419–20) and then, and in overpowering detail, a castle which he, as diabolic hero, must storm, possess, sack:

> His drumming heart cheers up his burning eye,
> His eye commends the leading to his hand;
> His hand, as proud of such a dignity,

> Smoking with pride, marched on to make his stand
> On her bare breast, the heart of all her land;
>   Whose ranks of blue veins, as his hand did scale,
>   Left their round turrets destitute and pale.
>
> [ll. 435–41]

If we think the poem about sexual passion, we shall again collapse into laughter at the absurd language. Tarquin puts his hand on Lucrece's breast much as Napoleon must have pointed to Russia on the map. The language makes sense only if rhetoric, and more especially feudal rhetoric, is the subject of the poem. Tarquin finally tells Lucrece that because "nothing can affection's course control" he must "embrace mine infamy." The force *we* have seen in the poem is not affection but language, and he is doomed to embrace his own infamy because it has been within him all the time.

The poem has become, by this point, clearly a study in dramatic motive. It should not surprise us, therefore, that Tarquin's attempt to persuade Lucrece, and her reply, are both developed within a rhetorical reality. He argues, "The fault unknown is as a thought unacted." A feudal threat again, nameless bastardy: "Bequeath not to their lot / The shame that from them no device can take." It is the heraldic term he thinks of—"device." Lucrece replies that he has changed roles: "In Tarquin's likeness I did entertain thee. / Hast thou put on his shape to do him shame?" (ll. 596–97). He is not acting the king, she tells him at length, concluding again with a theatrical metaphor: "Think but how vile a spectacle it were / To view thy present trespass in another" (ll. 631–32). And, after only a few dozen lines more, he steps on the torch and, between lines 686 and 687, does the deed. The poem never describes it. Shakespeare stresses again that his subject is motive, not sexual passion, not an act but the psychic superstructure built upon it. Tarquin then slinks off in shame, the narrator comparing, in a complex figure (l. 715 ff.), *his hero*'s state of mind to a besieged temple, his soul the doyenne thereof.

Compare Tarquin's "desire" with Venus's in *Venus and Adonis*, and you see how complex a portrait Tarquin's is and how utterly asexual his passion. He falls in love with a feudal rhetoric, not a woman; falls, in an odd but real way, in love with himself.

His "lust" springs from his imagination as spontaneously as evil from the brain of Iago and for much the same reasons. Shakespeare begins with an undeniably serious motive and finds it, on analysis, more rhetorical even than Venus's substantial hunger.

The original title page of the poem, which read simply *Lucrece*, suggests that the poem explores less the rape than the Lucrece her rape reveals. She begins her self-revelation in a curious image: "She wakes her heart by beating on her breast" (l. 759), the first in a series of images which suggests self-exacerbated sorrow. Not one to "cloak offenses with a cunning brow," she wants night to stay forever. Then she excoriates it in a full-dress apostrophe, "O comfort-killing Night" (l. 763 ff.), which reveals the voice of outraged virtue resonating in a chamber of ego. Space and time must be annihilated to cover her disgrace: "O hateful, vaporous, and foggy Night, / . . . Make war against proportioned course of time" (l. 771, 774). The moon and stars must be ravished to keep her company: "Were Tarquin Night, as he is but Night's child, / The silver-shining queen he would distain; / Her twinkling handmaids too, by him defiled, / . . . So should I have co-partners in my pain" (ll. 785–87, 789). She again thinks of her face as a mask, her predicament as a story:

> Make me not object to the telltale Day.
> The light will show, charactered in my brow,
> The story of sweet chastity's decay,
> The impious breach of holy wedlock vow.
> Yea, the illiterate, that know not how
>   To cipher what is writ in learnèd books,
>   Will quote my loathsome trespass in my looks.
>
> The nurse, to still her child, will tell my story
> And fright her crying babe with Tarquin's name.
> The orator, to deck his oratory,
> Will couple my reproach to Tarquin's shame.
> Feast-finding minstrels, tuning my defame,
>   Will tie the hearers to attend each line,
>   How Tarquin wrongèd me, I Collatine.

[ll. 806–19]

We step back not simply from her echoing ego but from what she says. How has she wronged Collatine? She puts the problem in terms of feudal possession: "O unseen shame, invisible disgrace! / O unfelt sore, crest-wounding private scar!" (ll. 827–28). The excursus on the instability of possessions (l. 855 ff.) intensifies the question. Is sexual chastity, or honor, adequately described by the feudal cluster of metaphors? They describe a surface, a crest. And she is again vexed that her predicament is not *social*. To make the sin real, she has to confess it. This poem grows from a *demande*, of course, but as with Tarquin, the emphasis shifts: not, "Should she have given in?" but "Should she confess or shut up?" Lucrece herself cannot pose the problem so clearly. Carried away by her own eloquence, she bursts into an apostrophe to Opportunity. Absurd enough applied to Tarquin, as she does—he has *seized* his opportunity—it finds its real relevance applied to her, seizing the occasion to enjoy a good rant. The compulsive anaphora—one stanza begins uniformly with *Thou*, the next with *Thy* (l. 883 ff.), seventeen lines in three stanzas (l. 940 ff.) with *To*—tips the rhetorical explosion into something like comedy. She so obviously *enjoys* unpacking her heart with words. The poem acknowledges our suspicions openly at the end of the rant. She explodes with "Out, idle words, servants to shallow fools," and the reader returns a prompt "Just so."

Shakespeare then increases the comic distance by making language yet more self-consciously the subject: "Unprofitable sounds, weak arbitrators! / Busy yourselves in skill-contending schools; / Debate where leisure serves with full debaters; / . . . For me, I force not argument a straw" (ll. 1017–19, 1021). This is ridiculous and meant to seem so. And gets more so. After forcing the argument yet further, she plunges back into—*anaphora!*

> In vain I rail at Opportunity,
> At Time, at Tarquin, and uncheerful Night;
> In vain I cavil with mine infamy;
> In vain I spurn at my confirmed despite:
> This helpless smoke of words doth me no right.

> The remedy indeed to do me good
> Is to let forth my foul defilèd blood.
>
> [ll. 1023–29]

The non sequitur of the couplet is magnificent: "Words fail me.
I'll kill myself!" She vows "in vain" some more because, like
Pyrocles in the *Old Arcadia*, at the crucial moment she can't find a
knife. The language here is meant to be entirely opaque. The
point depends on it—what use in fact she is putting words to, the
process by which vanity translates sorrow into pleasure. She is
confused. She has lost her role. "Of that true type hath Tarquin
rifled me." She is hammering out a new one—martyr of chastity.
The logic of such a role is laughable but the language doesn't
speak as the voice of logic, it speaks as the voice of ego, of
identity trying to reconstitute itself.

We are meant to see a woman carried away as much by the
language of feeling as by feeling itself. In the process, she exposes her former selfhood. It was entirely rhetorical. She was
only a role; that gone, she is as good as dead: "O, that is gone for
which I sought to live, / And therefore now I need not fear to die"
(ll. 1051–52). She must kill herself, she thinks, to prove she did
not betray that role. She must die, that is, to prove that she had
lived, that the role was genuine. We are now as far from sincerity
and serious identity as can be. Shakespeare makes the point
clear: the force of dramatic identity is stronger than life itself.
Lucrece's alternative to suicide does not seem so dreadful to us.
Let her learn a little hypocrisy. Let her learn to balance two roles
at once, develop a self in some way independent of circumstance,
recognize that she possesses such. But she must find this alternative the real fate worse than death *just because she has been
conceived as a study in rhetorical, dramatic personality*. Her suicide
makes sense only on such a premise. If her "honor" were a *means*
to preserve the family, if it were the tool of personality, not
identical with it, then she could continue, as best she might, to
uphold the family. But the point of life is to play the role. The role
comes first, its use second.

Lucrece's "virtue" comes to mean, just as does Isabella's in
Measure for Measure, the dramatic pleasure and assurance of

playing a role. In creating Lucrece as in creating Tarquin, Shakespeare began by equipping them with the most serious of motives, only to find, as the fundamental reality of his portraits, a rhetorical self. In both cases, the analysis is carried out through feudal imagery. Surely this is part of his point. He anatomizes the feudal, aristocratic conception of identity. It is egotistical: Lucrece sees herself everywhere she looks, just as Tarquin does. It is dramatic, not complex. And, as Lucrece's behavior goes on to illustrate at length, it is sentimental. It generates feeling for the sake of feeling. And the more sentimental she becomes, the further back Shakespeare stands from the opaque rhetoric.

Day comes and Lucrece, who had spent on Night's damnation an outrush of breath Shakespeare compares to Mount Aetna erupting (l. 1040 ff.), now damns the coming of day. Again the poem voices our reflection: "Thus cavils she with everything she sees" (l. 1093). Is it "true" grief which follows? If so, all grief, not only Lucrece's, is at heart sentimental, demands and resolutely creates a full, satisfactory dramatic equivalent. Grief must be public to be true. So Lucrece disputes with all she sees, "to herself all sorrow doth compare; / No object but her passion's strength renews" (ll. 1102–03). She must keep sorrow fresh and biting, stave off even the assuagement time and exhaustion bring. She enshrines this in a telling figure, compares herself to Philomela:

> And whiles against a thorn thou bear'st thy part
> To keep thy sharp woes waking, wretched I,
> To imitate thee well, against my heart
> Will fix a sharp knife to affright mine eye;
> Who, if it wink, shall thereon fall and die.
> These means, as frets upon an instrument,
> Shall tune our heartstrings to true languishment.
>
> [ll. 1135–41]

"True languishment" here begins to sound false.

Lucrece shows herself increasingly in love with her own virtue: "My body or my soul, which was the dearer / When the one, pure, the other made divine? / Whose love of either to myself was nearer / When both were kept for heaven and Collatine?" (ll. 1163–66). Heaven and Collatine seem valuable largely as the occasion for Lucrece's virtue. She begins her posthumous life in other men's minds with a will-and-testament topos (l. 1181 ff.), then cries a little, joined by a maid who cries to keep her company (l. 1236). The poem takes pains to voice our own thoughts again (l. 1254 ff.) that Lucrece is not to blame, before it returns to her sentimental grief. It is not real unless fully and oft expressed: "that deep torture may be called a hell / When more is felt than one hath power to tell. / Go get me hither paper, ink, and pen" (ll. 1287–89). When she writes to Collatine, the muse does not fail her: "First hovering o'er the paper with her quill. / Conceit and grief an eager combat fight; / What wit sets down is blotted straight with will. / This is too curious good, this blunt and ill" (ll. 1297–1300). Yet the note she finally writes is plainness itself. What's going on? Shakespeare seems to describe eloquence as a natural impulse, primary, one which has to be *suppressed* in favor of clarity. The muse shares the "true grief," in some sense creates it.

Lucrece now becomes an actress admitted: "the life and feeling of her passion / She hoards, to spend when he is by to hear her, / When sighs and groans and tears may grace the fashion / Of her disgrace" (ll. 1317–20). The poem pursues this theme relentlessly. Even the groom who takes the letter (l. 1345 ff.) is reproached for being a bad actor.

Lucrece finally wearies of grieving and looks around, "pausing for means to mourn some newer way" (l. 1365). She hits upon a sentimentalist's dream, "a piece / Of skillful painting, made for Priam's Troy" (ll. 1366–67). A perfect choice—rape, siege, huge, dramatic, artificial, flat, as conceited as the poem itself. Lucrece pounces on it with delight. The painting is full of faces, of masks, and Lucrece searches among them "to find a face where all distress is stelled" (l. 1444). Only the mask is real. She pities Hecuba; the painter had heaped woes upon her but given her no mouth to speak. She has it. *She'll play Hecuba.* " 'Poor instrument,' quoth she, 'without a sound: / I'll tune thy woes with my lamenting tongue' " (ll. 1464–65). Shakespeare's poem at this point veers toward his own craft, toward the uses of drama. What's Hecuba to her, she to Hecuba? Her rehearsal declares: "Why should the private pleasure of some one / Become the public plague of many moe? / Let sin, alone committed, light alone / Upon his head that hath transgressèd so" (ll. 1478–81). Lucrece, not Helen, wears the mantle of this argument. She takes it on herself to reenact the whole poem: "So Lucrece, set awork, sad tales doth tell / To pencilled pensiveness and colored sorrow: / She lends them words, and she their looks doth borrow" (ll. 1496–98). She plays the siege of Troy. She plays *all* the parts, we come to see, because she sees herself not as Helen but as *Troy!* As Priam trusted Sinon, "So did I Tarquin; so my Troy did perish." She has found a role big enough even for her elephantine ego.

She has now practiced enough and begins readying her last big scene. She knows that timing is everything:

> Here with a sigh as if her heart would break
> She throws forth Tarquin's name: "He, he!" she says,
> But more than "he" her poor tongue could not speak,
> Till after many accents and delays,
> Untimely breathings, sick and short assays,
>   She utters this: "He, he! fair lords, 'tis he
>   That guides this hand to give this wound to me."
>   [ll. 1716–22]

Even Jung might Freudianize that culminating narcissistic stab. She makes love to herself for the last time.

To make *Lucrece* a poem beyond doubt about dramatic identity, an exploration of rhetorical life, Shakespeare ends it with two displays depending neither on Tarquin nor Lucrece. Lucretius expresses a grief as dramatic and self-centered as his daughter's: " 'Daughter, dear daughter!' old Lucretius cries, / 'That life was mine which thou hast here deprivèd. / If in the child the father's image lies, / Where shall I live now Lucrece is unlivèd?' " (ll. 1751–54). Collatine bathes in Lucrece's blood and "counterfeits to die with her a space" (l. 1776). Then, no longer to be kept from "heart-easing words," he "begins to talk." The two mourners next proceed to a grief contest: " 'O,' quoth Lucretius,

'I did give that life / Which she too early and too late hath spilled.'
/ 'Woe, woe!' quoth Collatine. 'She was my wife, / I owed her, and
'tis mine that she hath killed' '' (ll. 1800–03). Brutus, thinking
this grief contest as silly as we do, decides it is time to resume his
sanity, "clothe his wit in state and pride, / Burying in Lucrece'
wound his folly's show" (ll. 1809–10). Brutus's late appearance
has puzzled scholiasts but it could scarcely be clearer. He represents the kind of personality Lucrece could not adjust to, the
complex self that uses a role without becoming it. Through his
mouth πράγματα not δόγματα finally speak:

> Why, Collatine, is woe the cure for woe?
> Do wounds help wounds, or grief help grievous deeds?
> Is it revenge to give thyself a blow
> For his foul act by whom thy fair wife bleeds?
> Such childish humor from weak minds proceeds.
> Thy wretched wife mistook the matter so,
> To slay herself that should have slain her foe.
>   [ll. 1821–27]

The sentimentalism ends just as the sentimental rhetoric does,
and Brutus provides the control for both. He is not out of place,
his appearance sudden. He is inevitable.

It is usually neither sensible nor legitimate to read one poem as
rehearsal for another. But a masterpiece invites such prophetic
attention and rewards it. *Lucrece* does not, let me hasten to add,
present itself as a rough draft of anything. Shakespeare's two
masterpieces are both *polished*, diabolically so. But *Lucrece* does
prophesy things to come. Shakespeare reflects on the nature of
an historical event, on the feudal aristocracy the poem courts; he
reflects on the uses of art; he sets out above all the range of styles
and attitudes toward style his kind of poetry will require. It is
this last point, the kind of stylistic attention he solicits, which
Lucrece especially strives to make. Let me deal with these topics
in order.

Tarquin's rape and Lucrece's suicide changed the nature of
Roman government, got rid of the kings. Shakespeare examines
the crucial event and finds, at its base, δόγματα not πράγματα,

not circumstances but attitudes, narcissism, romantic pleasure. Both Tarquin and Lucrece live in the future and tread the present as a stage. Shakespeare concludes from this that the present is intrinsically dramatic, that the dramatist, in staging history, need not fret about destroying its verisimilitude. *Lucrece* teaches that history happens on a stage to begin with. Just this reflection lies behind the history plays, and prompts, as we shall see, the choruses in *Henry V.* It is a theory of history Shakespeare shared with Cervantes. And the Ovidian exposure of Rome's theatricality was to premise the Roman plays. In history so construed, of course, speeches offer not less verisimilitude than narrative but more.

The gesture of courtship embodied in *Lucrece* strikes the modern reader as ambiguous. The poem abounds in feudal language and in acceptable aristocratic sentiments: subject high, style polished, proverbial wisdom unremitting. *Lucrece* has presented a surface sufficiently conventional and sufficiently reflective of critical naivete to masquerade for a long time as suitable for noble dedication. But it ends far from the political banalities that float on its surface. Shakespeare is not least Ovidian in his political statement. Naive feudal role playing, he warns, is no longer adequate. Nor is the naive feudal self. It has become suicidal, as Lucrece so amply demonstrates. A new *kind* of personality is needed for governance, the integrated personality Brutus symbolizes. Rhetorical display may be needed as mask but is no longer tolerable as indulgence. A governor must be self-aware and self-conscious about language. And so Prince Hal is put through his rhetorical education at the hands of the master sophist Falstaff. The governor needs a sense of theatre but he cannot, like Richard, be stagestruck. Shakespeare teaches these lessons as both dramatist and bourgeois. And, like that other bourgeois expert in courtship, Geoffrey Chaucer, he teaches through a poetry which can be read as totally conventional or totally the opposite. Both Tarquin's act and Lucrece's stem from a *demande,* an aristocratic pastime. But motive also comes from event, from commonsense behavior, from the dog that does not bark. Its absence in *Lucrece* warns that the aristocratic view omits

this half of motive at its peril. Lucrece's response is very aristocratic and very silly. Shakespeare makes both points.

   Lucrece as art critic need not detain us. She uses the painting
as reflection from her own thoughts, holds the mirror up to
Lucrece. Shakespeare staked out the opposite, critical detachment, as the goal of our poetic paideia. His readers would run
from narcissistic absorption to Ovidian detachment. His own
poem was designed as a mirror and has worked beautifully as
one. But his plays work this way too, offer simplistic morals for
those who need them. A generic verdict seems manifest: a reflective surface forms part of any work of literature, shows how it fits
into its own time, comes to terms with expectation. It is part of
the ingratiation of Shakespeare's address that he supplies a narcissistic stimulus with such willing ease, refrains politely from
overt challenge. Such may have been the manner of the age. The
strategy of surplus moralizing occurs again and again in Renaissance literature, and, just as frequently, an answering critical
simplicity. The people in Renaissance poems often fool themselves too, as here. Modern thinking about language thinks it a
prison. Shakespeare dwells concomitantly on its rich resources
of illusion, on our ability like Lucrece to make a new self from a
painting and The Method. *Lucrece* seems to conclude that art is
not in essence different from life. They inhabit the same spectrum of symbolic behavior. Shakespeare did not anticipate an
audience of disinterested, disengaged critics. At least not many
of them. People use poetry in all kinds of ways. Part of *Lucrece*'s
gesture as masterpiece is to stake out the theoretical extremes.

5

Superposed Poetics: The Sonnets

I

From the two views of life I've called rhetorical and serious there devolve, I've suggested, two corresponding poetics. Since Shakespeare's sonnets superpose these two poetics one upon the other, it may be useful to review the differences between them. Western poetics descend from Aristotle, and for Aristotle poetry was serious. We don't know what he said about comedy but, since he complains in the *Poetics* that at first it was not taken seriously (ἡ δὲ κωμῳδία διὰ τὸ μὴ σπουδάζεσθαι ἐξ ἀρχῆς ἔλαθεν [1449a37–1449b1]), perhaps he would have remedied this deficiency. His discussion of tragedy intertwined it with seriousness in a way lasting from that day to this. Tragedy imitates an action first and foremost serious: ἔστιν οὖν τραγῳδία μίμησις πράξεως σπουδαίας (1449b24–25). The word σπουδαίας, usually rendered "heroic," points not to a specific pattern of behavior but a different kind of self. Else makes my point in his commentary on ἢ σπουδαίους ἢ φαύλους (1448a2):

1. The dichotomy is moral, but not in the Platonic, much less in a Christian sense.

2. It denotes, not virtue and vice as states, but two different attitudes toward virtue. The σπουδαῖοι are those who strive for it, who spend their lives, and if necessary lose them, for the prize of *aretê*. The φαῦλοι are those who do not. They are not the vicious but the "no-account," those who spend their lives making money, or "having fun," or both.

3. Thus the σπουδαῖοι are those who take themselves and
   life seriously and therefore can be taken seriously; the
   φαῦλοι are those who do not and cannot.
4. The dichotomy is, by the nature of the case, absolute and
   comprehensive. All men *who act*—i.e., all men engaged
   in the practical life—are necessarily either σπουδαῖοι or
   φαῦλοι; there is no room for a third class.[1]

Serious man and rhetorical man, nicely distinguished. Serious
poetic, like tragedy itself, premises a central self; rhetorical poetic premises a social self whose behavior splits into two parts—
persuasion and pleasure. We might think such a rhetorical poetic, if admitted at all, a contextual poetic, an enclosing pa-
renthesis for formalist theorizing. Or as positing two defining
extremes of theoretical purity, each *more* not less real than the
intervening spectrum of compromises. Any serious poetic,
though it purposes sooner or later *aut prodesse aut delectare*,
insists on both at once and integrally related. A rhetorical poetic
does the opposite. It accommodates each in a pure state. It charts
ground both above and below serious poetic. Above, it allows
propaganda, teaching, rhetorical purpose unalloyed; below, it
allows delight, pure entertainment. Neither, for serious poetic,
ranks as "literature." The propagandistic extreme of self-serving
includes psychoanalytical coordinates as well. One extreme of
the rhetorical poetic points outward, toward politics and the
state; the other inward, toward self and the psyche. It is a commonplace that classical rhetoric and poetic were the same. In this
respect, not so. Poetic has defined itself essentially in terms of
seriousness. Rhetoric has charted different ground.

Serious poetic insists the poet keep faith with some vision of
experience, realistic or apocalyptic. He must want to share this
vision. And must have felt it. So Horace famously *si vis me flere,*
dolendum est / primum ipsi tibi (Ars Poetica 102–03). A poet may
write to eat but this remains incidental to keeping the faith. A
rhetorical poetic allows the whole range of sordid motive—

1. Gerald F. Else, *Aristotle's Poetics*, p. 77.

money, spleen, urge to shine, narcissistic posturing—as inter-
pretive categories. So too with the category of pure play. From a
serious point of view, this category is yet worse. A serious poet
does not play games just for his own amusement. He will know
moments of exaltation if he is lucky; he will by definition know
many of despair; but he cannot just delight. No pot-boilers,
then, and no games.

A poetic not built on a central self can have no plot, of course,
in the Aristotelian sense. Probability judgments in literature
depend on a central self. So the Aristotelian preference for prob-
able impossibilities over vice versa. Serious poetic insists that a
causal pattern be traced in experience by holding the coattails of
a single self. Or it dramatizes the impossibility, or exorbitant
price, of doing so. It does not matter which; both are equally
serious. The difference is not grounded on a theory of knowledge. The rhetorical poetic, too, admits patterns, but it admits
too many. It finds them impositions on, not expositions of,
reality. So it need not relate them, fuse them. It is *all* episodes,
those episodes Aristotle so disliked. It leaves order up to us,
remains aleatory. It does not finally care how we put things
together.

Style must never show for the serious poetic because that
means (1) someone is propagandizing us or (2) someone is having a good time for no good reason. Likewise, style and subject
must cohere into a decorum. Just the opposite for play poetic. It
aims at style/subject discontinuities. It depends on puns and
other false wits. It fails to honor metaphor as a god-term, ignor-
ing it altogether or cooking up outrageous ones.

If tragedy serves as reference-genre for serious poetic, a peculiar genre for which we might borrow "tragicomedy" (a mislead-
ing term probably, since tragedy and comedy are both *serious*
genres) serves for rhetorical poetic, a genre which, instead of
combining serious tragedy and comedy, stands back to consider
the merits of each. The sonnets are tragicomedy in this sense.
Such documents by nature come to us enmeshed in topical reference and local allegory. They are mixed up with life. A serious
critic must precipitate out this topicality straightaway, insist that

such things, if present, make no difference, for the serious critic must rigorously separate art from life. The term μίμησις implies such a distinction, of course, as well as the idea of beginning and end. The rhetorical poetic, with no plot, need worry about neither. It can play games with our expectation, or ease into fiction, as Renaissance prose narrative often does, behind a screen of prefatory apparatus. But it finds beginnings and endings equally a matter of convenience. Part of rhetoric's confounding, pouring together, of art and life is a willingness to define private audiences and play with them. So Shakespeare made plays which address two different plays to two different audiences at once. And rhetorical documents often use the bizarre or grotesque, ignore probability. Since they acknowledge no separate referent reality, they need not defer to it.

Nor need they be concerned with changes in scale. The unities have known their critics but their argument fits sensibly and easily into the serious poetic. Scale must not show. Conventional distortions indeed know no natural limitation, as Johnson insisted in the 1765 *Preface to Shakespeare*, but only if they are consistent. The conventions of scale must never themselves become objects of contemplation. Scale aims at a coherence such attention destroys. This is what Aristotle is trying to get at in *Poetics* 1450b, when he insists that beauty consists in size and arrangement: τὸ γὰρ καλὸν ἐν μεγέθει καὶ τάξει ἐστίν. For a rhetorical opposite, one need think no further than *Gargantua and Pantagruel*.

The Aristotelian poetic is premised on order. Morse Peckham, in *Man's Rage for Chaos*, has sought to overthrow this premise by insisting that art aims to disorder not order. It tries to break up and challenge experience, make us put it back together in different ways. It provides a gymnasium for the imagination. Peckham argues that art works by cognitive tension, confronting us with conflicting orchestrations we must sort out. It aims to expand our reality, to explain more accurately what happens when art and beholder interact. But that is just it. Explain. A poetic of play asks only that we enjoy. Thus the documents which use rhetorical coordinates can play games of order or disorder, balance and unbalance. They can use either for its whole range of nefarious applied purpose. The reconstructing and re-creating reader of the last few years develops clearly from Peckham's conception of the perceiver's role, a role terribly serious as well as infinitely difficult. But neither the order/disorder dispute nor the reader/text dispute growing from it change the Aristotelian premises of the discussion. Both seem to offer help with rhetorical documents but both can carry us only so far. They go further toward play than before only to pull further back.

To restrict literature to the serious critical reader is a possible, even legitimate restriction, but a big one. It leaves out not only the common reader but most uncommon ones as well. Is a rhetorical poetic necessary? What is it good at describing? Just its two extremes, avowed purpose and avowed purposelessness. It charts human self-serving. The element of play deserves special stress. Art works as a check on purposive experience. It reminds us of the inevitable playful, and hence self-serving, ingredient in experience. It can thus be moralized, at least negatively: it teaches how and how often we mask pleasure with high-minded purpose. Art acts as perpetual reminder of our resources of pleasure, pleasures beyond purpose. Such resources are there, if we are clever, to enhance, invigorate purpose, but they do not exist to do so. They exist in themselves, as a treasury of human resource. A poetic of play, then, allows for a radically un-Aristotelian reader, one who responds in nonserious ways.

II

The world does not always coincide with our images of it. This discontinuity presents problems—the area of serious poetic. But it also presents opportunities to become rich and to rejoice—the area of rhetorical poetic. Seriousness would preclude play and vice versa. But Shakespeare shows every sign, in the sonnets as elsewhere, of having felt and understood both. Rhetorical and serious poetic differ *essentially*, in pattern of expectation, not in a particular text. One can read any text seriously, philosophize the funny papers, explicate pop music. Or one can relish Homer, lose oneself in the romance. Texts, too, can invite one kind of attention or another. The sonnets systematically invite both kinds at once. We find here the alternating —☐— narrative pattern discussed earlier, but collapsed in on itself. They open with an exhortation to share oneself. Taken as a whole, though, they exhibit the liveliest awareness that the one element in art truly untranslatable into another language is its fundamental selfishness. We can see this ambivalence most easily in the vexed problem of order.

How the best kind of serious criticism might deal with it Stephen Booth's brilliant *An Essay on Shakespeare's Sonnets* has shown. He argues that the 1609 Q order, however it got that way, makes us *uneasy* as we pass through it, leads us in and out of differing, often contradicting orientations, tones, styles, at a bewildering rate. Shakespeare will stay with one subject or tone for a sonnet, or two or three, then turn the world upside down. The sequence re-creates *in us* the radical orientative unease the sonneteer himself feels. The sonnets re-create the world as a gymnasium of the imagination. Within serious coordinates, Booth is right, brilliantly so. But what if we read with a rhetorical expectation? If the order makes us uneasy, we rearrange it.

Here, as often with rhetorical documents, critical history lends external support to the need for rhetorical coordinates. From the beginning—from Thomas Thorpe perhaps—readers have itched to rearrange the sonnets. Such rearrangements please only the rearrangers. Obviously all the rearrangers cannot be right. Yes they can. The sonnets present orderless order, *invite* rearrangement. *All* the rearrangers are right. Aleatory composition— allowing a performer re-creative latitude—is not after all a modern invention. It was the customary proceeding for much Elizabethan music. Rearrangement, for the serious reader, is illegitimate. It makes the world too simple, especially since Shakespeare took so much trouble to make it ambiguous. Surely that is the point. Shakespeare took no trouble one way or the other. *We* do so. The sonnets invite us to specify our own poetic, examine our own pattern of expectations. To trigger this response, Shakespeare did not have to do anything but write the poems and gather them hugger-mugger together. The present order does abound in cognitive tension. So will any other, if we seek for it. Try the experiment with a revised order, Brents Sterling's for example or, as one of my students did, with one random-generated by a computer. Or accept each sonnet as a separate experience, neglect the context. Shakespeare offers an anthology. Pluck the flowers one by one.

Shakespeare often writes about the form he writes in. Does some such reflection on the nature of lyric emerge here? The sonnets represent the lyric anthology in its purest form because they pose most clearly its central formal question. What is the basic unit of order? What is the referential "event" you need before you can begin to think about order? What are you ordering? Now all the sonnets are, in some ways, identical and inter-changeable. In other ways, they differ completely. A reader must reflect on his own expectations, his preconditions for seeing. He is invited to meditate on the nature of plot.

Do the sonnets tell a story? Not a clear one, but the invitation for *us* to make up a story is clear enough. Here, like the medieval allegorists of Ovid, the silliest readers have been the wisest. What a cast the sonnets offer! Why not make up a story to suit your taste? No other assumption really makes sense of the son-nets' fragmented biography and topical reference. A sonnet se-quence is a poor vehicle for telling a story. Of course. But, as the sonnets' critical history demonstrates, it can stimulate all kinds of stories. A story, though, means a plot and plot demands the consistent self, for sonneteer at least, which the sonnets, in their multiple tergiversations, take pains to deny. We are made to see the price paid for plot. Lyric meditation unearths multiple selves hard to fit into plots. We are urged to make up a plot or, if we want, pointedly refrain from doing so.

Shakespeare's superposed strategies come especially clear when we consider the golden youth and the first seventeen sonnets. The sonnets issue plenty of invitations which legitimize biographical speculation. Private audience, manuscript circula-tion, publication pirated, obvious address to a single youth, sonnet series as social courtship. These all demand rhetorical coordinates, enact the poet's private plea for advantage. Yet so much does the youth evoke if not embody disinterested love, so many are the Renaissance commonplaces touched, from friendship to the parable of the talents, that serious coordinates are triggered equally. Shakespeare, like Plato, builds his serious encomia on thoroughly rhetorical grounds. And to this perplexity add a rhetorical coup for the first seventeen. Shakespeare came to the sonnet game when it was old and had to galvanize somehow a worn-out repertoire of Petrarchan clichés. He does so not by varying them but by shifting the sexual object to which they refer. In a stroke Petrarchan metaphor is renewed. A new area of serious reflection on love and sexuality opens up. The great extension in range of Shakespeare's sonnets, moving far beyond the begging mode to love accomplished, sealed, grown old, love Platonic and love physical, emerges from this decision. A profoundly serious gesture, then, but also a brilliant rhetorical one. Masterpiece psychology again. An act, first, of self-revelation, confession, and second of exceptional technical acumen; as a serious act it is outgoing, philosophical, moral, as a rhetorical gesture, a selfish masterstroke.

A sonnet sequence is by its form a virtuoso act—any sonnet sequence. Can the sonneteer do it, go on? The challenge to be new, fresh, is a game of balance. How long can he keep it up? He denies himself all but a basic form, and then, like a tightrope walker with his balance bar, tries to make it across. The narrower the theme, the tougher the game. Shakespeare egregiously increases the odds; a praising mode but praising a man. What is there to say? What man cares whether another begets children? And *seventeen* sonnets on the same theme? Daring—what Robert Frost called "scoring"—runs all through the sonnets. We reenact Shakespeare's uncertainty, as Booth shows. But we also participate in his virtuosity, admire him, wonder at the immense pleasurable resources of language.

The golden youth proves tremendously *useful* to Shakespeare. He enables Shakespeare to strike a pose altogether different from the frustrated adolescent heated with Petrarchan cliché. The exercise in panegyric rhetoric masks a very different tone. Never has anyone been so praised and damned at once as the youth. The sonneteer seems to do all the giving—a nice presentation of self—but he manages to recoup much of his own. A courtly lover, he is also a brilliant character-assassin who crowns his strategy by vowing to make the youth's unnamed name, his nonentity, live forever. A lot of getting-even goes on in the sonnets. It does not weaken the serious meanings clustering around the youth. It just sits atop them. The parable of the talents is all very well, but Shakespeare serves himself too.

In the opening sonnets, in the 1609 order, our attention falls on rejuvenation as a theme but on language being rejuvenated at the same time. We must simultaneously look at the words and through them.

> From fairest creatures we desire increase,
> That thereby beauty's rose might never die,
> But as the riper should by time decease,
> His tender heir might bear his memory;
> But thou, contracted to thine own bright eyes,
> Feed'st thy light's flame with self-substantial fuel,
> Making a famine where abundance lies,
> Thyself thy foe, to thy sweet self too cruel.
> Thou that art now the world's fresh ornament
> And only herald to the gaudy spring,
> Within thine own bud buriest thy content
> And, tender churl, mak'st waste in niggarding.
>   Pity the world, or else this glutton be,
>   To eat the world's due, by the grave and thee.[2]

In a serious reading, it is the first line that surprises. Babies do not figure strongly in Petrarchan poetry. From the beginning, the sterility of courtly passion had preoccupied Shakespeare. He noticed above all the narcissism in the Petrarchan orchestration. He writes, then, a sonnet about his own narcissistic passion? No, he has it both ways. *His* passion stands opposite narcissism.

2. Ed. Douglas Bush.

Nothing in it for him but pure love. It is the youth who consumes himself in self-containment. The imagery reverses direction. Eye-beams, darting outward in standard operating procedure, now go backward: "But thou, contracted to thine own bright eyes." The *lady* usually oils the fires of love. The youth "feed'st thy light's flame with self-substantial fuel." As for "beauty's rose," its point is that it dies. It represents a commitment in the private life and these, like the people whom they bind, do not last.

The act of continuance Shakespeare asks comes from the public life. We may ask that human beauty be continued, but what has this to do with love? And why must the youth encapsulate within himself Petrarchanism's narcissistic sterility? "Thyself thy foe, to thy sweet self too cruel." Serious readings dwell on the parable of the talents; we are but custodians of ourselves. But often the first seventeen sonnets argue nonsensically. They seem to aim for bewilderment, logical outrage. The sonneteer asks his male love to beget children, betray him with a woman in just the way later to call for reproach. The youth is given the attributes of both Petrarchan lover and Petrarchan beloved and then blamed for being narcissistic. Commentators have universally remarked that the youth, for all Shakespeare's praise, remains a shadowy figure. With good reason. More real, he would be less convenient. Shakespeare could not hang such contradictory arguments upon him. Not only the first seventeen sonnets work in this way, or the golden youth. The lady is a convenience too, as well as a tramp. Youth and lady fail to come together under serious coordinates but they make sense as rhetorical excuses, occasions for manipulation. What is outrageously contrived in the sonnets is less imagery than argument. Argument often becomes an intellectual prestidigitation meant to be seen as such, as with the homosexuality theme.

Sonnet 20 tells us, a bit late, that intellectual not physical homosexuality stands at issue. Scholars can relax; Shakespeare depicts only Renaissance friendship. But ought such friendship carry a full range and type of sexual jealousy, as in the sonnets? Shakespeare's love for the youth: if not homosexual, what is it?

We never learn. It emerges as both numinously idiosyncratic and
just plain hollow, not there, an excuse for effect. Both show in
sonnet 20 itself.

> A woman's face, with Nature's own hand painted,
> Hast thou, the master-mistress of my passion;
> A woman's gentle heart, but not acquainted
> With shifting change, as is false women's fashion;
> An eye more bright than theirs, less false in rolling,
> Gilding the object whereupon it gazeth;
> A man in hue all hues in his controlling,
> Which steals men's eyes and women's souls amazeth.
> And for a woman wert thou first created,
> Till Nature as she wrought thee fell a-doting,
> And by addition me of thee defeated
> By adding one thing to my purpose nothing.
> 　But since she pricked thee out for women's pleasure,
> 　Mine be thy love, and thy love's use their treasure.

Now this sonnet figures strongly in a serious reading of the
sonnets. "Use" is sexual knowledge and this Shakespeare re-
nounces. All the puzzlement about Shakespeare's possibly illicit
sexual proclivities ought to be relieved here. Not simply because
he says so but because it suits his rhetorical purpose much better
if the relationship is not physical, remains vague, rhetorically
convenient. In a sexual relationship, the Petrarchan imagery
could, with a little physical readjustment, find a home; with the
vague relationship, it stays up in the air and thus new. It can lend
itself to the kinds of word games exemplified by sonnet 20, with
its feminine rhymes and endings and its sexual puns.

The lady is an occasional piece, too. Look at sonnet 135:

> Whoever hath her wish, thou hast thy Will,
> And Will to boot, and Will in overplus.
> More than enough am I that vex thee still,
> To thy sweet will making addition thus.
> Wilt thou, whose will is large and spacious,
> Not once vouchsafe to hide my will in thine?

> Shall will in others seem right gracious,
> And in my will no fair acceptance shine?
> The sea, all water, yet receives rain still
> And in abundance addeth to his store;
> So thou, being rich in Will, add to thy Will
> One will of mine to make thy large Will more.
>   Let no unkind, no fair beseechers kill;
>   Think all but one, and me in that one Will.

This sonnet brings out the serious tut-tutting Elizabethan punning always generates. Yet if you read for "Will" the sonneteer, volition, sexual desire, and the male and female sexual organs, 135 turns out a bitter poem. "Since you sleep with the standing army, why not with me?" The pun anatomizes the sexual life from top to bottom. Superficial verbal ornament becomes profound metaphor for the degrading, exalting democracy of sexual life. But it still remains rhetorical ornament. Disinterested verbal pleasure sits atop the bitterness. Sonnet 135 shows with maximum compression Shakespeare's strategy of superposed poetics, the simultaneous insistence that we remain on the verbal surface and that we penetrate beneath it. Like the pun, it both insists that we take language seriously, and prevents our doing so.

At a higher level, we surprise the same double attitude toward verbal surface applied to time. On a serious level, the *aere perennius* arguments have been much rehearsed, yet the crucial distinction seldom drawn. Horace says *he* will last in his verse, just as Ovid in *Amores* 1.15 says *he* will survive in his. Shakespeare weasels. He again uses the youth to flatter himself. He writes to eternalize the youth, to eternalize beauty itself, not poor old Will. Thus the occasional sonnet which opines that when Shakespeare's arts of style decay into unfashion, the golden youth's golden youth will still shine bright. As arguments, of course, both kinds of sonnets are absurd. Sonnet 81 is the most famous:

> Or I shall live your epitaph to make,
> Or you survive when I in earth am rotten.
> From hence your memory death cannot take,
> Although in me each part will be forgotten.

Your name from hence immortal life shall have,
Though I, once gone, to all the world must die.
The earth can yield me but a common grave
When you entombèd in men's eyes shall lie.
Your monument shall be my gentle verse,
Which eyes not yet created shall o'erread;
And tongues to be your being shall rehearse
When all the breathers of this world are dead.
  You still shall live (such virtue hath my pen)
  Where breath most breathes, even in the mouths of men.

A monument to nothing. Where does the famous irony go?
Shakespeare misapplies his topos absurdly. The argument
Shakespeare develops points to a beauty beyond verbal surface,
to the youth, beauty itself, we are told at length. Yet the Horatian
topos insists that only the verbal surface lasts. Again the double
invitation. Look at the verbal surface; that's all there is. Look
below the surface; the surface means nothing. The paradox is
implicit—Shakespeare once again reflecting on his form, the
lyric anthology. Itself a collection of self-contradictory presents,
it inevitably looks at past and future. It pleads, in its arguments,
for the evanescence of the present but by the allegory of its form
sees life as but a series of presents.

Sonnet 81 thus celebrates the sonneteer and his power, but less
honestly than Horace. The additional complexity flows from the
need to include the youth—to attack as well as praise him—and
the need to do the same for language. The poem's statement
about time emerges so obviously we may overlook it. Documents
using rhetorical coordinates often veer toward mutability as a
theme, tend to find verbal surface the only reliable constant. To
make the point the surface has to show. For Spenser, antique
diction authenticated the allegory. For Shakespeare, obvious
verbal artifice is varied by the sonneteer's continual denial of
verbal artifice, his claim to gaze upon the thing itself. So in 55.
What kind of monument is it? *Odi et amo*, hate and love both
maximally strong and both at the same time. Lovers' eyes see
another and see themselves, and for just this reason Shakespeare
needs both poetics.

The rhetorical view of the world knows only a continuous present because it denies a central self. We can, thus, change roles absolutely, play another, enter the present moment without trailing clouds of past self. We become another creation. The sonnets say this often enough, and the form itself implies it: new sonnet, new self. Again, this continued re-creation of self erects a far more eloquent monument to sonneteer than to youth. But each sonnet, by re-creating a self, reaffirms the sonneteer's existence, tends to accrete substance for a central self. The sonneteer wants us to think his self a constant too, lasting from pose to pose. Some good thinking about the sonnets has allegorized, in a Freudian way or otherwise, the "cast" of the sonnets as aspects of the sonneteer's self. We might call them part of an ideal self, and thus construe the sonnets as an anatomy of self under sexual pressure, much like the middle books of *The Faerie Queene*. Such a thesis provides the most comprehensive serious explanation of the sonnets' theme. But if the sonneteer wants to bring his selves together, he also enjoys leaving them apart, role playing for its own sake. Again, Shakespeare has it both ways.

And naturally the clash between the two selves and hence the two poetics becomes a subject for sonnets, most famously, I suppose, for 116:

> Let me not to the marriage of true minds
> Admit impediments; love is not love
> Which alters when it alteration finds
> Or bends with the remover to remove.
> O, no, it is an ever-fixèd mark
> That looks on tempests and is never shaken;
> It is the star to every wand'ring bark,
> Whose worth's unknown, although his height be taken.
> Love's not Time's fool, though rosy lips and cheeks
> Within his bending sickle's compass come;
> Love alters not with his brief hours and weeks,
> But bears it out even to the edge of doom.
>   If this be error, and upon me proved,
>   I never writ, nor no man ever loved.

Is the final couplet paradoxical? Doesn't it rather make two different kinds of statements in the same words? If "nor no man
ever loved" is a private statement, topical reference, private
audience, it means one thing. If a public statement—not "I never
loved any man" but "No man ever loved anybody"—then it says
something else. The couplet illustrates perfectly the sonnets'
characteristic reasoning. The "proof" runs this way. "If such
ever-constant love is a delusion, I never writ. But since I have
manifestly writ, then it must be true." Reality, the chain of
reasoning, the only undeniable premise, however absurd, is the
act of writing. Style, the act of writing, again forms both center
and surface. Not writing the truth, since he admits in line one of
115, "Those lines that I before have writ do lie," but the act of
writing. On this premise is built true love. Or, if writing again is
the only *undeniable* reality, if true love really is a delusion—and
the previous one hundred fifteen sonnets have shown Shakespeare's love shaken, removed, unfixed, full of nothing but
impediments—then, following the "logic," some other "I" must
have written them. No problem. One hundred fifteen other
"I's," at least, stand ready. Neither central self nor true love
finally supplies the referent reality. Shakespeare in sonnet 116
argues a case for rhetorical coordinates, as well as against them.
Amo ergo sum on the one hand; *Scribo ergo sum* on the other. Read
as a serious poem, it argues that the "star," love, is a necessary
assumption if the world is to make any sense. We must start with
some commitment. Why not call it Love. *Amo ergo sum.* Read
within rhetorical coordinates, it says that all you really start with
is the act of writing. *Scribo ergo sum.* The poem is about the
relation between the two poetics. A poem about defining
essence—the marriage of true minds—it yet leans on its words in
such a way, varying their sense with repetition, that essence
dwells first in words: Love, love; alters, alteration; remover,
remove. Is such a subject serious? It is and it isn't. The poem
seems at once the most profound and the most playful in the
sequence. Two different poems share the same words.

Again and again in the sonnets the most serious statement
comes through verbal artifice meant to show. Look at sonnet 138:

When my love swears that she is made of truth
I do believe her, though I know she lies,
That she might think me some untutored youth,
Unlearnèd in the world's false subtilties.
Thus vainly thinking that she thinks me young,
Although she knows my days are past the best,
Simply I credit her false-speaking tongue;
On both sides thus is simple truth suppressed.
But wherefore says she not she is unjust?
And wherefore say not I that I am old?
O, love's best habit is in seeming trust,
And age in love loves not to have years told.
        Therefore I lie with her and she with me,
        And in our faults by lies we flattered be.

The pun on "lie," from the second line to the last, encapsulates the essential duplicity of passion the poem seeks to describe. It also introduces a series of puns: made, vainly, simply, habit, told (homonym—tolled). Ploce, antanaclasis, a complicated kind of chiasmatic pronoun pattern (she not : not I / she is : I am), the suggestion of syllogism in "wherefore . . . therefore," the symphony of verbs *sentiendi ac declarandi* (swears, believes, lies, thinks, thinking, thinks, knows, credits, false-speaking, suppressed, says, loves, lie, flattered); all this is rhetorical manipulation and meant to show. The poem does not work in spite of its virtuosity but because of it. The virtuosity holds us always, in the sonnets, slightly at a distance, and thus enables us to move so abruptly from one tone or subject to another (from 128 to 129, for example) without an unendurable sense of fracture.

It is a mistake to argue that, finally, the sonnets are not tricksy, show-off, prestidigitous. Of course they are. They are also calculated to display the sonneteer in a favorable light, youth and lady in mottled shade. They also harrow a divided self, map the aggressive duplicity of passion. They seem especially conceived to deny Petrarchan sublimity and the central self that forms its major premise. How can they do all this at once? By superposing a rhetorical poetic on a serious one. The sonnets include enormous logical inconsistencies. The uncertainties and the manifest absurdities of the sonnets are meant to give us pause. Perception psychologists tell us it is impossible simultaneously to perceive an object and analyze our mode of perception. Something like this the sonnets ask us to do nevertheless. If the sonnets are more profound than other Elizabethan sequences, this profundity comes not simply from Shakespeare's decision to write, in maturity, of fulfilled love, or to widen his cast to an androgynous range. He also widens the range of attitudes demanded of the perceiver. Or rather, he brings to more precise focus the double poetic that the sonnet sequence as a whole worked within, he makes it part of his subject. For from Petrarch on, the sonnet sequence combined two extremes, a sublime goal and a game procedure, without reflecting on or perhaps even noting the enormous gap between them. Shakespeare both notes and reflects upon it. He sees that the form draws on two extreme, two opposed, theories of motive, and on the two theories of rhetoric and attitudes toward style appropriate to each. The sonnets thus share the main concern of *Venus and Adonis* and *Lucrece*, the nature of human motive.

Ransom's churlish article, "Shakespeare at Sonnets," stumbled over an important truth. What troubled Ransom, arguing that Shakespeare should have been more like Donne, was that the act of formal discipline seemed almost divorced from the subject. In a way it is, and meant to be seen so. Form and subject inseparable; form and subject divisible. Such is the sonnet-form allegory, a series of poems alike in form, utterly different as poems. Sublime and dramatic motive, serious and rhetorical, move forward on parallel tracks. The sonnets are a spontaneous outpouring of feeling. But never was feeling more prompted by a form already in being, a formal challenge. The fundamental parallelism the sonnets seek to enforce is, obviously, that between the lover and the poet. Both are outgoing, self-sacrificing, seek a fundamental commitment, a hermaphroditic union. Both are narcissistic, self-serving, seek a hermaphroditic self-sufficiency. Both pour out, dissolve the self. Both display and hence reinforce it. This fundamental duplicity both explains and justifies the strategy of double poetic. Again, the rhetorical style, like Shakespeare's puns, works best when most rhetorical, most opaque, most outrageous.

6

Superposed Plays: Hamlet

Shakespeare uses a variation on the sonnets strategy in *Hamlet*.
He writes two plays in one. Laertes plays the revenge-tragedy
hero straight. He does, true enough, veer toward self-parody,
as when he complains that crying for Ophelia has interfered with
his rants: "I have a speech o' fire, that fain would blaze / But that
this folly drowns it" (4.7.189–90).[1] But he knows his generic duty
and does it. No sooner has his "good old man" (Polonius's role in
the straight, "serious" play) been polished off than he comes
screaming with a rabble army. He delivers predictably and suitably stupid lines like "O thou vile king, / Give me my father"
(4.5.115–16). And the Queen can scarcely manage a "Calmly,
good Laertes" before he begins again: "That drop of blood that's
calm proclaims me bastard, / Cries cuckold to my father, brands
the harlot / Even here between the chaste unsmirchèd brows / Of
my true mother" (4.5.117–20). And just before the King begins to
calm him, to the villainous contentation of both: "How came he
dead? I'll not be juggled with. / To hell allegiance, vows to the
blackest devil, / Conscience and grace to the profoundest pit!"
(4.5.130–32). He plays a straight, hard-charging revenge-hero.

Against him, Ophelia reenacts a delightfully tear-jerking
madwoman stage prop. The King mouths kingly platitudes well
enough ("There's such divinity doth hedge a king . . . "
[4.5.123]), comes up with a suitably stagey, two-phase fail-safe
plot, and urges the hero on ("Revenge should have no bounds").
And the whole comes suitably laced with moralizing guff. So the
King plays a Polonius-of-the-leading-questions: "Laertes, was
your father dear to you?" Laertes, with unusual common sense,
returns, "Why ask you this?" And then the King is off for a dozen

1. Ed. Willard Farnham.

129

Polonian lines on love's alteration by time: "Not that I think you did not love your father, / But that I know love is begun by time . . ." 4.7.109–10). Only then can he get back to, as he phrases it, "the quick o' th' ulcer." And the Queen plays out a careful scene on the brookside where Ophelia drowned. And wrestling in Ophelia's grave, Hamlet, annoyed at being upstaged by Laertes, protests, "I'll rant as well as thou." And, as superb finale, Laertes, at the fencing match, stands there prating about honor with the poisoned rapier in his hand. The poisoner-poisoned motif releases the Christian forgiveness that forgives us, too, for enjoying all that blood. *Hamlet* offers, then, a story frankly calculated to make the audience as well as the compositor run out of exclamation points.

Hamlet obligingly confesses himself Laertes' foil. "In mine ignorance / Your skill shall, like a star i'th'darkest night, / Stick fiery off indeed" (5.2.244–46). It is the other way about, of course. Laertes foils for Hamlet. Shakespeare is up to his old chiasmatic business, writing a play about the kind of play he is writing. The main play overlaps as well as glossing the play criticized—again, a strategy of superposition. Polonius plays a muddling old proverb-monger, and a connoisseur of language, in the Hamlet play, as well as good old man in the Laertes play. Ophelia, though sentimental from the start, is both more naive and more duplicitous in the Hamlet play; and so with the King and Queen, too, both are more complex figures. Shakespeare endeavors especially to wire the two plots in parallel: two avenging sons and two dead fathers; brother's murder and "this brother's wager"; both Hamlet and Laertes in love with Ophelia; both dishonest before the duel (Hamlet pretending more madness than he displays when he kills Polonius), and so on.

Now there is no doubt about how to read the Laertes play: straight revenge tragedy, to be taken—as I've tried to imply in my summary—without solemnity. We are to enjoy the rants as rants. When we get tears instead of a rant, as with the Laertes instance cited earlier, an apology for our disappointment does not come amiss. We are not to be caught up in Laertes' vigorous feeling any more than in Ophelia's bawdy punning. We savor it.

We don't believe the fake King when he maunders on about Divine Right, the divinity that doth hedge a king. We don't "believe" anybody. It is not that kind of play. For explanation, neither the ketchup nor the verbal violence need go further than enjoyment. The more outrageous the stage effects, the more ghastly the brutality, the more grotesque the physical mutilation, the better such a play becomes. Shakespeare had done this kind of thing already and knew what he was about. Such a vehicle packed them in. Just so, when part-sales were falling, would Dickens kill a baby.

The real doubt comes when we ask, "What poetic do we bring to the Hamlet play?" As several of its students have pointed out, it is a wordy play. Eloquence haunts it. Horatio starts the wordiness by supplying a footnote from ancient Rome in the first scene, by improving the occasion with informative reflection. Everybody laughs at Polonius for his moralizing glosses but Hamlet is just as bad. Worse. Gertrude asks him, in the second scene, why he grieves to excess and he gives us a disquisition on seeming and reality in grief. The King follows with *his* bravura piece on grief. Everybody moralizes the pageant. The Hamlet play abounds with triggers for straight revenge-tragedy response. The whole "mystery" of Hamlet's hesitant revenge boils down to wondering why he doesn't go ahead and play his traditional part, complete with the elegant rants we know he can deliver.

The rhetorical attitude is triggered not only by obvious stylistic excess, as we have seen, or by *de trop* moralizing, but by talking about language, by surface reference to surface. This surface reference occurs at every level of the Hamlet play in *Hamlet*, as well as, of course, throughout the Laertes play. Polonius plays a main part here. His tedious prolixity ensures that we notice everyone else's tedious prolixity. And his relish of language, his speech for its own sake, makes us suspect the same appetite in others and in ourselves. The Queen's rejoinder to the marvelous "brevity is the soul of wit" speech in 2.2 could be addressed to almost anybody in the play, including the gravedigger: "More matter, with less art."

Everyone is manipulating everyone else with speechifying and then admitting he has done so. Every grand rhetorical occasion seems no sooner blown than blasted. Polonius offers the famous Gielgud encore about being true to oneself and then sends off Reynaldo to spy and tell fetching lies. The King plays king to angry Laertes then confesses to Gertrude that he has been doing just this. Ophelia is staked out to play innocent maiden so Hamlet can be drawn out and observed. *Hic et ubique.* Is she a stage contrivance or a character? What kind of audience are we to be? Everyone is an actor, Hamlet and his madness most of all. The play is full of minor invitations to attend the surface, the theme of speaking. Even the ghost has to remind himself to be brief—before continuing for thirty-odd lines (1.5). Theatrical gestures are not simply used all the time but described, as in Hamlet's inky cloak and windy suspiration for grief, or the costuming and gesture of the distracted lover, as the innocent Ophelia describes Hamlet's visit:

> My lord, as I was sewing in my closet,
> Lord Hamlet, with his doublet all unbraced,
> No hat upon his head, his stockings fouled,
> Ungartered, and down-gyvèd to his ankle,
> Pale as his shirt, his knees knocking each other,
> And with a look so piteous in purport
> As if he had been loosèd out of hell
> To speak of horrors—he comes before me.
> . . . .
> He took me by the wrist and held me hard.
> Then goes he to the length of all his arm,
> And with his other hand thus o'er his brow
> He falls to such perusal of my face
> As 'a would draw it. Long stayed he so.
> At last, a little shaking of mine arm
> And thrice his head thus waving up and down,
> He raised a sigh so piteous and profound
> As it did seem to shatter all his bulk
> And end his being. That done, he lets me go,

> And with his head over his shoulder turned
> He seemed to find his way without his eyes,
> For out o'doors he went without their helps
> And to the last bended their light on me.
>
> [2.1.77–84, 87–100]

This might have come from an actor's manual. Do we take it as such, respond as professional actors?

The Hamlet play turns in on itself most obviously when the players visit. Dramatic self-consciousness retrogresses a step further as the tragedians of the city talk about themselves doing what they are just now doing in a play depicting them doing just what. . . . The debate is about rightful succession, of course, like both the Laertes and the Hamlet plays. "What, are they children? Who maintains 'em? How are they escoted? Will they pursue the quality no longer than they can sing? Will they not say afterwards, if they should grow themselves to common players (as it is most like, if their means are no better), their writers do them wrong to make them exclaim against their own succession?" (2.2.338–44). Who are the children in the "real" plays? Hamlet had invoked a typical cast a few lines earlier (314 ff.) such as *Hamlet* itself uses and stressed that "he that plays the king shall be welcome." Hamlet will use the play, that is, *as a weapon*, the propaganda side of rhetorical poetic, to complement the Polonius-pleasure side. But before that, there is a rehearsal, for effect, to see whether the players are good enough to play the play within the play. Here, even more clearly than in the Laertes play, we confront the connoisseur's attitude toward language. Polonius supplies a chorus that for once fits: "Fore God, my lord, well spoken, with good accent and good discretion" (2.2.454–55). This to Hamlet, a good actor, as Polonius was in his youth. They proceed in this vein, nibbling the words; "That's good. 'Mobled queen' is good."

The main question pressing is not, How does the feedback work? What relation is there, for example, between rugged Pyrrhus and Hamlet, or Laertes? Or what relation with the King, who also topples a kingdom? And why is Hamlet so keen to reach

Hecuba? The main question is, How does all this connoisseurship affect the "serious" part of *Hamlet*? *Hamlet* is one of the great
tragedies. It has generated more comment than any other written
document in English literature, one would guess, reverent, serious comment on it as a serious play. Yet finally can we take *any* of
its rhetoric seriously? If so, how much and when? The play is full
of the usual release mechanisms for the rhetorical poetic. And, at
the end, the Laertes play is there as stylistic control, to mock us if
we have made the naive response. But what is the sophisticated
response?

Hamlet focuses the issue, and the play, the plays, when he
finally gets to Hecuba. He who has been so eager for a passionate
speech is yet surprised when it comes and when it seizes the
player:

> O, what a rogue and peasant slave am I!
> Is it not monstrous that this player here,
> But in a fiction, in a dream of passion,
> Could force his soul so to his own conceit
> That from her working all his visage wanned,
> Tears in his eyes, distraction in his aspect,
> A broken voice, and his whole function suiting
> With forms to his conceit? And all for nothing,
> For Hecuba!
> What's Hecuba to him, or he to Hecuba,
> That he should weep for her? What would he do
> Had he the motive and the cue for passion
> That I have?
>
> •[2.2.534–46]

Hamlet makes the point that dances before us in every scene.
Dramatic, rhetorical motive is stronger than "real," serious motive. Situation prompts feeling in this play, rather than the other
way round. Feelings are not real until played. Drama, ceremony,
is always needed to authenticate experience. On the battlements
Hamlet—with ghostly reinforcement—makes his friends not
simply swear but make a big scene of it. Laertes keeps asking for
more ceremonies for Ophelia's burial and is upset by his father's

hugger-mugger interment. Hamlet plays and then breaks off ("Something too much of this") a stoic friendship scene with Horatio in 3.2. The stronger, the more genuine the feeling, the greater the need to display it.

The answer, then, to "What would he do . . . ?" is, presumably, "Kill the King!"? Not at all. "He would drown the stage with tears / And cleave the general ear with horrid speech" (2.2.546–47). He would rant even better. And this Hamlet himself, by way of illustration, goes on to do:

> Yet I,
> A dull and muddy-mettled rascal, peak
> Like John-a-dreams, unpregnant of my cause,
> And can say nothing. No, not for a king,
> Upon whose property and most dear life
> A damned defeat was made. Am I a coward?
> Who calls me villain? breaks my pate across?
> Plucks off my beard and blows it in my face?
> Tweaks me by the nose? gives me the lie i'th'throat
> As deep as to the lungs? Who does me this?
> Ha, 'swounds, I should take it, for it cannot be
> But I am pigeon-livered and lack gall
> To make oppression bitter, or ere this
> I should ha' fatted all the region kites
> With this slave's offal. Bloody, bawdy villain!
> Remorseless, treacherous, lecherous, kindless villain!
> O, vengeance!
>
> [2.2.551–67]

Hamlet is here having a fine time dining off his own fury, relishing his sublime passion. He gets a bit confused, to be sure: saying nothing is not his problem. If somebody did call him villain or pluck his beard it would be better, for his grievance would then find some dramatic equivalent, would become real enough to act upon. But he enjoys himself thoroughly. He also sees himself clearly, or at least clearly enough to voice our opinion of his behavior: "Why, what an ass am I! This is most brave, / That I, the son of a dear father murdered, / Prompted to my revenge by heaven and hell, / Must like a whore unpack my heart with words" (2.2.568–71).

Hamlet is one of the most appealing characters the mind of man has ever created but he really is a bit of an ass, and not only here but all through the play. He remains incorrigibly dramatic. Do we like him because he speaks to our love of dramatic imposture? Because his solution, once he has seen his own posturing as such, is not immediate action but more playing? "I'll have these players / Play something like the murder of my father / Before mine uncle" (2.2.580–82). Playing is where we will find reality, find the truth. The play works, of course, tells Hamlet again what he already knows, has had a spirit come specially from purgatory to tell him. But that is not the point. Or rather, that is the point insofar as this is a serious play. The rhetorical purpose is to sustain reality until yet another dramatic contrivance—ship, grave scene, duel—can sustain it yet further.

We saw in the sonnets how a passage can invoke opaque attitudes by logical incongruity. Something of the sort happens in the scene after this speech, the "To be or not to be" centerpiece. Plays flourish within plays here, too, of course. The King and Polonius dangle Ophelia as bait and watch. Hamlet sees this. He may even be, as W. A. Bebbington suggested,[2] reading the "To be or not to be" speech from a book, using it, literally, as a stage prop to bemuse the spyers-on, convince them of his now-become-suicidal madness. No one in his right mind will fault the poetry. But it is irrelevant to anything that precedes. It fools Ophelia—no difficult matter—but it should not fool us. The question is whether Hamlet will act directly or through drama? Not at all. Instead, is he going to end it in the river? I put it thus familiarly to penetrate the serious numinosity surrounding this passage. Hamlet anatomizes grievance for all time. But does *he* suffer these grievances? He has a complaint indeed against the King and one against Ophelia. Why not do something about them instead of meditating on suicide? If the book is a stage prop, or the speech a trap for the hidden listeners, of course, the

2. "Soliloquy?," *Times Literary Supplement*, 20 March 1969, p. 289.

question of relevancy doesn't arise. The speech works beautifully. But we do not usually consider it a rhetorical trick. It is the
most serious speech in the canon. But is it? It tells us nothing
about Hamlet except what we already know—he is a good actor.
Its relevance, in fact, may lurk just here. The real question by this
point in the play is exactly this one: *Is* Hamlet or not? Or does he
just act? What kind of self does he possess?

The whole play, we know, seeks authenticity, reality behind
the arras, things as they are. Hamlet, we are to assume, embodies
the only true self, the central self amidst a cast of wicked phonies.
The play, seen this way, provided a natural delight for both the
Victorians and the existentialists; their sentimentalism about the
central self ran the same way. Yet the question really is whether
Hamlet is *to be*, to act rather than reenact. Much has been written
on the Melancholy-Man-in-the-Renaissance and how his problems apply to Hamlet. Much more has been written on Hamlet's
paralysis. Yet, how irrelevant all this commentary is to the real
problem, not *what* Hamlet's motive is but *what kind of* motive.
Why can't he act? Angels and ministers of grace, he does nothing
else. Polonius, Rosencrantz and Guildenstern, Laertes,
Claudius, all go to it. But Hamlet never breaks through to "reality." His motives and his behavior remain dramatic from first to
last. So, in spite of all those bodies at the end, commentators
wonder if *Hamlet* amounts to a tragedy and, if so, what kind.
Hamlet lacks the serious, central self tragedy requires. We are
compelled to stand back, hold off our identification, and hence to
locate the play within rhetorical coordinates, a tragicomedy
about the two kinds of self and the two kinds of motive.

We see this theme in that Q_2 scene (4.4) where Fortinbras and
his army parade, with seeming irrelevance—at least to many
directors, who cut it—across the stage. They parade so that
Hamlet can reflect upon them. The theme is motive. The scene
begins as a straightforward lesson in the vanity of human
wishes. They go, the Captain tells Hamlet, "to gain a little patch
of ground / That hath in it no profit but the name" (4.4.18–19).
Hamlet seems to get the point, "the question of this straw," the
absurd artificiality of human motive, and especially of aristocra-

tic war, war for pleasure, for the pure glory of it. But then out
jumps another non sequitur soliloquy:

> How all occasions do inform against me
> And spur my dull revenge! What is a man,
> If his chief good and market of his time
> Be but to sleep and feed? A beast, no more.
> Sure he that made us with such large discourse,
> Looking before and after, gave us not
> That capability and godlike reason
> To fust in us unused. Now, whether it be
> Bestial oblivion, or some craven scruple
> Of thinking too precisely on th' event—
> A thought which, quartered, hath but one part wisdom
> And ever three parts coward—I do not know
> Why yet I live to say, "This thing's to do,"
> Sith I have cause, and will, and strength, and means
> To do 't.
>
> [4.4.32–46]

What has reason to do with revenge? His question—why, with
all his compelling reasons, doesn't he go on—is again well taken.
Shakespeare has carefully given him the realest reasons a revenge hero ever had—father murdered, mother whored, kingdom usurped, his innocent maiden corrupted in her imagination. The answer to Hamlet's question marches about on the
stage before him. As usual, he does not fully understand the
problem. It is the Player King's tears all over again. Fortinbras's
motivation is sublimely artificial, entirely dramatic. Honor. It
has no profit in it but the name. Hamlet cannot act because he
cannot find a way to dramatize his revenge. Chances he has, but,
as when he surprises Claudius praying, they are not dramatic.
Claudius is alone. To fall upon him and kill him would not be
revenge, as he says, not because Claudius will die shriven but
because he will not see it coming, because nobody is watching.

So, when Hamlet continues his soliloquy, he draws a moral
precisely opposite to the expected one. Again, logical discontinuity triggers stylistic attitude:

Examples gross as earth exhort me.
Witness this army of such mass and charge,
Led by a delicate and tender prince,
Whose spirit, with divine ambition puffed,
Makes mouths at the invisible event,
Exposing what is mortal and unsure
To all that fortune, death, and danger dare,
Even for an eggshell. Rightly to be great
Is not to stir without great argument,
But greatly to find quarrel in a straw
When honor's at the stake. How stand I then,
That have a father killed, a mother stained,
Excitements of my reason and my blood,
And let all sleep, while to my shame I see
The imminent death of twenty thousand men
That for a fantasy and trick of fame
Go to their graves like beds, fight for a plot
Whereon the numbers cannot try the cause,
Which is not tomb enough and continent
To hide the slain? O, from this time forth,
My thoughts be bloody, or be nothing worth!

[4.4.46–66]

He sees but does not see. In some way, Fortinbras represents where he wants to go, what he wants to be, how he wants to behave. But he doesn't see how, nor altogether do we. If ever an allegorical puppet was dragged across a stage it is Fortinbras. Yet he haunts the play. His divine ambition begins the action of the play; he gets that offstage introduction Shakespeare is so fond of; he marches to Norway to make a point about motive; and he marches back at the end, inherits Denmark. Yet he stays cardboard. It is not real motive he represents but martial honor much rather.

Shakespeare sought to give *Hamlet* a pronounced military coloration from first to last. The play begins on guard; the ghost wears armor; Denmark is a most warlike state. Military honor is the accepted motive in a Denmark Fortinbras rightly inherits.

Honor will cure what is rotten in Denmark, restore its proper values. Hamlet cannot set the times right because he cannot find in martial honor a full and sufficient motive for human life. Hamlet, says Fortinbras, would have done well had he been king, but we may be permitted to doubt it. He thinks too much. Yet honor and the soldier's life provide the model motive for *Hamlet*. All his working life, Shakespeare was fascinated and perplexed by how deeply the military motive satisfied man. It constituted a sublime secular commitment which, like the religious commitment, gave all away to get all back. Hamlet's self-consciousness keeps him from it, yes, but even more his search for real purpose. Chivalric war—all war, perhaps—is manufactured purpose. Hamlet can talk about clutching it to his bosom but he cannot do it, for there is nothing *inevitable* about it.

Military honor is finally a role, much like Laertes' role as revenge hero. Both roles are satisfying, both integrate and direct the personality. But once you realize that you are playing the role for just these reasons, using it as a self-serving device, its attraction fades. As its inevitability diminishes, so does its reality. War and revenge both prove finally so rewarding because they provide, by all the killing, the irrefutable reality needed to bolster the role, restore its inevitability. Thus Shakespeare chose them, a revenge plot superposed on a Fortinbras-honor plot, for his play about motive. They provided a model for the kind of motive men find most satisfying; they combine maximum dramatic satisfaction with the irrefutable reality only bloody death can supply. In the Elizabethan absurdity as in our own, men kill others and themselves because that is the only real thing left to do. It is a rare paradox and Shakespeare builds his play upon it.

But even death is not dependable. We can learn to make sport of it, enjoy it. So the gravedigger puns on his craft. So, too, I suppose, Fortinbras laconically remarks at the end of the play: "Such a sight as this / Becomes the field, but here shows much amiss." Death's reality can vanish too. All our purposes end up, like the skull Hamlet meditates on, a stage prop. It is not accidental that the language which closes the play is theatrical. Hamlet even in death does not escape the dramatic self. When the bodies are "high on a stage . . . placèd to the view" Horatio will "speak to th' yet unknowing world," will authenticate the proceeding with a rhetorical occasion. Hamlet's body, Fortinbras commands, is to be borne "like a soldier to the stage, / For he was likely, had he been put on, / To have proved most royal."

Nor is it accidental that Hamlet kills Polonius. The act is his real attempt at revenge, Polonius his real enemy. Polonius embodies the dramatic self-consciousness which stands between Hamlet and the roles—Avenger and King—he was born to play. But Polonius pervades the whole of Hamlet's world and lurks within Hamlet himself. Only death can free Hamlet. Perhaps this is why he faces it with nonchalance. Much has been said about Hamlet's stoicism, but how unstoical the play really is! Honest feeling demands a dramatic equivalent to make it real just as artifice does. Stoicism demands a preexistent reality, a central self beyond drama, which the play denies. Stoicism is death and indeed, in *Hamlet,* the second follows hard upon the avowal of the first. We have no choice but to play.

And so Hamlet chooses his foil and plays. I have been arguing that the play invokes rhetorical coordinates as well as serious ones. It makes sense, if this is so, that it should end with a sublime game and the triumph of chance. Hamlet never solves his problem, nor does chance solve it for him, nor does the play solve it for us. No satisfactory model for motive, no movement from game to sublime, is suggested. Hamlet can finally kill the King because the King thoughtfully supplies a dramatic occasion appropriate to the deed. And Hamlet can kill Laertes because dramatic motive has destroyed naive purpose. And vice versa. But Hamlet cannot get rid of his dramatic self, his dramatic motives. The duel allegorizes the quarrel between kinds of motive which the play has just dramatized. And the duel, like the play, is a zero-sum game. Interest for both sides adds up to zero. The play leaves us, finally, where it leaves Hamlet. We have savored the violence and the gorgeous poetry and been made aware that we do. We have been made to reflect on play as well as purpose. We have not been shown how to move from one to the other. Nor that it *cannot* be done. We are left, like those in the play, dependent on death and chance to show us how to put our two motives, our two selves, together.

Shakespeare as a mature playwright is not supposed to be an opaque stylist. The great unity of his mature tragedies is a style we look through, not at. The gamesman with words fades out with the nondramatic poems and early infatuations like *Love's Labor's Lost*. *Hamlet* shows, by itself, how wrong this view of Shakespeare's development is. The play depends upon an alternation of opaque and transparent styles for its meaning. The alternation almost *is* the meaning. *Hamlet* is a play about motive, about style, and thus perhaps, of the mature plays, an exception? I don't think so. Where Shakespeare is most sublime he is also most rhetorical and both poetics are likely to be present in force. To illustrate such a thesis would constitute an agreeable task. The lines it would follow are clear enough. They would yield explanation of the double plot more basic than the comic/serious one. They would render the comic/tragic division altogether less important than it now seems.

In play after play the same stylistic strategy illustrates the same juxtaposition of motive, of play and purpose. Richard cannot learn the difference. Hal must. Lear can play the king but he has never *been* a king. *Antony and Cleopatra* juxtaposes not only public and private life but two poetics and two selves. The double plot becomes, over and over, a serious plot-poetic and a play plot-poetic. The fatal innocence of Shakespeare's characters turns out, over and over, to be innocence about the real nature of their motivation. All through the *Henriad* political rhetoric must be *seen* as rhetoric. Egypt is meant to be *seen* as more wordy and more metaphorical than Rome. *Romeo and Juliet* depends on our seeing the Petrarchan rhetoric as such, else we will mistake the kind of play it is, a play where death authenticates game. Lear on the heath, that centerpiece of Shakespearean sublimity, alters his outlines considerably within rhetorical coordinates. Shakespearean tragedy may come to seem, as in *Hamlet*, a juxtaposition of the two motives with a hole in the middle, with no way to connect them. The comedies collapse them. And the problem plays and romances try to make a path between the two, see them in dynamic interchange. The two things that obsessed Shakespeare were style and motive, and his career can be charted coherently from beginning to end in terms of their interrelation. In this he typifies the stylistic strategy of the Renaissance as a whole. The real question of motive lay beyond good and evil. It was the principal task of the self-conscious rhetorical style to point this moral. Human flesh is sullied with self-consciousness, with theatricality, and these will be the ground for whatever authentic morality any of us can muster.

7

The Self as Middle Style: Cortegiano

Il Libro del Cortegiano unites in a single document most of the stylistic configurations discussed thus far. The conversation is built upon a series of speeches, and takes its meaning from their relation to the layers of context enclosing them. The book is self-conscious about language from the beginning; style and usage are discussed as such, transcended also in a final, or perhaps semifinal, sublime *Altitudo*. Castiglione employs generic layering to prohibit any single-orchestration coziness. He leads us in several directions at once. *The Courtier*, though obviously in the mirror-of-princes tradition, displaces the stress slightly—with a tacit shrug at real princes—from the prince onto his courtier, and then displaces it further by discussing the court lady sympathetically. Castiglione invokes the shade of ideal *res publica* too, of Plato's *Republic* as well as Xenophon's mirror, the *Cyropaedia*. He stands, as well, self-consciously in the Ciceronian shadow of *De Oratore*—fairly enough, considering his debt to it. Thus he offers a rhetorical treatise, too. Much of the Ciceronian borrowing comes in a section on comedy which recalls the joke book. But a persistent philosophic concern balances this frivolity, moves *The Courtier* toward Platonic dialogue. The anatomy of love and sexuality recalls the *Symposium* especially. Indeed, Castiglione's structural thinking may have started there. A philosophical treatise, then, as well as a political and educational one, it is also a basic etiquette handbook, superficial only in theorizing about the social surface. So often has *The Courtier* been called aristocratic that we might stress this last bourgeois purpose, concern with getting the social surface right. An aristocrat does not ponder the surface so. He floats on it. Again generic tension: aristocratic lightness contends with bourgeois didacticism. Castiglione casts himself as a social historian too. His book portrays an Urbino vanished, an Urbino almost golden. All the basic historiographic questions—what we can know of the past, how and why we know it—suggest themselves and find implicit answers. *The Courtier* becomes, considered as history, almost a "faction," a fiction from real life, halfway between life and art. Past and present, self and city, poetic and historic reality, all work together.

The basic preoccupations of the commentary again indicate a document built on the rhetorical view of life: tone, seriousness, structure. How are we to take such a book? When is it serious? How does Bembo's sublimity follow from the frivolities preceding? Castiglione invokes the broadest range of serious topics and considers them in a frivolous temper and tempo. He makes, as with *Gargantua and Pantagruel,* a book which is no one single thing, he calculates a form which prohibits specialization. Yet the subject is clear and clearly in the title, an exercise in definition: all things lead toward defining the courtier. Castiglione reveals his theme by placing the whole of *The Courtier* in a matrix of game. Seriousness, thus deliberately posed, must become the main concern. It is all a game—"the best game that could possibly be played." But, since "game" is never defined, neither is the tone of what follows. Motive, sublimity, love, decorum, all come to share a common ontological peril. And the courtier they create—is he the image of Western man or a social butterfly? Can Castiglione have posed this question by accident? He seems deliberately to juxtapose two fundamentally opposed orchestrations of reality, the two conceptions of man we have been considering, rhetorical man and serious man, the rhetorical and the serious views of the world. His strategy juxtaposes them to create a new definition of seriousness, a model of motive for a renewedly self-conscious Western man.

The Courtier reports a game. We can think of games as essentially separate from life (comment on, preparation for, whatever) or as quintessential, human culture itself a game. The first is a serious view, obviously, and the second rhetorical. We can read *The Courtier* with either assumption. In the first, the game will remain just that, a game. The possibilities for the courtier will remain exercises in possibility. No opinion, however serious in itself, will be advanced seriously. All figure as counters in a debating game. The aim will be not truth but rhetorical victory. All motives will be game motives, rhetorical, *ad hoc* and *ad hominem*. The grand design strives but to pass time, to entertain, please, embroider an idle hour. Castiglione means to urge this view upon us. The courtier game is not the first game suggested. The game begins with a game to select the worthiest game, the game "piú degno di celebrarsi in questa compagnia."[1] Emilia's motives for suggesting *her* game are suitably rhetorical and self-interested: little blame and less labor. And the object of the game is suitably ludic: to suggest the game worthiest to be played, most entertaining. Thus the *motive* for the proposals is ludic, to win the game of suggesting the game. The suggestions, like everything else in *The Courtier*, run the gamut from Cesare Gonzaga's moralizing, "Let each confess a characteristic folly," to fra Serafino's demande, "onde è che le donne quasi tutte hanno in odio i ratti, ed aman le serpi"—why all women hate rats and love snakes.

After Ottaviano's suggestion halfway between, Federico Fregoso advances the winner—forming the perfect courtier, "esplicando tutte le condizioni e particular qualità che si richieggono a chi merita questo nome" (1.12). It pleases Emilia and the Duchess—whereupon everyone agrees that this is the best game that could be played ("il piú bel gioco che far si potesse"). *The Courtier* is rich in such subtle qualifications. They like the game because the Duchess and Emilia like it. And why do these two ladies like it? Because it flatters them. *The Courtier* can tell us how to flatter without seeming to, and no better illustration than here. The game is the best, because the most *flattering*, the most narcissistic, that could possibly be played. They will *always*, whatever they say, talk of themselves.

Thus motive has been qualified at two removes before the game begins. Emilia, to start it, qualifies motive yet further.

---

1. 1.6. All quotations are from *Il Libro del Cortegiano*, ed. Vittorio Cian, 4th ed. rev. (Florence [1947]).

Ludovico is selected as master of ceremonies, πατὴρ λόγου, for rhetorical rather than serious purposes, because he will certainly be contentious ("perché, dicendo ogni cosa al contrario, come speramo che farete, il gioco sarà piú bello"). He accepts in just this spirit. He will not put off his task a night and think. That would constitute the wrong kind of challenge, tax diligence rather than quickness of wit. Instead he will improvise. If with approval, he will have won a bigger bet unprepared; if not, he will be excused by not having given the matter previous thought (1.13).

He continues, in a remarkable speech, to push the matter even further into the game sphere: "dico, che in ogni cosa tanto è difficil conoscer la vera perfezion, che quasi è impossibile; e questo per la varietà de' guidicii." An ideal is impossible and it is not, and anyway it is all a matter of opinion. People differ not only with each other but with themselves: "Né io già contrasterò che 'l mio sia migliore che 'l vostro; ché non solamente a voi po parer una cosa ed a me un'altra, ma a me stesso poría parer or una cosa ed ora un'altra." The matter could not well be rendered more conjectural and frivolous than this extended and involved narrative machinery renders it.

The rhetorical context perseveres. We never forget that each speaker speaks in attack or defense, from egotism. Everyone impugns everyone else's motives as a matter of course as well as of jest. Nearly every speech begins or ends with laughter, and most aim to evoke it. Arguments are held lightly, as counters, shields, weapons. Much debate has contested what Castiglione "really thought" about the issues at stake. Manifestly such an environment makes it impossible to know what *anyone* really thinks. This is a game, not life. Nobody is serious, except perhaps Bembo, who loses control and floats upward like a gas-filled balloon.

If we come to *The Courtier* with a serious referent reality then, and a serious referent self, we shall find a narrative carefully prepared and consistently sustained as a game, a rhetorical contest. The behavior *within* the game is completely rhetorical, of course. Pose, not central self, victory not truth, pleasure not improvement, prevail. Pleasure is the presiding deity. Every time the discussion, silly or significant, threatens boredom, Emilia or the Duchess cuts it off. We are free, of course, to take the opinions expressed as seriously as we choose. But the narrative, by definition of the game, can offer no help. If you want to take a game seriously, that is your probably tedious business.

If we approach *The Courtier* with rhetorical coordinates, however, a curious transformation comes over it. The game of courtier, far from being one they "have never played," becomes one that they play every day. The game becomes *realistic*, a straightforward mimesis of a dramatic reality. Now Castiglione encourages us to apply rhetorical coordinates as much as he encourages serious ones. *The Courtier* is, after all, a portrait of aristocratic Urbino. Games are taken to be its most characteristic reality. Urbino succeeds at these things much better than other places. Clearly Urbino's ideality in some way emerges from the idea of game. Serious life, war, and politics aim at creating the climate of aristocratic leisure in which such activities flourish. They provide the justifying activity for the state. Furthermore, the very narcissism of the game encourages us to apply rhetorical coordinates. The players talk about themselves, about the ideal forms which they wish their lives to approximate, and these all amount to a dramatic reality and a dramatic self. Their game is reflexive, an anatomy of their everyday lives, a game about a game. Thus, paradoxically, we come to take the arguments themselves *seriously*. There is no "as if" about them. We are being admitted behind the scenes. This game is special. As Castiglione emphasizes at the beginning, a special mood of festivity prevails. We might call it group confessional, therapy. So emerges the special typicality, as it were, of this game, and the reason why a game is chosen as Urbino's characteristic activity: the game symbolizes the kind of seriousness Castiglione sees Urbino as representing, the characteristic seriousness, he suggests, of human life.

We are invited, then, to read *The Courtier* in two ways at once. The two ways stand fundamentally opposed. Castiglione's narrative strategy aims to bring all that he discusses under this double gaze. Can we hold both ways of seeing in the mind at once? *The Courtier* trains us. It does so by rapid temporal alternation, by continually switching back and forth. The speeches in *The Courtier* are often long, long enough at least to catch us up in matter rather than rhetorical stance. Then we are pulled back into the argument, laughed at, scorned, whatever. We recoil into a rhetorical world, only to be caught up again in serious reality. Thus on a small scale the oscillation works—if we read seriously. If rhetorically, the opposite happens. We are always returned to seriousness when we return to rhetorical interchange, to game when we return to matter. Castiglione has taken the speech-narrative-speech alternation and superencrypted two contrary patterns of expectation above it. They might be diagrammed thus:✕◯◯◯◯✕.As a result, we move continually in and out of seriousness, stay always in motion. We never adopt one relation to the world without lively awareness that we might have adopted the other.

Such a narrative method by nature discourages static analysis. You can see only half the process at once. You must keep moving. And the whole process will be isomorphic only with the whole book. (This is one reason why Castiglione wants the structure open-ended and repetitive, and ends by recalling *another* conversation the following night.) If you isolate a part of it, fail to reckon in the whole narrative context, you will not understand that part. It is a long book and the duration of real time required to read it, as with *The Faerie Queene* or *Clarissa*, makes a difference. It takes time to train us as we pass through. For we are asked to learn not a pattern of concepts—of whatever sort—but a skill. Reading *The Courtier* is like learning to ride a bicycle, not like learning about Renaissance Platonism. Critical analysis, though needed, defeats its own purpose and *The Courtier*'s. Worry about *how* you ride a bicycle and you fall off. So, here, Castiglione tries to teach us a skill, an intuitive not a conscious, considered response. No surprise, this. The theme of intuitive judgment, intuitive response, runs through *The Courtier* from first to last. To think about response inevitably spoils it. Yet it must be thought on. Castiglione solves the paradox by putting it in motion, alternating nature and nurture concurrently. No real syncretism is involved. That would degrade the interaction. Oscillation is recommended, not blending. Such a process wars with logic, of course, as it is intuition's business to do. As we read we are not always to remember how we read it. Again like *The Faerie Queene*, *The Courtier* requests a selective forgetting. And to be understood, it demands our repeated experience of itself. It trains us in intuitive knowing, in a skill. What is known is not a collection of objects but a corresponding process. Thus *The Courtier* is by design no one thing. Castiglione seeks to build a dynamic not a static model of man and his society. And so the problem of structure, of narrative context, looms so large. Here is where, how, the process is created.

We become, put through Castiglione's course, the prime pupils of Western literature. The two fundamental categories this literature seeks to express here find their fundamental, alternating pattern. Our experience in reading is designed to parallel the courtier's experience at court. We too alternate serious and rhetorical views, learn and forget, pose spontaneously, develop a talent for, a skill in, living.

Castiglione makes this clear enough. He bludgeons us at the beginning with his central concept—*sprezzatura*. The term's manifest absurdity—a certain carefully rehearsed and prepared spontaneous unrehearsedness—disappears if it describes a process taking place over time. A skill. The company is talking about grace (1.25). Cesare Gonzaga asks Count Ludovico how it can be acquired. The Count replies by invoking rhetorical coordinates: "Obligato non son io . . . ad insegnarvi a diventar aggraziati, né altro; ma solamente a dimostrarvi qual abbia ad essere un perfetto Cortegiano." He has undertaken not to teach grace but only to model a perfect courtier. Having reinvoked the rhetorical coordinates he transcends them to discuss seriously how to teach grace, or rather whom to steal it from: "cosí il nostro Cortegiano averà da rubare questa grazia da que' che a lui parerà che la tenghino. . . ." Then comes the famous passage on sprezzatura, the art of concealing art, of unaffected affectation:

Ma avendo io già piú volte pensato meco onde nasca questa grazia, lassando quegli che dalle stelle l'hanno, trovo una regula universalissima, la qual mi par valer circa questo in tutte le cose umane che si facciano o dicano piú che alcuna altra: e ciò è fuggir quanto piú si po, e come un asperissimo e pericoloso scoglio, la affettazione; e, per dir forse una nova parola, usar in ogni cosa una certa sprezzatura, che nasconda l'arte, e dimostri, ciò che si fa e dice, venir fatto senza fatica e quasi senza pensarvi. Da questo credo io che derivi assai la grazia: perché delle cose rare e ben fatte ognun sa la difficultà, onde in esse la facilità genera grandissima maraviglia; e per lo contrario, il sforzare, e, come si dice, tirar per i capegli, dà summa disgrazia, e fa estimar poco ogni cosa, per grande ch'ella si sia. [1.26]

But having thought often already about where this grace comes from, excluding those who were born with it, I find one universal rule, which seems valid to me above all others in human affairs, whether in acting or speaking. That is to flee as much as you can—as if it were a very rough, perilous rock—affectation. And, to coin a new word perhaps, to observe in all behavior a certain *sprezzatura*, so that art is hidden and whatever is said and done seems without effort or forethought. From this, I believe, a great deal of grace comes. Everyone knows the difficulty of unusual, well done things, and so ability in such things causes very great wonder. To labor, on the other hand and, as who should say, to drag forth by the hair of the head, seems most ungraceful and makes us disesteem something, however marvelous it may be.

A rationale for hypocrisy certainly, within serious coordinates at least. Rhetorically, it is honest posing. Castiglione wants both. Affectation is not to be banished for romantic sincerity. In that sense, he obviously thought *nothing* natural to man. The alternative is a fully learned, complete possession of an attribute. We make it ours through the repeated acting out which naturalizes

it, makes it a completely learned skill. No paradox haunts spontaneity's being a skill. What else can it be?

Castiglione sets out in *The Courtier* to describe the courtier's
"parts," catalog his attributes. At the beginning, he is careful to
specify how they are to be possessed, the spirit in which they are
to be exercised. Sprezzatura retains the force of its parent verb. It
involves disdain. It declares, brags about, successful enselfment,
a permanent incorporation in, addition to, the self. It satisfies
because it publicly declares an enlarged self. One has *acquired* an
area of *instinctive* response. And the audience response certifies
it, makes it real. Thus the self is enriched, amplified, and as sign
of amplification comes the effortlessness, the sprezzatura. What
Castiglione has done here is to model the growth of the self, a
growth equally narcissistic, equally dependent on audience, on,
as G. H. Mead puts it, a "generalized other." Such a growth, as
Mead describes it in *Mind, Self, and Society*, indeed involves a
process, a continual interchange. Each individual must learn, in
addition to a symbolic vocabulary of word and gesture, how to
read his own gestures as others read them. He must, as he grows
up, through the repeated dramatic interchanges of socialization
learn how to reenact both the roles which constitute his own self
and the roles of others which respond to his own. He must grow
up, that is, as a miniature narcissistic drama. The success his self
will find, the fullness, the joy, will depend on how well he has
deposited the dramatic reality of his society within his own
personality. The hoary issues of sincerity fail to arise here because the model is dynamic not static, process not entity. The self
at any time comprises a series of experiences and potential experiences, drama enacted and yet to be. If Castiglione is a behaviorist, he is Mead's kind of behaviorist, a dynamic one. Man
cannot know naive response. Our attention starts out selective,
nature and nurture in dynamic alternation.

It follows that we cannot cut our selves loose from the society
which creates and sustains them. The pressure to do so persists,
to be sure, never more than now. Castiglione must come to terms
with it too, as we see in Bembo's Platonic sublimity. But the
model of self Castiglione invokes by his discussion and dramati-

zation of sprezzatura denies such radical sublimity, such an independent self. It is not forbidden. It is impossible.

Identity, the self, in such a theory proves then both process and skill. No eleatic substance informs it. A process, a drama, as Castiglione saw it, a game. Thus *The Courtier's* narcissistic form is not simply a happy choice. Given what Castiglione had to say, it is inevitable. If Mead is right, the creation of the self means continuous drama, and drama sustains the self once created. Such a conception of self does not advocate hypocrisy. It simply places it, shows it as part of a larger process. The self is many selves:

> We realize in everyday conduct and experience that an individual does not mean a great deal of what he is doing and saying. We frequently say that such an individual is not himself. We come away from an interview with a realization that we have left out important things, that there are parts of the self that did not get into what was said. What determines the amount of the self that gets into communication is the social experience itself. Of course, a good deal of the self does not need to get expression. We carry on a whole series of different relationships to different people. We are one thing to one man and another thing to another. There are parts of the self which exist only for the self in relationship to itself. . . . There are all sorts of different selves answering to all sorts of different social reactions. It is the social process itself that is responsible for the appearance of the self; it is not there as a self apart from this type of experience.
>
> A multiple personality is in a certain sense normal. [*Mind, Self, and Society,* p. 142]

Sincerity, then, full expression of the self, depends on the opportunities for expression society affords it. And so Urbino becomes the main character in *The Courtier.* Like the self, it emerges as process not entity. Its history must be literary, dramatic. Its essence can be preserved no other way.

Urbino is sustained by the same kind of skill which sustains the selves who compose it. The courtier game is played with

sprezzatura, and the game sustains the state. The game enshrines the state's ultimate purpose, an ideal individual. The
game supplies an ideal toward which the state moves, and, since
the ideal is social, by implication an ideal state as well. But
priority matters: Plato talks of a state; Castiglione talks of an
individual. Again, stasis and dynamism. Plato's ideal common-
wealth, like More's, strives for an ideal stasis. A conception of
self like Castiglione's—genesis and continuance—prohibits
such a stasis. Things must continue to change in order to continue to exist. The state, like the individual, must develop in
order to continue being itself. As Ortega reminds us in *La rebelión de las masas*, "La nación está siempre o haciéndose o des-
haciéndose. *Tertium non datur.*" The process must be reasoned
upon,   self-consciously   entertained,   yet   spontaneous—
inevitably a game and entertained as such. Yet its citizens must
be committed to it, citizens, not visiting anthropologists. Citi-
zenship, ideally, emerges from *The Courtier* as a skill much like
selfhood. The same technique is required—holding opposite
worlds in the mind at once. When the conversation turns to
serious themes, as it seems, in book four, Ottaviano poses the
hard question. Is the courtier useful, or an ornamental butterfly?
Castiglione's bitterness threatens to overflow the fictional measure just here. He casts the princes of his time as symbols of
human corruption ("poi che oggidí i principi son tanto corrotti
dalle male consuetudini, e dalla ignoranzia e falsa persuasione di
se stessi" [4.9]), and to their allegory of fallen man the courtier
must play an allegorical poet. Ottaviano's argument, as he develops it, insists that the courtier will affect politics by playing
poet-of-the-public-life, by connecting the good with the
pleasurable and thus bridging the gap in our fallen nature. Castiglione has not been sufficiently praised for thus prophetically
charting the dramatistic ingredient in the politics of a self-
conscious state. Whether Castiglione was monarchist or republi-
can seems irrelevant. Either form of government must make
terms with pleasure-loving sinful man. The crucial issue remains, how? Artful, well-directed flattery. No reader of *The
Courtier* ought be surprised. Artful flattery holds Urbino to-

gether. People continually stroke each other, put the best construction on events. They often, too, apply the worst
construction—and then soften this with flattery. The serious
reader demands a more vigorous accounting—moral confrontation, satiric scorn at least. Castiglione never allows it. He writes
about style as ingratiation. The courtier cannot change reality. It
will be a drama of some sort. He must become expert in drama, in
stylistic manipulation, so that it will be convincing drama.

The politician, then, will play both poet and critic by turns,
acting and assessing the acting of others. Such purely rhetorical
coordinates observe no difference between being and doing,
between active and contemplative life. In such a process, the
need for an either/or distinction evaporates and both poet and
critic assume their essential places in the state. Their roles,
though, reverse what proverbial wisdom requires. Poets supply
the day-to-day expertise, the needful conversions to pleasure;
the practical serious men design the Utopias, tell the state where
to go. Art is a necessity for man, but a practical not a theoretical or
ornamental one.

A poetic lurks in all of this, as in all political theory. Obviously
enough, it centers on pleasure. Literature's job, like the job of
The Courtier itself, seems to be reality-maintenance. Literature
maintains reality by continually rehearsing it. We are led to
conclude with Castiglione that politics is most often played for
its own sake, for fun, just to assure us that we are alive. Politics is
as literary as life, perhaps more so. It seldom "debates the issues" because the real "issue" is the act of debating. Literature
creates a similar reality but does not pretend so often to purposeful action. The politician as poet and critic must stay alert, skillful, in continually moving from purpose to game, serious to
rhetorical coordinates, as circumstances require. He must know
in his bones what to take seriously, when to play and maintain
reality, or to be serious and destroy in order to rebuild it. The
game sphere provides the home of pleasure. The job of literature,
like the job of politics, is to harmonize and space these journeys
home and to fructify them. For both literature and politics, the
self represents a more efficient version of the state. The back-

and-forth motion is quicker. In this respect, indeed, we might parallel art and self. Both embody condensed, more efficient versions of the public polity, the process on a reduced scale. We must beware of thinking the individual stabler, less a process, than the state because on a smaller scale. The self is no more or less an entity than the state.

The self emerges from *The Courtier*, then, as aesthetic rather than moral entity, as a matter, finally, of taste. Castiglione depicts a self built from the outside in. To know people, we argue from the surface back, from the allegory of clothes and gesture, from the psychopathology of everyday life that men are largely known by. ("Vedete adunque che questi modi e costumi . . . fanno in gran parte che gli omini sian conosciuti" [2.28]. We are not born with an authentic central self. We try to create one. The central self is a skill, instinctive good drama. This does not imply a naive behaviorism—we are merely roles. We are a process which has its genesis in roles, but grows into a characteristically human combination of self-consciousness and skill. The central self is not a substance but an effect, successful process. Castiglione's comparison of this effect with grace exposes the point. We cannot strive for authenticity, for a real self. Like happiness, it seems to come *en passant*. We act in the world inevitably within a matrix of our own interests. We hope these will yield a genuine self, but no inevitability governs the process.

What misleads us are the occupational psychoses our purposes create in each of us. We are formed by our purposes, become the creation of our desires. Surely here emerges the morality in Castiglione's study of the surface. He wants to reverse the process, recommend purposes which will yield a central self. He becomes, seen thus, not scorner of the central self, but a chief defender and prophet. The whole courtier portrait is calculated to yield a central self, not, of course, through naive experience— in Castiglione's view there isn't any naive experience—but through knowledge of the surface. The central self is to be sought through self-consciousness, not around it. So Castiglione proceeds to rearrange purposive life to yield the rich self he wishes to portray. Resources for converting purposive life into game, and thus allowing it to create and reinforce a self, crowd around us. Man will not use them. He wants desperately to return to naive experience, to be a first Adam.

It is, then, a profound mistake to consider Urbino a leisure-class state. Urbino knows no leisure at all, just as self-conscious man knows no leisure in the world. He is either making or unmaking himself. *Tertium non datur.* What Urbino aristocrats *can* do is confront this calculus more directly than most of us do. But the calculus itself is undeniable: They have nothing to do but play games. Pure leisure. They make up games. The best game that can be played? The creation of an ideal self. They must then—*to be more themselves*, to raise the temperature of reality—imitate the ideal. Farewell leisure. It is of course an artificial goal, and narcissistic. But are our own "practical" purposes not both these to a fantastic degree? "O reason not the need," Lear agonizes under the whips of usefulness. We can, then, refute the charge that *The Courtier* presents a decorative, narcissistic, useless theory of identity simply by accepting this theory as a realistic imitation of life. Our purposes are more decorative and narcissistic, less purposive, than we want to admit. In a sense such narcissistic decoration is the most purposive of all. It sustains reality. Again, we don't want to admit this. Reality is *just there*, like the *self*. It needs no maintenance. Castiglione was not so soft-headed.

He thus plots out a full cycle of address to the world, a model for motive. We begin in pure play. We have nothing to do. We invent games to amuse ourselves. But the appetite comes in eating. These games grow purposive. We have become committed to purposes and these change us, form our self, invigorate it or deny it, stunt it. If the game maximizes our pleasures, enriches the self and fulfills it, renders it capable of genuine moral choice, it will be in truth the best game that could possibly be played. For goodness in Castiglione's world is an action too, process, not reified substance. Goodness must be enacted. It must form part of us, a skill not an external ethic. Castiglione wishes to internalize ethics, to transfer its domain, make it grow with the self rather than against it. He comes to terms with pleasure and he finds the final source of pleasure to be progressive enrichment of the self. I have been glossing a dictum of Whitehead's: "Style is the ultimate morality of mind." Castiglione chronicled the social surface but he also pondered it. He saw clearly that for self-conscious man ethics was, initially if not entirely, a matter of style. It would have to orchestrate ornament before it could plead to essentials because only by the orchestration of ornament could it create the essentials it would plead to.

Castiglione merits admiration not least for his steady resistance to satire, his reluctance to debunk. Material lies ready to hand in *The Courtier* for radical exposure of "real" motive, backstage debunking of Urbino. Castiglione sees further. He refuses to accept any single range of motive as referential, to interpret all others as only a disguised version of the referent, be this economic, psychoanalytical, religious. One might almost call him a "rebunker," concerned as he is to show how different ranges of motive can reinforce one another. All things can be known in terms of other things—and only thus: "Chi non sa che al mondo non saría la giustizia, se non fussero le ingiurie? la magnanimità, se non fussero li pusil animi?" (2.2). Part of his redefinition of seriousness comes as an understated, implicit war on dogmatism, on the robust confidence that life within a single orchestration engenders. He wants to credit the other fellow's reality, stands ready to embrace customs radically different from his own. He thus verifies rhetorical motive while he exposes it.

It follows, incidentally, from this willingness to entertain alternate realities that *The Courtier*'s comedy must be an unconventional kind. Theories of comedy fall into two categories, absolute and normative. In absolute theories, comedy is created by measuring, by whatever manipulation of time and space scale, an aberrant performance against "reality." This is serious comedy in its pure form and it can be serious indeed. All such theories depend on a preexistent serious reality and central self, and on a referent motive-system depending from them. Such a theory might be Fielding's theory, as expressed in the preface to *Joseph Andrews*: comedy exposes pretended motive. Or

Bergson's: the real nature of man is elastic and so inelasticity
seems comic. But what if no set of motives is more real than
another? What if inelasticity is as natural to man as elasticity—or
anything else? What happens to comedy without a referent reality? When it is denied its redefining complementary, tragedy?
Obviously it then invents a temporary god's-eye view, usually
called decorum, contingent external sanction, social norm. The
reasoning back to norm can remain the same and, since day-to-
day dealings with reality remain largely normative, comic power
remains unimpaired. Castiglione's characters entertain a
number of normative arguments, exhortations to observe *una
certa onesta mediocrità.* But the mean is not an entity. It constitutes an empty category. It balances extremes, a moment of
poise. It cannot be discussed except in terms of the extremes
creating it. Again, process, oscillation. It thus needs comic excess
in order to exist. The long section on comedy in *The Courtier*
exemplifies as much as it theorizes. The comic corrective the
extremes supply does not reveal the norm, it creates it. Folly is
not just a diversion. It is a necessity. The middle path is then a
skill like the self, a path among follies. So in *The Courtier* folly is
almost cherished. A dynamic rather than a static model of the self
inevitably produces this effect, throws the defining locus outward toward the defining extremes. The decorous norm is a *path*,
hedged by the extremes at every point.

The Courtier, then, contains two theories of comedy corresponding to its two conceptions of reality. For serious reality,
comedy is a corrective and the measure by a preexisting norm.
Rhetorical comedy makes the process two-way. It accepts the
measurement against norms. More fun lies that way. Comedy in
The Courtier is fundamentally therapeutic, aims to *esilarar l'animo*
and make us forget our troubles. The laughter emerges from a
process of comparison circular, inevitable, and partly disin-
genuous. We reify the norm because it is more fun to do so, it
puts more zest into our laughter. But we can—and at some stage
should—reverse the polarity and admit the extremes as referent
preexisting reality. The theory of comedy thus parallels in structure a theory of normative clarity in verbal utterance.

An apologist for rhetorical comedy would then stress comedy as pleasure rather than ethical restorative. Whether the comic theory be based on superiority, ambiguity, incongruity, or sudden deliverance, what takes our interest is the pleasure of the change. A norm may be inverted, that is, for pleasure rather than ethical measurement. A balanced view, a seriousness both rhetorical and serious, would alternate the two emphases, stress norm as product of both search for truth and search for pleasure. Normative judgments recur more commonly because they give more pleasure. Some such awareness may explain the lightness of Castiglione's touch, his reluctance to laugh aggressively. He is trying to establish a norm—and so by definition reform—but he wants to marshal the resources of social pleasure as well.

We can extract from the book's thinking about comedy a sketch not simply of a single norm, but of how to hold norms of any kind. Clearly, for Castiglione, language and behavior can be considered in the same terms. In both a norm, but a dynamic norm, ought to prevail. So the conversation on antique diction in book one suggests that Tuscan words should be known but seldom used. Extremes should enter as suggestive shadow, suggest meaning by their absence. Ludovico specifies for the courtier full and traditional verbal skills, which is to say fundamentally contradictory and confusing ones. So he insists (1.33) that antique diction by itself cannot avail. We must have thought: "for to separate thoughts from words is to separate soul from body." Yet there must be good words and in good order, and with suitable gesture. Yet not too heavy, but expressed "sensibly in everything, with readiness and a lucid fullness . . . making every ambiguity clear and plain." Yet metaphorical when necessary, coined words if need be. Yet not so as to dazzle. And so on. We confront again the paradoxes of normative clarity. The style Ludovico describes is the successful style. It possesses no formal content at all. Anything can be permitted that works. Both the courtier and his speech come forward as normative portraits formed by extremes, and teachable only by imitation. Both advance a paradoxical ideal, visible invisibility. The style must be seen in order to work. In order to work, it must not be noticed. What Castiglione has done is to define the middle style, to show it as dynamic rather than empty. He emerges as the great apologist for the middle style. If the successful self consists of a process, a dynamic interchange, so does the middle style. It has no discrete formal content. It is an attitude, a skill. The oscillation from one kind of self to another finds parallel here in the oscillation from word to concept and back. Just as the successful self has built into its creative apparatus a "generalized other," so the mature stylist has internalized his own sense of decorum, poise between extremes. Sprezzatura means the same thing for both verbal style and life-style. It means success. Like verbal clarity, it is an artificial state, projects an idiosyncratic moment of poise. Just so with successfully presenting a public self. Oddly enough, what has seemed central to seriousness for verbal style has seemed frivolity itself for life-style, yet "sincerity" means the same thing in both: successful illusion.

So close stand the two kinds of style that Castiglione may be used to exemplify a typical Renaissance process: personality theory formed on the analogy of rhetorical theory. Or, put another way, the progressive realization that all rhetorical theory implied—close under the surface—a theory of personality. The style was indeed the man. And the man was less a work of art, as Burckhardt thought him, than a work of rhetoric. The parts of speech and the "parts" of a man could be discussed with the same vocabulary, within the same theory of decoration. For both man and speech, Castiglione provided, in addition to a set of specific ornaments, a theory of ornament. He showed how, working inward from the circumference, ornament defines an essential man, supplies a center.

But the self can be authenticated in the opposite way, by positing a center through sublime exaltation. Castiglione's decision to include this choice has puzzled posterity. What relation does Bembo's soaring hymn to love bear to the sophisticated comedy preceding? As with the *Phaedrus,* how can we connect the discussion of style with that of love? The obvious answer talks about the styles of love. Such talk exists in *The Courtier* but it does not interest Bembo. It is just this he flees. He yearns for a retreat from, transcendence of, all style. He wants to confront essence rather than process, pure subject.

We are left on our own in assessing Bembo's sudden inspiration. He is heard with profound attention but also with comic interruption, Signor Morello playing that role stoutly by insisting that old men can still make love. Bembo is not challenged as to his arguments, except by the whole of *The Courtier* preceding. The speech ends *The Courtier* but it does not end the debate. That will resume the next night, and continue, presumably—since the debate allegorizes culture, represents our self-reflexive efforts to understand ourselves—forever. We are left to construe Bembo's oration as we choose; we can soar with him or stay on the ground. To soar is tempting. *The Courtier* then becomes something like a complete spectrum of human involvement in the world, our full model for motive. We begin in pure play, at leisure, debating for the fun of it. We get progressively more caught up in the game. It becomes ever more serious, modulating from surface ornaments to essential attributes of self, politics and the public life, love and the private. The self becomes ever more serious, finally moving from the game sphere to sublimity, from process to essence. The book and the enselfing process the book describes thus find a proper conclusion, end in apotheosis. A parallel development in style moves from early preoccupation with surface to final transcendence of it, moves from the world's mortal beauty to an indwelling immanence beyond style. The ritual of love serves here as paradigm for the whole stylistic address toward life. The book then moves from a closed circle of play to a certification of self beyond it. It carries us as far as words can go and then, like Bembo, leaves the remaining rungs of the ladder to each of us alone. The concluding mysticism is designedly ecumenical, equal parts Christianity and Platonism. It absolves us of self-consciousness, pours the self into a union beyond human contrivance. It leads us out of the wilderness of game.

We may thus think of Bembo's mysticism as completing what has gone before or as contradicting it. Castiglione takes pains not to force the issue. If we want a god's-eye view, a perspective from the eighth sphere, he provides one, takes us at least as far as man can. If we doubt such a perspective exists, we are free to view Bembo as the author of *Gli Asolani*, an outstanding spokesman of fashionable Platonism—another spokesman for another style. *The Courtier* is a game in which people entertain theories because the theories entertain them. Platonism earns no exemption. If Bembo wants to heat his mind with incredibilities, the conversational framework proves wide enough to contain him. But it does not certify him, any more than it certifies any other attitude. Bembo's search for the center may lead to heaven or to heavenly sentimentality. We choose our own compass points. *The Courtier* shows us how to leave process for essence, but, like Chaucer's *Troilus*, it does not itself do so. Sublimity can be thought of as a skill as well as a transport. It may lead back to game as well as out of it.

Castiglione frames his book in a context which intensifies our choice rather than simplifying it. He characterizes his task, in the opening letter to Don Michel de Silva, as erecting a pious memorial to Urbino, and at the beginning of each book he includes a proleptic necrology. Castiglione frames the whole *Courtier* in the pathos of death and time. Here is a final seriousness if you like. One seems in *The Courtier* always looking into a warm and brightly lit room, into youthfulness, from a cold, dark old age outside:

> Però dei cori nostri in quel tempo, come allo autunno le foglie degli alberi, caggiono i suavi fiori di contento, e nel loco dei sereni e chiari pensieri entra la nubilosa e torbida tristizia, di mille calamità compagnata; di modo che non solamente il corpo, ma l'animo ancora è infermo; né dei passati piaceri riserva altro che una tenace memoria, e la imagine di quel caro tempo della tenera età, nella quale quando ci ritrovamo, ci pare che sempre il cielo e la terra ed ogni cosa faccia festa e rida intorno agli occhi nostri, e nel pensiero come in un delizioso e vago giardino, fiorisca la dolce primavera d'allegrezza. [2.1]

Here, only the Hoby translation will do:

Therefore the sweete flowers of delyte vade away in that season out of our harts, as the leaves fall from the trees after harvest, and in steade of open and cleare thoughts, there entreth cloudie and troublous heavinesse accompanied with a thousand heart griefes: so that not onely the bloud, but the minde is also feeble: neither of the former pleasures receiveth it any thing els but a fast memorie, and the print of the beloved time of tender age, which when wee have upon us, the heaven, the earth, and each thing to our seeming rejoyceth and laugheth alwaies about our eyes, and in thought (as in a savorie and pleasant Garden) flourisheth the sweete spring time of mirth. . . .

Yet this passage is a rhetorical chromo, too ("Pagina bellissima; ricca, vasta, armoniosa, soavamente accorata," as one critic calls it), and *The Courtier* certainly teaches us how to whittle rhetorical chromos down to size. We cannot rest easy in pathos either.

Castiglione seems a decorative rather than an essential Platonist. Bembo may be right, but perhaps he is not, perhaps the only finality is old age, death, and the sadness they bring. Carefully, then, as Castiglione imitates the structure of the *Symposium*, he finally chooses an opposite strategy: the seriousness of *The Courtier* remains man-made. It finds less the footprint of God Bembo seeks than the ambiguous, posing, and imposing footprints of man.

8

The War between Play and Purpose: Gargantua and Pantagruel

Gargantua and Pantagruel seems to observe rhetorical coordinates almost too scrupulously. It overlays an intermittent, obviously capricious narrative with an overpoweringly self-conscious style. It repeatedly makes style, words, its subject, and considers them as objects, as things. Composed in broken times; installments appearing, as with *Tristram Shandy*, when the author wanted them to appear; fated, until death or posthumous reviser took over, to go on forever; written in declared, if not actual, haste and carelessness by a shameless posturing clown; attacking along the two extremes rhetoric observes, propaganda and play; full of speeches in ambivalent contexts; looking to a reality overwhelmingly literary, moving in a world of books; continually taunting and trapping the reader; observing no time but a continuing present; working by scene rather than narrative progression; betraying_in style and image a pronounced concern with oral modes of address—it seems the perfect rhetorical document. It is not least so in refusing to be any one thing, to find a center in a single genre, however broadly defined. It works in the opposite way, invokes the patterns of expectations for every genre, seemingly, that ever was. It plays games with genre. Its author wants to prove that, like Pantagruelion, he can do everything. Rabelais comprehended the narrative resources of his time, tried to control the full weight of his written and oral past. Such a Herculean endeavor renders us self-conscious about narrative form. We must soon, in such a spectacular world, notice our own spectacles. We become and remain perpetually aware of our own narrative assumptions. What is a character? An event? What do you mean by story? Well, *c'est selon*. We are always aware of the terms upon which we enter into the narrative. Thus the generic babel works, like stylistic excess but on a greater level of magnification, to render the surface opaque.

Gargantua and Pantagruel offers a whole property-room full of masks. It starts with a chronicle. "Comment . . . Comment . . . Comment." The simplest of narrative forms, one unrelated event after another. The chronicler expects to be believed: "et, si ne le croyez, le fondement vous escappe!"[1] He consults original sources ("les anciens pantarches, qui sont en la Chambre des Comptes à Montsoreau" [1.8]) and remains scrupulously on guard against anachronism ("Et n'estoit poinct froncée, car la fronsure des chemises n'a esté inventée" [1.8]). Yet Rabelais really does chronicle carefully, if unmethodically, the customs of his day; he takes fine-grain photographs of the social surface.

Other kinds of historical discourse are invoked as well. We at times find the narrative-speech-narrative pattern. So Janotus's memorable oration asking the return of Notre Dame's bells (1.19), Gallet's harangue to the feasting King Picrochole, Panurge's speech to the sheep as they jump overboard in book four, his encomium of debt, and more. These speeches are often ironic or comic in tone or context, but no more so than many in Thucydides or Livy. And the speeches themselves, from school-men's chop-logic to humanistic Ciceronian pomposity, seem historically accurate. So, too, with the local history, or local mock-epic perhaps, as in the cake bakers of Lerné episode, which uses nearly half of book one to allegorize a family quarrel over riparian fishing rights.

Rabelais overlaps his generic invitations. If the cake bakers reenact a provincial epic, Epistemon's descent into hell (2.30) provides full-scale, if comic ("O ma muse, ma Calliope, ma Thalie" [2.28]), epic. Epistemon finds down there a not-very-epic Lucianic dialogue. He is healed by a Panurgian bit of codpiece-warmed mumbo-jumbo that slides us into yet another Rabelaisian genre, the medical treatise. The healing intention runs through *Gargantua and Pantagruel* from first to last. It can

1. *Oeuvres Complètes*, ed. Pierre Jourda, 2 vols. (Paris, 1962), 1.4. All subsequent quotations are from this edition.

become almost sacramental, as in the prologue to book four ("C'est l'Evangile, on quel est dict, *Luc*, 4, en horrible sarcasme et sanglante derision, au medicin negligent de sa propre santé: 'Medicin, o, gueriz toymesmes' "), and then trail off into a list of medical treatises. The battle scenes often absurdly superpose medical treatise and the traditional gory detail of romance ("Soubdain après, tyra son dict braquemart et en ferut l'archier qui le tenoit à dextre, luy coupant entierement les venes jugulaires et arteres spagitides du col, avecques le guarguareon, jusques es deux adenes" [1.44]). Or it may sometimes mask as Scripture and preach or slide off into a game of "Begats": "Et le premier fut Chalbroth, / Qui engendra Sarabroth, / Qui engendra Faribroth, / Qui engendra Hurtaly . . ." (2.1).

Grail-romance, the search for a holy bottle, finally draws out into a major narrative thread. And there is plenty of romance in *Gargantua and Pantagruel*, blood and gore *partout*, ritual boasting, battle scene and suitable prefatory prayer (2.29), as well as attenuated variations like the live chess match. Yet ritual instruction to listen for *Trink*, the holy word, "with only one ear" turns into talk about a one-eared bottle or homely liquor jug and back into everyday. Only this perpetual sliding off into another world, another kind of discourse, remains constant in *Gargantua and Pantagruel*.

The opening section of book one, Gargantua's education, comprises a humanist *speculum principis* against which to see Pantagruel's different education in book two. But again, we are always sliding out of that orchestration into another. Thus, when we come to Gargantua's games, we get an accurate anthropological catalog of games-current (217 of them, M. Jourda tells us, "presque tous en usage au xviᵉ siècle"). And the word-heap catalogs form priceless deposits for the philologist as well—and off we slide into another genre, the treatise on, perhaps epic of, the French language in the Renaissance. *Gargantua and Pantagruel* is a rhetorical treatise too, one of the great discussions, as well as examples, of prose style. Its breadth and range, suitably reassembled and interpreted, can stand comparison with Quintilian. And the more encyclopedic it becomes in other areas (joke book, parody of the decretals) the more valuable its stylistic commentary grows. And from the joke book it is an easy trip to the picaresque, a spirit which enters *Gargantua and Pantagruel* specifically through Panurge but seems to inform the whole. The narrator, from his first direct address, holds us in his spirit of *sans culottisme*. His genre seems almost a mountebank's spell, holding us by never-ending talk.

This generic dizziness by no means exhausts the expectations *Gargantua and Pantagruel* evokes. Utopia, philosophic-dialogue/drinking-party à la *Symposium*, scholarly debate, sophistic display, digest and compendium, all surface at one time or another. What do they add up to?

Are we to allegorize this self-conscious generic bouillabaisse? To argue, as Michel Beaujour does in *Le Jeu de Rabelais*, for example, that by declaring war on genre, Rabelais declares war on the social structure genres represent? Or find master-coordinates, a genre to include all these, even should this prove only a genre of generic confusion? Might, that is, a pattern emerge from the juxtapositions, a continuity from the discontinuities? Or, conversely, are we to discard these serious expectations and simply "Enjoy"?

Why bother to make sense of it? The narrator has not. But we cannot afford a similar luxury—and Rabelais knew it. We cannot read just for the fun of it. The mixed form is problematic by nature, draws us in. To enjoy, we must know. To enjoy more, know more. Our laughter depends on comparisons, discontinuities, absurd contrasts of style and subject, situation and topic. The more we try to keep our patterns of expectation straight, the funnier the narrative gets. Our own pleasure draws us in. Our laughter depends on trying to make sense of the senseless. The most open form turns out to be the least. We must enter *Gargantua and Pantagruel's* world on Rabelais's terms. We try to make sense of his world and feel foolish doing so. We seem to be offered an alternative—only enjoy—which involves remaining silent, failing to specify the sources of our enjoyment. Even if you think that Rabelais and his narrator are only playing games with forms of discourse, still you have begun, by so thinking, to take Rabelais's generic cornucopia seriously, begun to resist *Gargantua and Pantagruel*'s declared invitation.

Gargantua and Pantagruel makes the same point on two other levels. Besides the narrative invitation, we confront an allegorical and a stylistic one, both working in the same way. The allegorical invitation is perhaps the stronger. Rabelais reinvites us to penetrate to the heart of his mystery at intervals throughout. The allegorical impulse, in this respect, rather resembles the impulse to bawdy innuendo. It is synergistic. Once such an atmosphere of expectation has been created, all is drawn into it. No cigar, to borrow Freud's familiar example, remains just a cigar. So with the allegory. The *more* puzzling and discontinuous, arbitrary or grotesque an event, the more strongly do we suspect hidden meaning. Thus Rabelais invites us to reweave his loose ends for him.

What meaning, for a trivial example, lurks beneath Eusthenes' trick with the water glasses at the end of 2.27? Sometimes the narrative takes allegorical interpretation as subject—so the ring the lady sends to Pantagruel in 2.24. The last words of Christ inside the ring? What do we make of that? Or consider the Abbey of Thélème. Its name, the Abbey of *Will*, releases conflicting allegorical responses. It is obviously a positive ideal, yet *will* rings all the alarm bells—and rightly so. For there is nothing in the rest of *Gargantua and Pantagruel* to support the bland assurance that, if you leave well-bred people together alone, all will be well. The very war from which the Abbey's construction stems disproves the assumption of its founding. How far are we supposed to allegorize? How much to notice the contradictions between allegorical and literal level?

It is in the first three prologues that Rabelais most insistently asks his central question. "Avés vous bien le tout entendu?" (2.1). The first opens with Alcibiades' comparison of Socrates and the Silenus box from the *Symposium. Three* kinds of comparison are solicited: (1) *Gargantua and Pantagruel* is like the *Symposium*; a convivial drinking party but preoccupied—the whole saturated in joking and, with Alcibiades' interruption, in real drunkenness—with the most profound issues; a philosophical tent pitched on rhetorical ground. Above all, Rabelais plays off against the *structure* of the *Symposium*—a gradual penetration into central truth itself. (2) The Silenus box provides an emblem for the book to follow. Gaily decorated on the outside ("pinctes au dessus de figures joyeuses et frivoles") to make people laugh, but containing within rare unguents ("fines drogues comme baulme, ambre gris, amomon, musc, zivette, pierreries et aultres choses precieuses" [1. prologue]). (3) And Socrates himself, with his homely appearance and divine truth beneath, is drawn into the Rabelaisian style, his unprepossessing exterior ("le reguard d'un taureau, le visaige d'un fol, simple en meurs, rustiq en vestimens") hiding a divine wisdom, a drug "celeste et impreciable."

Is this a portrait of Rabelais? Of *Gargantua and Pantagruel*? Lest we miss the point, Rabelais waves it again, concluding, "C'est pourquoy fault ouvrir le livre et soigneusement peser ce que y est deduict" (1. prologue). We must not remain content with laughter, must press beyond it, "à plus hault sens interpreter ce que par adventure cuidiez dict en gayeté de cueur" (1. prologue). The reward: "en icelle bien aultre goust trouverez et doctrine plus absconce, laquelle vous revelera de très haultz sacremens et mysteres horrificques, tant en ce que concerne nostre religion que aussi l'estat politicq et vie oeconomicque." And then comes the passage mocking the foolish allegorizers of Homer and Ovid. Don't do it to Rabelais's *livre seigneurial*, which took no more time than that spent eating and drinking, these being—switch—extensive and allegorically significant activities in *Gargantua and Pantagruel*, of course. And—switch again—somebody says his works smell of wine, are not serious, but—the general phrase of Rabelaisian defiance—"bren pour luy!" Sainéan remarks early on in *L'Influence et la Reputation de Rabelais* that "Rabelais et son livre ont été au cours des âges, l'objet d'étranges déformations et d'interprétations singulières." Doesn't he *invite* them? Of course they are mocked too. He returns at the end of book one to allegorical interpretation. What does the Abbey of Prophecy mean, Friar John asks. The perpetuation of Divine Truth ("le decours et maintien de verité divine"),

Gargantua replies. Not at all, says the Monk, only a tennis match ("De ma part, je n'y pense aultre sens enclous q'une description du jeu de paulme soubz obscures parolles").

The alternating invitations to allegorize and to laugh at allegorizing continue in the prologue to book two. We are first bidden, in language that recalls Christ's in the Gospels, to leave our dearest concerns and to cleave to this Book. "Et à la mienne volunté que chascun laissast sa propre besoigne, ne se souciast de son mestier et mist ses affaires propres en oubly, pour y vacquer entierement sans que son esperit feust de ailleurs distraict n'y empesché . . ." (2. prologue). But we have been deceived. The title Rabelais recommends is not his book, but his source, the original *Grandes et inestimables Chronicques.* The form of recommendation is just as in book one, for his own book, but now all turned to mockery. He goes on, in a passage Sterne later found useful, to recommend the book as a poultice, here for toothache. Thus, in a new way, he both does and does not recommend allegorization of a book both his and not his. Again, at the end of book two, he returns to seriousness: "Si vous me dictes: 'Maistre, il sembleroit que ne feussiez grandement saige de nous escrire ces balivernes et plaisantes mocquettes,' je vous responds que vous ne l'estes gueres plus de vous amuser à les lire" (2.34). But he and his pleasure-loving readers "sommes plus dignes de pardon q'un grand tas de sarrabovittes, cagotz, escargotz, hypocrites, caffars, frappars, botineurs, et aultres telles sectes de gens. . . . " He concludes with a Lucianic exhortation to hug everyday life, the literal level, and enjoy it, "vivre en paix, joye, santé, faisans tousjours grande chere." Clear enough. But then the coliphonesque closure announces the end of a book by "M. Alcofribas, *abstracteur de quinte essence."*

And what is to be made of the prologue to book three, where Rabelais likens himself to Diogenes rolling his tub before the siege of Corinth? The figure of Diogenes allegorizes the problem of whether to allegorize. It can be just a joke, a juxtaposition of two word-heaps, the first what "les aultres" do, the second a catalog of tub-thumps. Thus when Rabelais compares himself to Diogenes, they both play buffoon. Or does the whole allegorically satirize the foolishness of war preparations and war—that is, make a very serious statement? The serious/comic bifurcation, that we may be perfectly clear, is then emblematized by the story of a half-black and half-white slave. This illustrates—well, one is not quite sure whąt, but something to do with seriousness.

Rabelais has been often praised for his realism, his accurate social reportage. He plunges us into physical realities, into a physical and linguistic mass of overwhelming power. We are immersed in physicality, flesh, excrement, objects, stuff. But at the same time, we are invited repeatedly to allegorize, to take nothing at its face value. It is not simply a question of what or how to allegorize. Is the birth of Gargantua a parody of the birth of Christ? Is Pantagruel "un geant socialiste"? Some allegory seems undeniable. Eusthenes is force; Carpalian, quickness; Epistemon, good sense; Panurge—well, it gets a bit harder, but shrewdness for a start. And the papal satire of the cinquième livre cannot be mistaken. Or the topical allegory of the cake bakers. At the other extreme, some *merde* is nothing but *merde*. But in the middle we are on our own or, worse, invited to allegorize and then mocked for it, beaten until we cry and then beaten for crying. There seems a great hole in the middle of Rabelais's discourse; it seems a sandwich without the meat. We have a literal level of physicality, folk custom, shit, piss, words as things, as objects like building blocks or, more wonderfully, like frozen fish. Atop this level sit the strongest and most complex invitations to allegorize. But the two levels, often, either have very little to do with one another or deliberately clash. We contemplate substance, and mind acting on substance, but no body to the interactions. Both categories seem to be closed, self-subsistent.

In this respect, *Gargantua and Pantagruel* seems very like *The Faerie Queene*. The two poems, in fact, resemble one another in striking ways. Both, written and published over a long period of time, stood subject to the changes in attitude and mood age brings. Both depend heavily on literary allusion, and notable, often notably displaced, borrowings. Both remain unfinished.

Both are built up by scenes, allegorical panels, and tend to let the story take care of itself. With Rabelais as with Spenser, one rarely forgets a scene but often where that scene occurs. Both, though seemingly visual, resist successful illustration. The text does not permit visual equivalents. Both use the same strategy of complex, overlapping generic invitations. Both call for agility, intuitive good sense about when and how to allegorize. Both use styles calculatedly opaque, incantatory. Both are styles of word rather than of syntax, styles that depend on a poetic diction. Both are immensely learned and in both, beneath the learning, lurks a mythical level of folk motif and popular iconography, above all of blood, physical violence, and continual sexuality. Both find characterization a useful tool but not an overpowering obligation. Both lend themselves with remarkable ease to analysis by psychoanalytic coordinates, whether Freudian dream or Jungian archetype.

I catalog these similarities because Rabelais's realism, like Nashe's, has been unduly emphasized. It makes less than half the story. *Gargantua and Pantagruel* seems to share far more with a poem like *The Faerie Queene* than with any novel, ancient or modern. Rabelais felt just Spenser's self-conscious fascination with allegory as a way of knowing. It seemed to him both foolish and the only real way of knowing, the only human kind of meaning. Both men tried to redeem allegory as a method in much the same way Shakespeare redeems Petrarchanism in the sonnets, by a rhetorical coup. For both, this included a whole range of syncretistic techniques: for Spenser, antique diction; for Rabelais, slang. But both aimed to reconstruct the same method of knowing and of writing. Curiously, both are "realists" in the same way. Many scenes in both just "are," exist beyond any interpretable framework. Think of the sybil scene or Raminagrobis, and then of Despair's Cave and Britomart skewering Marinell. Both works abound in scenes no allegory seems fully to explain. The allegory rather excuses, ties together, panels of self-sufficient grotesque detached from concept or moral. And above them, allegory hovers more as a self-pleasing exercise than as a real effort to explain. Both seem most alike in leaving this hole at the center of experience. Both invite us to lose ourselves on a vast but vacuous plain.

We have surprised this hole in the middle of experience before, most notably in the *Metamorphoses*. There, too, a mythic, almost primitively participated level of experience underlies a very sophisticated allegorical apparatus above, the second trying without marked success to interpret the first. Perhaps the long poem built on rhetorical premises inevitably creates this effect. Such an effect goes a long way to explain *Gargantua and Pantagruel's* unusual critical history, the split between the *école historico-allégorique* and the prophets of the unashamed flesh or, more recently, of the unashamed word. Michel Beaujour, in his brilliant but intensely serious essay, dismisses the whole critical history of *Gargantua and Pantagruel* as doomed from the start: "Toute tentative d'interprétation est vouée à l'échec, comme le prouve ce tissu de contradictions et de sottises qu'est l'histoire de l'exégèse rabelaisienne" (*Le Jeu de Rabelais*, p. 26). Beaujour, like Mikhail Bakhtin—the only previous scholar to escape his housecleaning—insists on *Gargantua and Pantagruel* wholly as a myth of language. The invitations to allegorize must be refused. The book is a carnival. Rules don't apply. There are no meanings, only words. Thus the *exégèse rabelaisienne*, after embracing one half of its object for centuries, now embraces the complementary simplifications, the other half. But it is only when both *Gargantua and Pantagruel's* invitations are accepted that the narrative strategy can work. That hole in the middle we must fill. And we must remain aware that *we* fill it.

Beaujour thinks all previous commentators, all the allegorists, wrong. It would be closer to Rabelais's way of proceeding to think them all right. Or at least partially so. They all supply meanings, rush to interpret. All are right to do so, and the more right, the more foolish. My favorite volume in the Library of Saint Victor's—how often have we all read and written it—is *Des Poys au lart, cum Commento. Of Peas and Bacon, with a Commentary*. In the prologue to book one, Rabelais numbers this among the "livres de nostre invention" along with *Gargantua* and *Pantagruel.* He too plays commentator, and commentator on himself. All of us yearn to translate mythic reality, the world that just is out there, into terms that we can understand, feel comfortable with. An arbitrary procedure to be sure. Nothing intrinsic connects fable and allegorical interpretation. Nothing ever does. Rabelais points to a general conclusion. People always use fables for their own purposes, see in them what it suits them to see. What does the central motif of book three—Panurge's search to know his postmarital horns—illustrate if not this? The methods of interpretation all are preposterous enough. The world wants to convince Panurge that he will be a cuckold, for that is what previous experience has trained it to see. So its interpretations all converge on this. Panurge wants to see the opposite future and so of course he does. Allegory's great advantage as a way of knowing is that you need allegorize only as much as suits your argument. The rhetorical documents' fondness for aleatory composition, for building in chance, surfaces here in another way. The rhetorical habit of mind, and of composition, must obviously be a useful strategy for the aleatory composer. We are asked to realize and rearrange—notes, orchestration, myths—as we wish to, to collaborate in making meaning. Some rearrangements will seem better than others because we have been taught to look for them. But we must, in such an aesthetic, acknowledge the final source of meaning. It lies in our patterns of expectation as much as in the work of art releasing them.

Fundamental to Rabelais's narrative strategy—and I think to Spenser's—is the impossibility of direct, nonsymbolic experience. Both try to re-create it self-consciously, but this obviously cannot be the same thing as primitive, participative, "unscientific" reality. It is to indicate just this inevitable difference that both poets use the arcane vocabulary and repetitive syntax of incantation. They want to invoke a reality they cannot address directly. Direct address would destroy it, translate it into concepts, allegorize it. (Thus, as the clever students of Spenser always find out, glossing arcane words seems to destroy them. Their meaning *is* their unfamiliarity.) Self-conscious myth must preserve a special language, as Ovid saw as well as Spenser and

Rabelais. But such language can only remind us that what it points to, by the nature of language, it cannot describe. The figure of secret center runs, in one form or another, throughout *Gargantua and Pantagruel*. The allegory of the holy bottle yields finally a central meaning—Trink—which is a center in words themselves. But these only throw us to the surface again, a surface we must allegorize.

Perhaps it is now clear why, even at its most powerful, Rabelais's genuine form was burlesque and not satire. Rabelais speaks from the midst of nonsense, not standing outside it. He shows a remarkabl willingness, even compulsion, to mock the things he most values. Think of the pain Greek must have cost him. He mocks his own knowledge of it mercilessly. His allegories are finally no more reliable than the next man's. It is not that we lack reference points. We are given too many.

Rabelais's story thus needs its allegorists and commentators. It could not exist without them. Rabelais built their responses in. And they—it should be we—intensify the comedy, complete it. This is not to belittle Rabelais's many historical and allegorical exegetes. Many students of Rabelais are doubtless so learned as not to need an intervening reality of textual and explanatory apparatus, but Rabelais expected most of his readers to depend on those notes. Never was a text so carefully arranged to require interpretation, demand diligent grooming from generations of commentators. Rabelais himself has made annotation of *Gargantua and Pantagruel* irresistibly comic, often the funniest thing on the page. For example, in chapter thirty-seven of book one, he mocks the commentators by inventing a mythical commentary, the *Supplementum Supplementi Chronicorum*. This, of course, requires a comment from the present commentator, M. Jourda: "Titre de fantaisie. Rabelais se moque des auteurs de commentaires" (1.37). The commentator can be depended upon—it is his job—to literalize the text. So when Panurge says (2.18) "mist de cul," the editor glosses "et obligés à se rasseoir." This does not explain the text, it translates it. The editor's kind of attention is always necessary for *Gargantua and Pantagruel* and always beside the point. So, during a drunken conversation, right after a parodic allusion to Christ on the cross (*sitio*) one of the conversants offers—"Lans, tringue" (1.5). The editorial counterpoint comes in suddenly from another world: "Y avait-il, parmi les invités de Grandgousier, un lansquenet? Le mot fait écho à celui du Gascon: Lagona, edatera!" Or, a page or two before, the perfect scholarly footnote. Still in the drunken conversation; the text is "Ceste main vous guaste le nez" ("That hand of yours is spoiling your nose!"). The commentator seeks an allegory beneath superficial nose-picker: "Le nez est rouge parce que la main lève trop souvent le verre." Sometimes the explanatory note seems almost part of the score. I am not selecting M. Jourda for special attention except inasmuch as, since he is so good an editor, he makes the point more strongly. An editor's commentary often—always?—finds itself essentially at odds with his text, especially a poetic one. This discontinuity fits Rabelaisian comedy perfectly. Yet another effort to explain what explanation can only translate, never explain.

If Rabelais mocks his readers, then, he mocks himself too. He mocks all of us. We all want to confront reality directly and we all confront an intermediate symbolism. In literary terms, we want to read the text, and find ourselves doomed to read commentators on the text, and then the commentators on those commentators. The text exists no more than reality does, just out there. You can't get there—at least not directly—from here. One wants to think Rabelais revenging himself on past commentators by mocking future ones. But, again, he speaks from amidst the throng. His own fame, as much as any other writer's, depends on the humorless commentator. In fact, as he must have seen, more so.

Gargantua and Pantagruel attains its natural form, then, becomes its real self, only when visibly surrounded by its allegorists. The notes enhance the comedy, they do not distract from it. They recall the terms under which all of us enter the world of Gargantua and Pantagruel. These terms are, like the generic juxtapositions poised above them, essentially contradictory and unfair. We are invited to allegorize. But this is an investment. We must, in future, defend it or feel foolish. Sainéan

quotes La Harpe to this point: "Ceux que rebutoit son langage
bizarre et obscur ont laissé là Rabelais comme un insensé; ceux
qui ont travaillé à le déchiffier ont exalté son mérite en raison
qu'il leur avoit coûté à entendre." We are trapped into humor-
lessness. And then mocked by a work demanding a rhetorical
poetic.

Can there—we have asked it before—be such a criticism? Isn't
criticism by its nature serious? It must allegorize, seek explanations, be purposive. How can it address itself to a work which
makes war on purpose in the name of play? *Gargantua and Pantagruel* demands both a serious poetic and a play one, the two
held in alternation. Thus held, both tend to become its subject as
well as the method of its understanding, tend to merge into a
satire on informative discourse. Rabelais defends pleasure from
a purpose always moving in on it. This is done, as we have seen,
by games with genre, narrative form, and allegory. But it is done
most clearly on the level of style, the third of the three levels of
self-consciousness Rabelais keeps in continual interaction.

Everywhere Rabelais parodies the purposive pretentions of
discourse, advances instead its playful, self-pleasing nature.
Janotus de Bragmardo's immortal oration to recover the Notre
Dame bells does just this. The oration goes forward entirely as
entertainment, irrelevant and ornamental. Gargantua has already (1.18) decided to return the bells. And it succeeds brilliantly in oratory's central purpose—to entertain. Everyone
laughs and then "ensemble eulx commença rire Maistre Janotus"
(1.20). Janotus is not, as usually thought, a parody of the bad
orator. He is a good orator. Rabelais likes him. He has got his
values straight, "bon vin, bon lict, le dos au feu, le ventre à table
et escuelle bien profonde" (1.19). He talks for sensible reasons.
Provided he gets his sausages, he does not care who laughs at
him. He'll join in, as we've just seen. The scene does parody
schoolmen's discourse, to be sure. But Rabelais points out how
to enjoy it. Janotus manages to find the real rhetorical
purposes—play on the one hand, sausages on the other—
beneath the pretensions to profundity.

Rhetoric is usually irrelevant or practically useless in *Gargan-*

tua and Pantagruel. The speeches occur at crucial moments but they never change anything. Even the prime sample of humanist eloquence which follows hard upon Janotus's *joyeuse harangue*, Gallet's Ciceronian speech to Picrochole, turns out to be ineffective. To the brilliant peroration ("Quelle furie doncques te esmeut maintenant, toute alliance brisée, toute amitié conculquée, tout droict trespassé, envahir hostilement ses terres, sans en rien avoir esté par luy ny les siens endommagé, irrité ny provocqué? Où est foy? Où est loy? Où est raison? Où est humanité? Où est craincte de Dieu?" [1.31]) Picrochole returns only, "Come and get them. They'll bake some cakes for you." ("Venez les querir, venez les querir. Ilz ont belle couille et molle. Ilz vous brayeront de la fouace." [1.32].) Gallet's *sentiments* are unexceptionable, but irrelevant. This is Rabelais's point. The speech's function remains the same whether the matter be sense or nonsense. The whole speech assumes the status of Frere Jean's swearing: "Ce n'est (dist le moyne) que pour orner mon langaige. Ce sont couleurs de rethorique Ciceroniane" (1.39).

Gerard J. Brault has recently noticed the ambiguous placement of Gargantua's famous letter to his son. Its celebration of learning's great new age follows hard upon the Library of Saint Victor's and it has been suspected that the letter is no more seriously intended than the library. Not at all. The letter is serious, can be so, just because of its placement. The placement seems yet more perilous than critics have noted. The first part of the letter talks about posthumous fame, and stands under pressure from Saint Victor's. But the second part talks about the polymath ideal, the *abysme de science*, and especially language training. And this is attacked by what follows, the meeting with Panurge (2.9). Here, the polyglot ideal is undermined as purposive, but reinforced as play. So the letter is enveloped by ironic commentary. But we must read it seriously in itself or we fail to see the alternation Rabelais sets up between purposeful and play discourse. The letter was written from Utopia but it was sent into a different world. We must dismiss neither.

Otherwise, we misinterpret the joke as it develops. Pantagruel goes on to pose as a wise man. (He has been aided in his role of polymath Solomon because, as noted at the letter's beginning, his bigger brain can hold more.) Pantagruel's behavior as judge develops directly from his father's abuse: "Pantagruel, bien records des lettres et admonitions de son pere, voulut un jour essayer son sçavoir." So he goes into the streets and "les mist tous de cul." So great does his reputation grow that he is asked to judge a case, Baisecul versus Humevesne, odd enough to have become unsolvable. He burns the written evidence, hears oral pleading, and then offers an opinion as nonsensical as the case, and all are satisfied. How can we allegorize this? Is Pantagruel as mindless as they? Or is his nonsense self-conscious and strategical? ("Eh bien, Messieurs, dist Pantagruel, puisqu'il vous plaist, je le feray; mais je ne trouve le cas tant difficile que vous le faictes. Votre paraphe *Caton*, la loy *Frater*, la loy *Gallus*, la loy *Quinque pedum*, la loy *Vinum*, la loy *Si dominus*, la loy *Mater*, la loy *Mulier bona*, la loy *Si quis*, la loy *Pomponius*, la loy *Fundi*, la loy *Emptor*, la loy *Pretor*, la loy *Venditor* et tant d'aultres sont bien plus difficiles en mon oppinion" [2.13].) How do we read this legal babbling? Is Pantagruel's characterization consistent? Or does he change into one of the fools? I'm not sure. But we must clearly preserve our idea of referential discourse, because this is what galvanizes the joke. The letter talks of an onset of self-consciousness and that we must take seriously, for it founds the comedy. It permits us to turn folly to pleasure. We can, as here, function in the world on the world's terms. Pantagruel's judgment amounts entirely to a gesture of style, a dramatic effect, a role. He plays it to the hilt and wins, leaves his audience "tous ravys en admiration de la prudence de Pantagruel plus que humaine." To see the role style plays, we must preserve a base in serious referential discourse. The seriousness must remain serious so the humor can make us laugh.

The extremes of style and referential discourse are pulled yet further apart, and the joke improved, when Panurge debates Thaumaste using gestures only. The stress here falls on Thaumaste's purity of motive. He comes a long arduous way, "rien ne estimant la longueur du chemin, l'attediation de la mer, la nouveaulté des contrées." He wishes to transcend the limits of both conventional wisdom and conventional debate, debate by signs only. The following debate makes the standard repertoire of rhetorical gesture into an abstract painting, pure play with forms. Words can never be completely purified of meaning and so they are done away with. What remains is the framework of play, of and for its own sake. Thaumaste and Pantagruel cannot see this, of course. They still mimic the language of referential purpose. But it is really Panurge's game. He prepares by spending the night drinking with the pages, prepares for pleasure by pleasure. In what follows (2.19) we literally reenact the debate ourselves, spell it out with our fingers. Panurge begins by sticking his thumb in his nose and wiggling his fingers ("Panurge soubdain leva en l'air la main dextre, puys d'icelle mist le poulse dedans la narine d'ycelluy cousté, tenant les quatre doigtz estenduz et serrez par leur ordre en ligne parallele à la pene du nez, fermant l'oeil gausche entierement et guaignant du dextre"), a sublime gesture which leaves Thaumaste dumb with delight, "ravy en haulte contemplation."

All of this allegorizes the pure pleasures of discourse. Debate is reduced to challenge, aggression, scorn, victory, defeat, admiration—in other words, to pleasure. Thaumaste and Pantagruel appear ridiculous not because they enjoy these delights but because they pretend to seek sublime truth. And truly think they truly do. But if the pleasures of discourse are allegorized, so is the need of words, of referential discourse, of trying to say something. If truth goes beyond words, it will go beyond sense. The search for sublimity turns into play. Thus we may say that the debate carries to its limits the search for a high style, the style seeking beyond words a transcendent truth. It constitutes Rabelais's comment on what happens when we cease to be self-conscious about words, self-conscious both about their meaning and about their agonistic delights. The subject is certainly wisdom, how knowledge is held, but Rabelais does not simply attack. He issues his customary invitation to allegorize. The audience tries to figure out what is meant just as we do. We can never surmount our urge to find significance—even after we find thumb in nose and fingers waving in the air. We are not

meant to discard our desire for seriousness but to see more
clearly the conditions under which it must be pursued. Every
debate shows in abstract outline the agonistic pleasures which
inform it. We have learned to see *through* the subject, or rather to
look only *at* the surface of the debate. It is part of our education as
rhetorical connoisseurs. This hardly means we will never cherish
a serious subject again. Rabelais does not think knowledge impossible. He only would remind us how it is—and must be—
held, held always by human beings, with their own desires and
purposes. Rabelais works here to split off means and ends, to
show how means always threaten ends. This is done not to urge
the predominance of either, but rather to reanimate their relationship.

Carnival is not all Rabelais wants to depict. He struggles to
build a full and fully dynamic model of human motive, and the
war on serious purpose forms only part of this. It is this beginning and ending in play, the whole traverse through game and
sublimity, that Rabelais comically models in the Thaumaste debate. And, more largely, in the satire on learning that runs from
the Library of Saint Victor's to the Thaumaste debate and beyond
to Bridoye's *alea judiciorum*. And on a yet larger scale, as we have
seen, in the whole allegorical invitation of *Gargantua and Pantagruel*, culminating in the Divine Bottle. Sublimity and the center
always, when pressed to the extreme, become play and the
surface.

Gargantua and Pantagruel's structure, if it has a single one,
comprises a series of these models—in concept all the same—
superimposed one on the other, but not all in phase. What from
one point of view is game will be play from another and sublime
from a third. Every stage of the model is thus made pregnant
with every other. The model seems always to move, to be
dynamic in essence. And it models meaning as well as motive.
Meaning grows out of play and gradually distances itself from it,
rarefies itself back again into play. Rabelais does not thus attack
seriousness alone, any more than he apotheosizes carnival
license at the expense of social order. The peace, order, and
decorous gravity of Thélème haunt *Gargantua and Pantagruel*,

just as the pure prose of reason, the world truly imaged in words, haunts the style. Rabelais displays the whole model at work and not in Utopia only—that is, not only in a single cycle—but with many overlapping simultaneous cycles. Rhetorical and serious coordinates, the two poetics, oscillate continuously as we move through the narrative.

This explains, I think, what seems Rabelais's share in the basic disingenuity of satire. Most satirists—Juvenal offers the best example—gain their power by exposing human fondness for pretending a serious purpose when seeking only play. Yet the satirist himself, and the more so the better he is, does just this himself. He pretends to reform, but his zest betrays him. He *likes* to castigate. His motive is a play one too. The great satirist sympathizes with his targets. He stands one of them. Rabelais recommends all the stages of the process, of the model for motive, but he gains his satiric power, his laughter, by juxtaposing discontinuous phases from different models, laughing first at play from a serious point of view and then vice versa. He thus manages both to gain the full range of comic effect and to avoid the fundamental Juvenalian inconsistency. The humorist takes carnival as reference; the satirist, atonement. Rabelais has it both ways, embraces first one then the other. The alternation of play and purpose observes no temporal priority. We are tempted to demand that pleasure precede knowledge, that we must savor the fable before we can allegorize it. We must be filled, satisfied, before we can think. It is true, but it is true too that such pleasure depends on the need to know and is conditioned by it. The process is just that, a continuous process, however and whenever we break into it.

The games Alcofribas plays commemorate this endlessness. They are always moving from play to purpose. Alcofribas starts out to amuse himself, then plays games to amuse us and then moves into a seriousness destined to return to play. We are not allowed to simplify the model, omit any part of it. The generic babel and the continual allegory stress purpose at the expense of play and then play at the expense of purpose, and so too with the style. The discourse, the verbal surface, does not need the apologies required twenty years ago. Rabelais forces awareness of words as things, objects, ends as well as means, just as he does with body vis-à-vis mind. The parallel is obvious. We are not to leave the body behind in a transcendent high seriousness. It remains always there. Nor are we to look through words to a transcendent truth beyond them. Our noses are rubbed over and over in both word and body. Both are ends in themselves and we continually use them as such. The pressure to forget body and word must be resisted. Body and word supply boundary conditions for whatever seriousness we pretend to.

When we recognize this, however, when we become self-conscious about these limitations, we have already begun to reflect seriously. Rabelais would defend the pleasures of language and the human body against the purposefulness always moving in on them. Verbal play comes, as much as defecation, drinking, and eating, to stand for the day-to-day pleasures ambition always wants to sacrifice. Rabelais aims to dispel fear, the fear of failure and nonconformity that any single, serious orchestration of reality inevitably generates. Thus he wages a continuous warfare with the pretensions of the public life. Thus Epistemon gratifyingly reports that hell turns great and small upside down. Thus Rabelais shatters the psychic superstructures built atop sex, reduces it, as Panurge does with the Parisian lady and the new Parisian walls, to degrading physicality. The sure sign that *means*, the constraint and distortion of words, have been forgotten is dogmatic opinion. The sure sign that the body has been forgotten is inflexible dignity. Rabelais wars against both.

Most of Panurge's pranks cherish dignity as their object, aim to fracture the social surface and the secure sense of bodiless self. Panurge always speaks for present pleasure, against ambition's careful usefulness. So he replies to an Alcofribas who asks of his pranks, "Et à quelle fin?": "Mon amy (dist il), tu ne as passetemps aulcun en ce monde. J'en ay, plus que le Roy" (2.17). The great set-piece of the war against purpose is Panurge's oration praising debt. Here all the topoi of good government are inverted to support social irresponsibility, present pleasure.

Again we are invited to allegorize seriously. Do not present pleasures provide the central concept permitting the whole apparatus to function, Panurge argues. The parallel stylistic effect controls conceptualization, never allows it to forget words. The endless debate about what Rabelais "really believed" might be qualified by a counterargument. He found nonnegotiable not *what* to believe but *how* to believe, how knowledge should be held, sublimity controlled. Absolute certainties must always transcend language and this leads, as Thaumaste shows, to mindless gesture.

Thus with both words and body Rabelais defends against encroaching purposefulness. This does not mean that he wishes to deny purpose, make all opinions the same. Nothing in the modern commentary would have surprised him more than Beaujour's insistence that *Gargantua and Pantagruel* makes no statements at all. It makes plenty. Conceptualization stands central to the model of meaning Rabelais wishes to depict and reanimate. Opinions are to be held, but held in a certain way. So too with the body: it looms so large in *Gargantua and Pantagruel* because the pressures against it were so enormous. So too with the defense of present pleasure. Medieval Christianity was future-oriented, but the Renaissance search for fame more so, and Protestant capitalism more so still. So honor is redefined in Thélème to exclude emulous striving. So everyone is made well-off, leisured. The carnival coordinates are by no means the only coordinates operating in *Gargantua and Pantagruel.* Thélème stands on neither carnival nor atonement but on a middle ground defined by these extremes. So much has been made of Rabelais's exuberance that his intense yearning for peace and quiet—and here he stands close to the More of *Utopia*—is forgotten. Rabelaisian joy is finally a disciplined pleasure, a cognitive discipline.

The inevitable movement toward seriousness is implied by the very defense of present pleasure. Concentrate on words and you begin to allegorize them, to think of their function. Pure pleasure remains voiceless. You cannot, finally, play with words purely, says Freud. Your own serious concerns will emerge. You can enjoy eating, drinking, and defecation, but when you start talking about that enjoyment you have begun to allegorize it. Thus *Gargantua and Pantagruel* comes to seem more and more a treatise about language. That kind of allegory currently pleases us. We are trapped, on the level of style, in the body and the body of words, in the same inevitable folly genre and allegory bring. We can hope not to escape the process but at least to become self-conscious about it.

Eric Havelock, in *A Preface to Plato*, argues that Plato's objection to Homer and the poets was an objection to orality, a brief filed in behalf of conceptual thought, mathematical generalization, an intellection beyond words. Does not *Gargantua and Pantagruel* echo such a struggle? The narrator poses as talker, we as listeners. The pace of the narrative and its diversions has been thought oral. Certainly the habits of oral presentation recur constantly. Catalogs, repetitions, proverbs, traditional anecdotes, all the apparatus orality developed to preserve by saying. And the narrator must continue to speak in order to exist. Garrulity sustains reality. Rabelais's sense of preserving and sustaining the past threatens to overwhelm him.

Cannot all this constitute an oral defense against conceptualization? Can one argue generally? Do the rhetorical styles always to some degree re-create this struggle between oral and abstract thinking? Might one consider *Gargantua and Pantagruel* as an attempt to both enshrine this struggle between orality and concept, play and purpose, and in some sense make peace between them? To see this struggle as ahistorical process? Is it a struggle inevitable to all art, this between play and purpose? Does art try always to oppose the forces of generalization, of future purpose, which threaten to denature experience? Trying sometimes, as in a fey, gamesome, nonrepresentational art, to insist on the sanctity of pure play, but inevitably drawn into purpose by the attention process just described? Might then *Gargantua and Pantagruel* encapsulate in a generalized form the structure basic to the history of art?

Rabelais, like Castiglione, argues for self as skill, process. He presents the self differently from Castiglione—the two form nice complements—but both aim for a golden mean that comes from self-conscious awareness of self as dynamic process. For both, skill with words models skill with everything else. For both, sincerity and genuine self require awareness of the self-pleasure in our purposes. *Gargantua and Pantagruel* emerges a gigantic primer to sincerity, a counterstatement—like other great verbal models of the Renaissance—to the clarity and neutral style of a later age. *Gargantua and Pantagruel's* attitude toward words bears a fundamental likeness to More's war on pride in *Utopia*. Both counter the tremendous force of dogmatic, of symbolic, valuation. Both fear it in general, think it pride. Both see that since it cannot be excised from human life—though More would have liked to—it must be controlled, tamed, discounted. Both feared the human propensity to insist on one's own symbols as inevitable, though Rabelais's suspicion here ran far deeper than More's. Both feared that the symbolic structures created by the nation-state would prove as dangerous as those of the religious state.

From this fear of symbolic envaluation flows Rabelais's dislike of agonistic games, games of competition. Roger Caillois, in *Les Jeux et les Hommes*, has isolated four types of games—agôn (competition), alea (chance), mimicry, and ilinx (balance). Rabelais wants always to turn games of competition into one of the other types. Chance, of course, runs throughout *Gargantua and Pantagruel*, from its aleatory structure to Bridoye's novel means of dispensing justice. Rabelais likes to turn contest into rite, or mimicry, by subtracting its end, as in the Thaumaste debate. This fondness for rite devoid of its religion, its sublime significance, is very Ovidian. Rabelais conceives game essentially as a technique to displace aggression, his own first of all. The whole of *Gargantua and Pantagruel* constitutes a displacement of this sort, a conversion of hatred and frustration into pleasure and game. As with Nashe, reserves of hostility betray themselves, though they come out harmless, a transformation Nashe could not manage. Rabelais succeeds by transforming his bloody impulses into a mechanical game—detailing just where the head was bashed—or into a game of scale, exaggerating a chronicle of slaughter to ludicrous numbers, excluding women and children, of course. The Rabelaisian emphasis on self-satisfaction in itself looms as irenic rather than aggressive, as an unwillingness to let others orchestrate your pleasures into their purposes, as a perpetual suspicion of high-mindedness. The Rabelaisian predilection to play with a style always defuses aggressive satire. Just as Rabelais seems finally a fastidious man, so, in spite of the violence, he seems a peaceful one. He would defuse aggression, as other kinds of purpose, by dissolving it into play.

Rabelais, then, no more than Castiglione, subscribes to the Renaissance cliché about man's unlimited future. A sense of inevitable limitation, of boundary conditions necessarily charted, is what *Gargantua and Pantagruel* aims to teach. No more can we speak of noble ambition and the search for fame. Both are pernicious, minatory. Rabelais wants far more to control than to encourage them. As for the cliché that seems to fit, Renaissance commitment to the world, it represents at best half of what Rabelais tried to say. He knew the world to be no more accessible without a symbol than a text without a commentator. If he mocks those who seek seriousness totally out of the world, he mocks those who seek it totally within the world as well. Like Chaucer and like Sterne, he remains a secular writer whose secular view suggests a religious one without insisting on it. His radical skepticism about the seriousness of the self and of human experience stands closer to Chaucer's than to anyone else's. Chaucerian too seems his insistence on a dynamic model for human envaluation. Envaluation is inevitable, essential, essentially humanizing. But it is always to be feared. Only play can control it. Some values are certainly better than others, but are any worth the vexations they cost—and we inevitably pay? "Car tous les biens que le ciel couvre et que la terre contient en toutes ses dimensions: haulteur, profondité, longitude, et latitude, ne sont dignes d'esmouvoir nos affections et troubler nos sens et espritz" (3.2).

Rabelais is thus neither wholly serious nor wholly rhetorical. *Gargantua and Pantagruel* tries to build, instead, a dynamic model for our perpetual movement between the two. Rabelais depicts the war between play and purpose, tries to harmonize it, chart it as single process. If he strives continually to defend play against the encroachments of purpose, he does so always in the name of right purpose, to defend the balance of human nature. "Life is free play fundamentally and would like to be free play altogether," Santayana reminds us in an essay called "Carnival." But it cannot be and Rabelais knew that it cannot. "The universe," he might have reflected, "embraces the same paradox. God is not constrained. He must have conceived the universe in a spirit of play. Should we be so surprised if it seems allergic to our purposes, purposeless?" Man, however, is a purposeful animal. Some purposes are better than others. No careful reader of *Gargantua and Pantagruel* can doubt which those are. Some games too are better than others, self-pleasing games better than agonistic ones. But about the process, the perpetual movement from play through game to sublime seriousness and back into game, Rabelais does not editorialize. He presents it, involves us in it, shows himself involved in it, purposeful champion of purposeless play. But he does not approve it or disapprove it, say anything at all about it. What is there to say?

9

The Dramatic Present:
Shakespeare's Henriad

I

The choruses, or prologues, in *Henry V* express, according to Alfred Harbage,[1] Shakespeare's dissatisfaction with theatrical resources inadequate to his epic theme. So the opening chorus:

> O for a Muse of fire, that would ascend
> The brightest heaven of invention;
> A kingdom for a stage, princes to act
> And monarchs to behold the swelling scene!
> Then should the warlike Harry, like himself,
> Assume the port of Mars, and at his heels,
> Leashed in like hounds, should famine, sword, and fire
> Crouch for employment. But pardon, gentles all,
> The flat unraisèd spirits that hath dared
> On this unworthy scaffold to bring forth
> So great an object. Can this cockpit hold
> The vasty fields of France? Or may we cram
> Within this wooden O the very casques
> That did affright the air at Agincourt?

But Shakespeare seldom used a chorus in his plays. Why here, where it *calls attention to* theatrical limitation? It pines for resources of spectacle Shakespeare never possessed and his audience never expected. "Piece out our imperfections with your thoughts": the Elizabethan audience did this without thinking.

1. Introduction to the play, Pelican text revised, p. 742.

They did not need reminding that the wooden O was not the vasty fields of France. "What childe is there," Sidney says, "that coming to a play, and seeing Thebes written in great letters upon an old doore, doth beleeve that it is Thebes?" Why does Shakespeare call our attention to the act of imagination *Henry V* demands, emphasize the contrivance of his own dramatic surface?

Discussions of historiography usually preoccupy themselves with the attitudes and procedures proper to the historian. Very little attention, I argued earlier, has been given to the reality re-created, evoked, preserved. It has been assumed to be just out there, to have certainly happened, all events "happening" in the same way and accessible to the same correct method, could it but be found. Whether or not Ranke practiced what he preached, *wie es eigentlich gewesen* could serve as motto for almost all methods, or philosophies, of historical investigation. It all happened in one way, whatever that way might be. Thus "method" or "interpretation of history" has come to stand for a tacit decision to acknowledge only those "facts" or "events" that fit one's framework.

The chorus in *Henry V* suggests a further reflection on historical event. How do you write the history of the rhetorical view of life? Motive is the causality of history. What if, as with dramatic motive, a principle of indeterminacy animates it? We cannot imagine an historian saying, "Well, he did it just for the hell of it." Nor, "He did it because he thought someone in his position ought to do something like that." Nor, "He thought that if he acted like a statesman people might mistake him for one." Scientific history must be fundamentally serious and purposive. It must assume—what other operating assumption can it go on?— that people do things for reasons and that these reasons make sense within a single orchestration of values that can be charted, if not always by the people involved, then by the recording historian. It follows that such history can record only serious reality. It cannot "see" the rhetorical ingredient of experience. It is notoriously bad at recording a style of life because, properly speaking, it cannot see it. It cannot address itself, in political history, say, to intuitive judgment. It always breaks this down, and thus distorts it, into its purposive factors. Scientific history postulates the reality it seeks. How else can you talk about accuracy? There must be something to measure against. Such history, or rather such a positivist attitude toward the past, never credits the surface of an account. It always tries to see through it. If the surface defines experience alien to the facts postulated then that surface is wrong.

This point develops in parallel to the argument for verbal style presented earlier. The modern view of "good history," if I can synthesize such a spectre, resembles "good prose style." The stylistic surface never shows. You look through to the shining fact. Yet the style is there, helps us to see. (The historian must feel his period, re-create it within himself, and make us feel it.) The great historians, if you read their prefaces, acknowledge that such an ideal is impossible—like perfect neutral prose, it is an empty category—yet always to be striven for. Historical fact, then, is like prose clarity. It is a final construction, a synthesis mistaken for a preexistent reality. And, as for prose style, the path to it lies through the fields of style, not around them. We see a prose style as "clear" inasmuch as we acknowledge, in some part of our brain, all the paths *not* taken, the configurations *not* set down, the words *not* used. So the historical fact seems real to us inasmuch as we recognize the kinds of facts that it is not, the other kinds of history that might be written. Both kinds of clarity depend on a pattern of ambient attention. Historical fact is thus a refinement, an extreme case, the product of a great many previous choices. The best or clearest history will make us aware of all those decisions without asking us to focus on them.

Shakespeare is approached as an historical dramatist by asking how he adopted or adapted history for the stage. This puts the problem backwards. He is not retelling dramatically a kind of history which could be told another way. He is putting forward a dramatic history which could be told only the way he has told it. And he tries hard to suggest that other ways of telling his story would yield other stories. So the chorus presents political myth, Virgilian epic, if you like. The play of *Henry V* pays another kind of fealty, a more Ovidian homage, to England, but in the process it becomes another story. It introduces other kinds of facts. The search for honor or fame or reputation—for the satisfactory second self, whatever form it takes—casts us, for posterity, as actor to audience. The theatre is not a medium to which this kind of history need be adapted, but rather the form from which it comes. At all events, the medium expresses its subject essentially, puts us, as audience, in that position historians agree is ideal. We participate in the process, feel it as well as comprehend it. So does the actor. He is not imitating a king kinging when he impersonates Henry V. He is imitating an actor acting. History can thus, in more than a manner of speaking, be re-created. Inasmuch as it was theatrical to begin with, observed dramatic coordinates when it first happened, it can be re-created absolutely, in real time. Furthermore, such re-creation will be absolutely scientific, loyal to its event. It will just construe event differently from scientific history.

In support of such a task, Shakespeare can muster only the imaginary puissance of language, and so he must use it in the most theatrical, the most rhetorical way possible. It must always call attention to itself. Thus, immediately after the heroic expectations conjured up by the chorus to act one, Shakespeare offers the wonderfully boring stiff-arm opening scene, two churchmen-politicians calculating how to pay off the new Mars-like Harry. And the second scene is longer and more tedious than the first. It is again a formal rhetorical occasion. It occurs, we come to perceive beneath the gorgeous language, to hoke up a sacred, unopposable excuse for invading France. Mars-like Harry has remembered his father's deathbed advice to busy giddy minds with foreign quarrels. Hal, as always in this play, (after he gets the tennis balls from the Dauphin; before Harfleur; before the battle) tries to hold someone else responsible. Here his "May I with right and conscience make this claim?" finds the Churchly quid pro quo—"The sin upon my head, dread sovereign!"—he wants to hear. Then Canterbury retails a second council chamber chestnut, the famous honeybees, "Creatures that by a rule in nature teach / The act of order to a peopled kingdom." Canterbury does all right while he remains for twenty lines in the bosom of the cliché, gilds the topos as the singing masons build their roof of gold. But when he applies it to the case in hand, he runs into trouble ("I this infer, / That many things having full reference / To one consent may work contrariously, / As many arrows loosèd several ways / Come to one mark . . ."), and, after some more waffling, concludes with the perfect non sequitur, "Therefore to France, my liege!" The clash of gorgeous language and absurd, irrelevant argumentation forces us to see the speech as speech. Whether Canterbury, or Shakespeare, believed it neither arises nor matters. We respond to it as a rhetorical weapon not as a political philosophy. The kingdom in act one *is* a stage. The cockpit can hold, if not the vasty fields of France, at least this kind of stylistic manipulation. Stylistic manipulation, language as authentication, mythmaking, is just its affair.

The discontinuity between chorus and act two looms yet greater; the second chorus begins pitched to yet a higher note than the first. "Now all the youth of England are on fire, / And silken dalliance in the wardrobe lies. / Now thrive the armorers, and honor's thought / Reigns solely in the breast of every man." The contrast with what immediately follows, Nym and his cheese-toasting sword ("I dare not fight, but I will wink and hold out mine iron"), is exquisite. And against the hyperlanguid Nym stands Pistol's fire (" 'Solus,' egregious dog? O viper vile!") about a real quarrel—over eight shillings.

The stage again provides a genuine location for the second scene; in it Hal stage-manages treason and its unmasking. He makes of the unmasking a dramatic device and a rhetorical argument, just as with the Salic Law and the honeybees. If we lean on the rhetoric, think about Hal's speech, it turns into fustian. Talk of betraying countries? What does he propose for France? As for pay-offs, what else has the Church rendered him? We must seek the authentic high style elsewhere. We find it, oddly, in Pistol; the genuine language for genuine grief; "No; for my manly heart doth earn. / Bardolph, be blithe; Nym, rouse thy vaunting veins; / Boy, bristle thy courage up; for Falstaff he is dead, / And we must earn therefore" (2.3.3–6). And for universal

suspicion: "Trust none; / For oaths are straws, men's faiths are
wafer-cakes, / And Hold-fast is the only dog, my duck. / Therefore Caveto be thy counsellor. / Go, clear thy crystals. Yoke-
fellows in arms, / Let us to France, like horse-leeches, my boys, /
To suck, to suck, the very blood to suck!" (2.3.45–51). Shakespeare makes the language of parody into the only genuine high
style, the only authentic sublimity, the play permits. Arnold
might have used it as a touchstone. By comparison Hal seems to
prate. How dare *he* call it treason?

Each chorus becomes more dubious and hollow, and more
impassioned, than the one before. So for act three:

> Thus with imagined wing our swift scene flies,
> In motion of no less celerity
> Than that of thought. Suppose that you have seen
> The well-appointed king at Hampton pier
> Embark his royalty; and his brave fleet
> With silken streamers the young Phoebus fanning.
> Play with your fancies, and in them behold
> Upon the hempen tackle shipboys climbing;
> Hear the shrill whistle which doth order give
> To sounds confused; behold the threaden sails,
> Borne with th'invisible and creeping wind,
> Draw the huge bottoms through the furrowed sea,
> Breasting the lofty surge. O, do but think
> You stand upon the rivage and behold
> A city on th'inconstant billows dancing;
> For so appears this fleet majestical,
> Holding due course to Harfleur. Follow, follow!

Here the chorus supplies the construction patriotic myth must
put upon the event, the construction we too, if sufficiently inat-
tentive to stylistic surface, will accept. In the process, Chorus
begins to sound like Pistol and Hal, in the Harfleur breach, even
more so: "Once more unto the breach, dear friends, once more,
. . . / Stiffen the sinews, summon up the blood, / Disguise fair
nature with hard-favored rage; / Then lend the eye a terrible
aspect: / Let it pry through the portage of the head / Like the brass

cannon . . . / On, on, you noble English . . ." (3.1.1–17). Hal is
performing again, and we eke out the performance with our
minds in a way Chorus has not imagined. If we are still fooled,
Bardolph comes along immediately after to refrigerate the sublimity: "On, on, on, on, on! to the breach, to the breach!"

The fourth chorus is longest of all. It begins with an extended
piece of epic scene painting and then moves to a proleptic portrait of the King on the Night-before-the-Battle:

> O, now, who will behold
> The royal captain of this ruined band
> Walking from watch to watch, from tent to tent,
> Let him cry, "Praise and glory on his head!"
> For forth he goes and visits all his host,
> Bids them good morrow with a modest smile
> And calls them brothers, friends, and countrymen.
> Upon his royal face there is no note
> How dread an army hath enrounded him;
> Nor doth he dedicate one jot of color
> Unto the weary and all-watchèd night,
> But freshly looks, and overbears attaint
> With cheerful semblance and sweet majesty;
> That every wretch, pining and pale before,
> Beholding him, plucks comfort from his looks.
> A largess universal, like the sun.
> His liberal eye doth give to every one,
> Thawing cold fear, that mean and gentle all
> Behold, as may unworthiness define,
> A little touch of Harry in the night.

[4.cho.28–47]

So should a king act. But what has this to do with Harry le Roy
stalking about incognito in Sir Thomas Erpingham's cloak? Or
picking quarrels with poor soldiers when they show a natural
dubiety about the King's motives, one the play itself amply
justifies? And that "cheerful semblance and sweet majesty,"
how does that fit "Not to-day, O Lord"? The Chorus offers one
picture, the orthodox one, and the play offers another. The

Chorus has become spokesman for the serious political myth, for the surface of history. It concludes:

> And so our scene must to the battle fly;
> Where (O for pity!) we shall much disgrace
> With four or five most vile and ragged foils,
> Right ill-disposed in brawl ridiculous,
> The name of Agincourt. Yet sit and see,
> Minding true things by what their mock'ries be.

By this point it is not altogether clear what are true things and what mockeries. Read the lines literally and Agincourt becomes a brawl ridiculous. It can fit into the wooden O because *it was played to begin with*. What it was like then is what it is like now. Shakespeare seems less concerned to dramatize history than to point out its intrinsic dramaticality. The scene was played for the dramatic pleasure of playing the scene.

On the night before the battle, after the King has abused his incognito yet again and quarreled with Williams, comes the great masterpiece of self-pity, the magnificent speech on ceremony. "Upon the king! Let us our lives, our souls, / Our debts, our careful wives, / Our children, and our sins, lay on the king! / We must bear all. O hard condition. . . ." The speech climaxes the *Henriad* argument. "O Ceremony, show me but thy worth!" Indeed. Ceremony motivates the long chronicle of usurpation and relegitimation Shakespeare has just chronicled. Montaigne supplies the gloss in "de la Praesumption" (2.17): "Nous ne sommes que cerimonie: la cerimonie nous emporte, et laissons la substance des choses: nous nous tenons aux branches, et abandonnons le tronc et le corps." There *is* no "substance of things" in *Henry V*. Hence the Chorus's ironical exhortations that we supply one. Hal dismisses the play's central value, its only substance. What is Agincourt if not a ceremony? He sees it thus himself in the most famous patriotic speech in English letters, the "happy few" war cry prefacing the battle. He defines the battle as a struggle not for victory but *for honor*, for ceremonial reward: "But if it be a sin to covet honor, / I am the most offending soul alive" (4.3.28–29). Those who disagree can leave.

And the battle is defined as history, the present redefined as a play with posterity as audience: "He that outlives this day, and comes safe home, / Will stand a-tiptoe when this day is namèd / And rouse him at the name of Crispian."

The last chorus begins: "Vouchsafe to those that have not read the story / That I may prompt them." But which story and what kind of prompting? Again we are offered the pageantry, the epic event, the official story. And if the apology for disunity of time and space seems labored—the King bounces from England to France like a Ping-pong ball—general epic elevation will yet carry us away. What follows is the most glaring non sequitur of all. Hal, having won the lady on the field of ceremonious battle, then mounts a make-believe wooing as if he were a private citizen. It is very cute but very fake. It concludes perfectly a play about the uses of ceremony. The chorus as Epilogue ends with an apology for "in little room confining mighty men" and with a quick glance forward, as climax and justification for all the patriotic glory, to the reign of Henry VI.

We might, in trying to find fitting premises for *Henry V*, think of our stylistic spectrum. At extreme left put the most "realistic" chronicle history, "Her Atheling cyning," one uninterpreted fact after another, and at the other end put Sir Walter Scott. Perhaps we can now agree that no place on the spectrum is any truer than any other, that they are all equally true to different kinds of truth. We may say "aspects" of truth, all adding up to Truth. We agree to *credit* the surface, not to penetrate it to a previously-agreed-upon reality. We thus restate the stylistic spectrum in terms of historiography. I do not object if historians wish to sign off here. They know their part of the spectrum and want to stick to it. But the spectrum makes a point. The past is as complex as the present. There is no absolute separation between art and life, and the style of the past can be reconstituted only through artistic means. The literary historian, like Livy telling of Lucrece, will not forget that fiction is part of history. What-might-have-been surrounds fact as clarity is surrounded by a penumbra of opacities not chosen.

I argued earlier that classical history, by observing a speech-narrative-speech-narrative alternation, tried to span something like this range of possibility. The alternation simplifies the spectrum, but at least aims at the whole of it. Classical historians were far more scientific, if our reference point be full human experience, than the nineteenth-century historians of carefully laundered, impersonally certified fact. The literary student must see that, though historians today content themselves with part of the spectrum, Western literature has never been satisfied with less than the whole story. It has never been happy as only literarily true. It has tried to cover as much of the spectrum as possible, to be true in as many ways as possible. If it cannot do it all at once, it imitates first one kind of truth and then the other. What strikes one about Western literature is its persistent radical impurity. It is seldom any one kind of truth for long. Even the purest genres range widely. This range obtrudes itself in fiction, where the oscillation from literal truth to fiction to pure romance occurs all the time.

Henry V spans the same range from certifiable fact to pure romance, and often piles one atop the other. Their relations, more complex than the set-piece speech-narrative-speech pattern, work in an equally complex structure of styles and attitudes toward style. Shakespeare did not portray *only* a dramatic reality (would it be possible?) but such a reality had to remain, so long as he was a dramatist, a central element in his conception of the past. His history engages in a complex imitation, not adapting for theatre a referent history or—the opposite simplification—borrowing for purposes of "literary truth" a few historical motifs. To read the *Henriad* aright, we must credit the surface, believe what it says. If we come to it with preconceived ideas—Shakespeare believed thus and so; the Age of Elizabeth saw the world in such a way; Henry V was the great patriotic king—we see only what we have come prepared to see. No premises about "fact" then, and no premises about style either. Of course we never shake free of premises absolutely, but the plays about Hal establish their stylistic controls as they go along. From them

comes a peculiarly rich mixture of rhetorical and serious self and
their two views of life. They concern us, too, because they
prophesy so strongly the many turns our dominant form of prose
fiction was to take. Cervantes, Fielding, Sterne, George Eliot,
and Joyce did not consider themselves historians without reason.

II

If *Henry V* looks at Agincourt
until it dissolves into a series of dramas, *Richard II* offers a series
of dramatic occasions that dissolve not only an event, the deposition, but a theme, the legitimation of power. Both event and
theme turn on a sense of theatre and the skillful identity flowing
from it. The crown is held by force of personality, legitimacy
becomes a matter of style. The play refuses to adopt Plato's
Symposium strategy, to look outward for authoritarian sanction
either thematic or stylistic. All its problems and all its solutions
are internally generated. It begins with a secular invocation of
God's will, a trial by combat. But the King interferes and from
then on only stylistic clues are offered. The demande the play
builds on—better a bad legitimate king or good usurping
one?—balances so nicely we must seek for guidance from the
style. Attempts to *think* the problem through lead nowhere.
Usurpation leads to civil war finally; the legitimate King leads to
civil war immediately. God has sanctioned Richard, but the
House of York had not always reigned. They usurped some other
and, after all, does not Bolingbroke think himself the scourge of
God? Richard insists no one can unking him and then literally
and figuratively unkings himself. The play offers two exquisitely
balanced rights and wrongs; between them intellection is
trapped. The play's political theory (alas for Divine Right)
remains irrelevant from beginning to end. If the play is about
sanction and legitimation, these are acts of drama and verbal
style, not acts of intellection.

A front-stage/back-stage alternation prevails throughout the
play, and renders style opaque from the beginning. The first

defiance scene is followed by a backstage interlude between Gaunt and the Duchess of Gloucester. The King is really the guilty party in the dispute: "God's is the quarrel; for God's substitute, / His deputy anointed in his sight, / Hath caused his death" (1.2.37–39).[2] The now hollow ceremony is then resumed, then the banishments come. These, which seem ex tempore, we later learn were planned. Then backstage again, this time with the King and Aumerle who, we learn yet later, did the actual killing of Gloucester. The ceremony is a charade from the beginning, and our suspicion, once aroused, remains. We are forever learning later what was "really" going on. The debate often stands ironically at odds with the event in other ways. In 2.3, York roundly scolds Bolingbroke before Berkeley Castle, laying the clichés of legitimacy thickly on. He will "remain as neuter." Then he adds, as laconic afterthought, the phrase that makes him of Bolingbroke's party: "So fare you well— / Unless you please to enter in the castle / And there repose you for this night" (ll. 159–61). Bolingbroke is not slow off the mark: "An offer, uncle, that we will accept." Or Richard in 3.3, asking in a long speech to see "the hand of God / That hath dismissed us from our stewardship" while Bolingbroke and his soldiers parade below. We never take anything at face value, but at what value to take it is never clear.

The language calls attention to itself in little as well as in large. All verse, lots of rhyme, the compulsive cluster of breath, speech, word, throat imagery, above all the punning. These continually call attention to stylistic surface, render style a theme. So Bolingbroke, the "Silent King," stands prisoner neither to language nor ceremony, functions in the world of deeds, while Richard has come to believe his own myth, to take it seriously. It is not his flatterers who trip him but his own absorption in words, ceremony, myth. Like the Chorus in *Henry V*, he accepts the public, serious definition of reality uncritically. This proves fatal. The play thus comes to be about the political uses of rhetoric and ceremony. Richard, paradoxically for one so self-

2. Ed. Matthew W. Black.

conscious, fails to be sufficiently self-conscious about language and social surface. This is a failure of stylistic awareness, the same failure that threatens the audience.

We are alerted time and again. So Gaunt's famous deathbed "scept'red isle" oration (2.1.31–68) is prepared for by an interchange on breath, air, tongues. We expect words, finally *air*, as Gaunt's opening pun ("Methinks I am a prophet new inspired / And thus, expiring, do foretell of him . . .") testifies. Concept is reduced to word and word to hot air much as Falstaff later reduces honor. Yet another rhetorical display piece which speaks to the Polonius in all of us, the speech also nicely summarizes the practiced politician's repertoire: first a torrent of proverbs, then a series of epithets (the *naming* strategy so strong in the *Henriad*), then the real business, the tax farming. After Gaunt's pun on "gaunt," Richard replies, "Can sick men play so nicely with their names?" This is for us. Language is always the issue. Never take it for granted. But it ought to remind Richard too, and does not. His attitude toward language resembles his attitude toward his role as king. He is aware of it but does not understand it. Identity judgments are like stylistic judgments, and he understands neither. He misses the speech's real point—how language can create or destroy that earth of majesty. The issue remains the role of language, an entity more substantial than the soil of England just leased out. Richard is not hearing. He stands on ceremony but cannot understand it. Stylistic contrast again makes the point. York is appalled at the seizure of Gaunt's lands and conveys his horror in two splendid speeches. Between them is sandwiched Richard's "Why, uncle, what's the matter?" The matter is words, and Richard cannot see them. His blindness is not to deeds but to words.

The same ironic juxtaposition of land and words infuses 3.2, the play's pivotal scene, where Richard falls on his knees to "salute" the earth of England, and his courtiers start laughing at him. Richard is usually thought too much a poet to be king. Isn't it just the opposite? He takes literally, seriously, what was meant metaphorically, rhetorically; he believes his own myth; he thinks like Chorus. It is very well to *use* myth. (Churchill remarks in *My Early Life*, "I had no idea in those days of the enormous and unquestionably helpful part that humbug plays in the social life of great peoples.") But it is fatal to believe it. You will then, as Richard shows in the rest of the scene, fall prisoner to events rather than manipulate them.

When the myth seems imperiled, Richard wants to discard it entirely: "Throw away respect, / Tradition, form, and ceremonious duty" (3.2.172–73). He is busy learning a new part, Poor Richard, without having understood the old. Kings do not stand exempt from the demands of humanity. Again, the myth has fooled him. Richard has no central self, no private self. When deposed, he must call for a mirror and smash it. Only by dramatizing his symbolic death can he make it real to himself. And he must overact his new role, too: "What must the king do now? Must he submit? / The king shall do it. Must he be deposed? / The king shall be contented. Must he lose / The name of king? A God's name, let it go!" (3.3.143–46). Only in his great concluding speech does Richard begin to constitute a private identity, the brain proving female to the soul to reconstitute the world out of imagination, sustain its external pressures with countervailing internal ones.

We need not chronicle the bypaths and indirect crooked ways by which Bolingbroke gets his crown to make the point. A silent king indeed, not fooled by words, he can play, use, a scene but does not mistake ceremonial rehearsal for power itself. One of the play's best comic scenes—*Richard II* does not lack comedy—is 4.1, when Bolingbroke faces the situation Richard met in the opening scene. But here, too many denouncers, too many challenges. The new flatterers fall over each other in challenging Aumerle until he runs out of detachable haberdashery ("Some honest Christian trust me with a gage"). Bolingbroke is not deceived. He ascends the throne, as he does everything else, "in God's name," but he never loses sight of power.

III

The realities of power, though, as they are pursued in the two parts of *Henry IV*, turn out as essentially dramatic as everything else. Shakespeare does not subscribe to the Thucydidean scheme—power on one hand, mythical certification on the other. The facts of power and the motive behind them turn out to be as mythical as the ornamentation publicly expressing them. These four plays seek to explain the violence merely chronicled in the *Henry VI* sequence. Shakespeare finds a Chaucerian answer—not individual but social tragedy. Violence and social instability are implicit in the way we constitute ourselves and the way society is itself. Deposition brings revolution, but so does legitimate monarchy. There are always plenty of motives for rebellion in these histories. Too many. They all add up to zero and social upheaval comes to seem finally gratuitous, a spontaneous, motiveless malignity. *Richard II* opens with a scene of bad governance; the vacillating self-dramatizing and self-satisfied King cannot control events. Disaster follows. *I Henry IV* offers, in its first act, a similar trial of governance. The King is decisive and sensible. Again disaster follows. Richard has the myth but not the skill to use it; Henry IV has the skill but not the myth. King Henry V has skill and myth too, new-minted though it be. He brings some kind of unity. It would seem to follow that the two plays about Henry IV concern themselves with how to hold and enself a myth, what motives lead to social violence and how they may be controlled.

These issues are focused on the personality of Hal. Shakespeare has written a mirror of princes but a dynamic not a static one. Hal must not *be* someone only, but act a role too. His self is less pattern than skill. He does not learn about human motives. He lives among them. The final shape of his personality and the forces shaping it comprise what Shakespeare learned about motive, about the mainsprings of history. His conclusion is not an optimistic one. You can direct violence, channel it, but you cannot eliminate it. If identity is dramatic, it will always be challenged, if not from outside then from within. To sustain itself, identity has, as we have seen repeatedly, to be played, defined by opposition, talked about to be fully felt. And so with the central self. The imagination creates it, must be capacious enough to reenact its own role and all those it touches. And this self thrives on drama. We are all propelled toward dramatic intensity, toward sublimity, because we feel more our self, both our selves. And the more these two selves struggle, the more alive we feel. Thus rebellion is implicit in how we create ourselves and how society creates itself. Rebellion can never be abolished, it can only be orchestrated. If history is essentially dramatic, drama is in a manner of speaking essentially evil. Or essentially fraught with evil promise. If you cannot contain it in England, you must lead it to France.

Things fall apart in *Richard II* because Richard remains a prisoner of the theatre. In *I Henry IV* this role is played by Hotspur. Henry IV is made one of Hotspur's admirers by the exigencies of a prodigal son motif which shows Shakespeare again writing about the form he is writing in. Which kind of prodigal, he asks, ought to be welcomed home? Hal answers the question; he admires, but he does not much imitate, Hotspur. Inelastic role playing was just what his father had learned a prince could not afford. Just after Poins and Hal play the "Francis!" trick, Hal revealingly changes subject in mid-speech: "That ever this fellow should have fewer words than a parrot, and yet the son of a woman! His industry is upstairs and downstairs, his eloquence the parcel of a reckoning. I am not yet of Percy's mind, the Hotspur of the North; he that kills me some six or seven dozen of Scots at a breakfast, washes his hands, and says to his wife, 'Fie upon this quiet life! I want work' " (2.4.94–100).[3] The play has already made the connection that sparks in Hal's mind. Hotspur's responses are mechanically predictable. Thus he can be manipulated, all-warrior though he be, by his uncle and Northumberland, as in 1.3 and again before the battle. He is Sincerity: "out upon this half-faced fellowship!" He incarnates the very theme of Honor's tongue in the sublimest sense of Honor. He can quarrel over dividing the promised land but he forgets the map of it.

Worcester and Northumberland must redeem their banished honors, restore themselves "into the good thoughts of the world again" (1.3.180–82), but they do this for their own purposes.

3. Ed. M. A. Shaaber.

Hotspur lives entirely in other men's minds, plucks bright honor from pale-faced moon or ocean floor all for present and future chronicles. He *does* better brook loss of life than loss of titles. His motive *is* pure, pure sublimity fallen over into pure play. He is always verging on nonsense or falling in: "If he fall in, good night, or sink or swim! / Send danger from the east unto the west, / So honor cross it from the north to south, / And let them grapple" (1.3.194–97). Pure chivalry, pure play; he is as doomed as Richard and as silly.

He gets parodied mercilessly by and in comparison with his opposite variation on *miles gloriosus*, Falstaff. "La parfaite valeur et la poltronnerie complète sont deux extrémités où l'on arrive rarement," La Rochefoucauld reminds us. They get together here. Falstaff is many things but above all honor's opposite. He lives in the flesh, and not in other men's minds. His catechism of the flesh establishes the only real present in these plays. He lives now. His trouble is bad reputation but it does not genuinely trouble him. He has been long adulated as the greatest English humor character. Is he a humor character at all? His *response* is infinitely flexible, hypocrisy itself. And there is nothing laughable or even comic about the central self this hypocrisy seeks to protect.

Falstaff is a very Rabelaisian character but not in his drinking, eating, and cursing so much as in his determined resistance to living by concepts. People are always trying to move in on him, make him serious, purposive, principled. He resists, like Rabelais, the massive tyranny of all the duties "honor" comes to represent. He can be cruel but we forgive him less because he is a good clown than because of the self that rhetorical clowning seeks to protect. He possesses the only genuine central self in the play. Here above all he stands opposed to Hotspur. We cherish him for it. It is not that he is sincere, dear heaven, but that he possesses a central self to be false to. He comes to represent, again like Rabelais, the private life. Unambitious, he alone in the play does not lust for violence.

Jolly Falstaff has too much dominated our thinking. He is not a comic character in the second part nor finally in the first. He *plays* a clown in the first part, just as he *plays* in the second a pathetic old man closer to his real self. But finally he remains beyond our feelings, pleasure trying to protect itself from all the concepts that would lure it to destruction. Like pleasure, he seems more used than using. Against honor, the voices of conscience and conscientious myth making, he hasn't much chance. Between those two extremes Hal must find his way, as the battlefield scene in the last act so neatly emblemizes. He must take Hotspur's honor from him but hold it with fresh self-consciousness. He must learn to distance both myths and their language. Here Falstaff comes in. He offers dramatic rehearsal, acts as a verbal sparring partner, plays his true role as Hal's schoolmaster in the rhetoric of everyday life, his taskmaster in the styles and textures of reality.

Hal learns to play his royal role without being absorbed by it, without forgetting its precarious dramatic construction. He learns, that is, to make history. This configuration of personality resembles the skill at self Castiglione's *Courtier* portrays. And the "honor" it seeks embodies a like skill, a similar oscillation between Hotspur's honor and Falstaff's. He must choose serious honor, finally, as a public man, but he holds it differently from Hotspur. Falstaff haunts the court he was banished from. His ghost takes the form of a stylistic self-consciousness questioning high style at every point. This is not to say that we always reject the high styles. But neither are we ever carried away. Hal and his father must legitimize their line, adopt a myth. This is the usual task of epic. It transfers power and sanction from past to present, Greece to Rome. These four plays conclude that such a transfer is indeed an epic task, a task for the imagination. Legitimation is dramatic, originally and persistently, because life is dramatic. Again, the invitation is extended in real time. The subject of the *Henriad* is epic, epic essentially as the description of a dramatic reality. It was, we know, Ovid who saw this truth first. The self-consciousness about style and motive bred into his imagination required a different kind of epic. So it was with Rabelais and Spenser, and here with Shakespeare. The epic clichés are ironic, the high style two-edged, because based on a naive epic self no

longer tenable. This is the problem for Bolingbroke and his son.
Political theory was needed, certainly. But what wove it into
authenticity was the ruler's dramatic and rhetorical skill, skill
finally in self. Drama legitimized and empowered the myth.

The movement from *Richard II* through *Henry V* reconstitutes a
cycle from legitimacy to renewed legitimacy, from disintegrating
to rejuvenated mythical sublime. It thus rehearses, in large, the
model for motive sketched earlier. It imitates on the level of
politics the process of envaluation mankind inevitably describes
in expressing and sustaining his complex sense of self. At the
same time it uses an oscillation of higher frequency to express the
model, to trigger the in-and-out process of viewing the self.
Whether the technique is front-stage/back-stage or blank-verse/
prose or high-style/low, it always switches our attention back
and forth from rhetorical to serious coordinates. The great advantage drama possesses for encapsulating the model for motive is
its manipulation of scale. Here again drama tends to fall over into
life, fictional time into real time. For manipulation of scale is our
primary way of knowing. It is the essential human way to change
the object without changing the nature of the object, and thus a
way for our theory of knowledge to build plural orchestrations
into itself. It is also, as Heraclitus seems to have noticed, our
customary way of distinguishing subject and object. Shakespeare's stylistic manipulations (perhaps those of the rhetorical
stylists generally) are games of scale like this. We are accustomed
to shifting from style to meaning, from pageant to myth, at a
certain speed, history to moral significance at a certain rate.
When we are slowed down, the object looks different. *It* slows
down. And this complementarity continues, up and down. Our
distance from experience varies. The extremes seem to be the
rhetorical and the serious coordinates. For serious reality, there
is a past and there are events and they can be narrated by
someone standing in a present separate from them. For rhetorical
reality, not so. All is present. And so, in these four plays, the
characters live in a true past inasmuch as they are essentially
dramatic selves and fixed only in the past. At the same time,

since their being is flux, they can know only a present and their drama is in real time. Shakespeare wants it both ways. And so the history play supplies an apt vehicle since such an alternative—the creation of a dramatic present—is essential to it. It follows that if you approach such a form conceiving being to be static, if you deny the dramaticality of the past, if you impose serious purposiveness upon it, you will distort it. You will take literally what was not meant to be taken so. You will locate yourself at a fixed distance from reality and the play will cease to work upon you. When Canterbury starts talking about those singing masons, the bees, building their roofs of gold, you will start talking about Shakespeare's hierarchical view of public order. You will impose a naivete of perception on the past which not even the most cloistered scholar could afford to impose on the present. If he did, like Don Quixote he would go mad.

Epilogue

"Man is not double," Plato insists in the *Republic* (οὐκ ἔστιν διπλοῦς ἀνὴρ [397E]). My attempt to explain our continuing taste for formal rhetoric has led to the opposite conclusion. It is only by supposing man's nature to be double that his invention of and appetite for rhetorical ornament can be made intelligible. The more one studies the ornamental, self-conscious, opaque styles, the more duple—if not duplicitous—man comes to seem. He likes to think himself intensely purposeful but often this is self-flattery. At least half the time his living is play, his motive dramatic and self-contrived, his self a role. It is to sustain this second man and second reality that rhetoric exists. As we have seen, a theory of rhetorical style will always invoke a theory of motive, a theory of identity, and a theory of knowledge. These will vary concomitantly and can be plotted on similar spectrums: a central self will bring with it serious motive and a scientific, measurable reality independent of man; a social self will act from role-sustaining motives in a dramatic reality.

In the first chapter, two possible tests were suggested, in passing, for this referent dualism. If it really prevails, critical disagreement on texts such as have been discussed should fall into a characteristic opposition, an archetypal pattern of misunderstanding. Serious coordinates should be found where rhetorical ones are required, and vice versa. I think that, in each case, such a pattern is observable. The reader—only he can apply the test fairly—is invited to see if such patterns exist for Renaissance texts. They certainly exist in later times: Victorian depreciation of Sterne and of *Tristram Shandy* is a perfect case in point. Such a pattern, if it is there, should serve not as disproving such conflicting commentary but rather as isolating the terms in which each side may be on target. Often a scholiast will isolate the right question brilliantly—for Renaissance studies C. S. Lewis is the prime example—but suggest an answer within the wrong coordinates. Seeing the pattern of disagreement allows one to extract the maximum benefit from such critical observations even while finally disagreeing with them.

The role of rhetoric in Western education has also been suggested as an area of possible confirmatory evidence. Again, the reader must himself inquire. The history of education ought to lend itself to analysis as recording the two selves in an oscillation of varying fruitfulness. The curriculum ought to share the fundamental structure of Western literature, the repeated oscillation between serious and rhetorical reality, between, as Whitehead calls them in *The Aims of Education*, periods of integration and periods of romance. We would expect to find, too, repeated instances of disputes carried on from seemingly disparate premises and about totally disparate conceptions of man. The continuing debate between professional training for a serious reality and progressive education through a curriculum of play provides a striking modern instance of such an opposition. There should be many more.

A third broad means of testing, obviously, is to ask what light our fundamental dichotomy, expanded as it has been through some exemplary texts, casts on the Renaissance more broadly conceived, and on the course of Western literature as a whole. Sketching an answer can be suggestive at best, but it may supply a context within which the reader can test for himself the truth and the usefulness of the theory.

Some light is cast, for a start, on the primary question of whether there was a genuine intellectual Renaissance at all, or only a stylistic revival of Ciceronian Latin. If we think of the humanist worship of style, its preoccupation with Cicero, as a rediscovery of rhetorical man, then the two kinds of Renaissance immediately collapse into one. The preoccupation with style takes its rightful place as genuinely revolutionary. No deeper rebirth can be imagined than man's recovery of half of himself. The growth of the city-state would not, in its implications, be more profound. As for the derivative question of whether there was a radical break between Middle Ages and Renaissance, surely that too may be answered by the stylistic preoccupation. The change from a central self, a Christian soul, to a rhetorical

Ciceronian self constituted indeed a fundamental break. But rhetorical man was not, of course, being discovered for the first time. He lurked in the medieval scene—as witness not only Chaucer but a broad range of texts, from Goliard poetry to a twelfth-century letter writer like Guy de Basoches—however strongly Christian dogma sought to proscribe him. Thus there was a change but nothing radically new.

And so it might be argued that the Renaissance infatuation with language, from Ciceronianism to the enriched vernaculars, was a central attribute, not a peripheral adolescent bumptiousness. It was both the sign of a revolution and its instigator. It testifies to a great hunger for the full complex Western self and its enriched model for motive. The movement from style to self was direct and immediate. Each implied the other. From this interdependence, several further implications derive.

First, the famous Renaissance celebration of man as endless possibility may need, as suggested earlier, some modification. To block out a full model for motive is to find boundary conditions, not to transcend them. Man is shut in, not opened out, describes a circular path. Rabelais, Castiglione, Erasmus, and somewhat differently More too, argue for a sense of man's inevitable limitations. Sublimity will always return to play and the cycle start over. There are no new worlds for man, no golden ages. Prospero cannot stay on his island and Iago will always lurk in our hearts. Man and his motives constitute a closed system.

His zeal for knowledge is similarly restricted, bounded by his limited capacity to absorb the past and by the weight and blindness that past inevitably bestows. It is necessary periodically to burn the Alexandria library down, to resist somehow, as Rabelais contends, the implacable purposefulness learning comes to represent. Our ways of knowing are not infinitely expandable, but only two, like our double self and the double reality it inhabits. Once you chart this primary oscillation, you have come to the end of man's world. There is no place else to go.

The Renaissance self as overreacher requires a similar qualification. As Shakespeare's sonnets show, this inner-outer dichotomy was felt to be too simple and too static. A more

complex, dynamic relationship was needed between self and
society, between the private and the public life, one that can
come only by recognizing man as rhetorical as well as serious.
Hamlet's stoicism was out of date, as *Hamlet* shows. The ego
running out of control usually falls into theatrical imposture long
before it arrives at world conquest. In this light, some traditional
judgments about Renaissance political philosophy may need
rethinking as well. It is a commonplace to observe, for example,
that Machiavelli in *The Prince* is a political realist—*the* political
realist—by whose side Castiglione seems a Platonic idealist. But
this verdict invokes serious coordinates only and is correct only
in terms of them. Within rhetorical coordinates, Castiglione
seems much the shrewder. Machiavelli assumes that all human
behavior is purposive, and thus his political advice is often
disproved by the very historical examples he adduces to support
it. Compared to Castiglione, his grasp of human nature sometimes seems shallow and simplistic.

Like *Utopia, The Prince* is bemused by a Platonic ideal—the
Republic's perfect stasis. Yet, in implication, the stylistic revolution moved in the opposite direction, toward a self-conscious,
self-correcting dynamic polis. This antithesis may explain the
conflict so common in Renaissance literature between the political theory explicit in a work and the political reality implicit in it.
In *The Faerie Queene*, for example, the governing design
applauds and celebrates Tudor centrality, the static vision. Yet
the image of man the poem creates is of a being by his nature
violent, incapable of stasis, forever flying off on tangents, sal-
vageable, if at all, only by radical self-consciousness about the
springs of his own behavior. For such a being, as Shakespeare
made clear in the *Henriad*, the static patterns of orthodox political
philosophy were useful largely as rhetorical glosses, counters in
a game forever changing. Ulysses can prate about "degree" in
Troilus and Cressida, but he would have been a fool to believe in
it.

The biggest readjustment in our traditional thinking about the
Renaissance, however, perhaps comes in a commonplace so
common that it may escape our notice—the difference between

good and evil. If the humanist endeavor finally amounted to the placing of style, and the study of style, in the larger context of human behavior, the final result of that reorientation was the protean figure of Iago, a figure created to suggest that the genesis of evil is stylistic, rhetorical, lies in action which aims only to rehearse and sustain the self, in behavior for its own sake. The primal dichotomy for behavior would seem to be less passion and reason, or good and evil, than rhetorical and purposive, serious motive.

Surely it was an awareness, however vague, of this distinction which prompted so many Elizabethan dramatists to feel that dichotomizing passion and reason did not, even though it was supposed to, carry them to the end of their story. The very nature of drama, as we have seen, implies a dichotomy more fundamental still. The revolution in style led to a revolution in ethics deeper than has been suspected. Pondering on dramatic motive leads us to conclude that a great deal of human behavior is simply not in the traditional ethical dimension at all. This seems to me a revolution equal in scope and implication to the Copernican one. The age was forever stumbling across this discontinuity but did not always know what to make of it.

Little wonder. What is implied, finally, is a redefinition of ethics which still preoccupies us. The literature of the Renaissance, at its best, points directly to these uneasy intersections between dramatic and ethical motive. It is always concerned to point out, as it does so often with its irrelevant proverbs, that the standard ethical machinery is no longer adequate, that a new dimension of explanation has appeared on the scene. Thus the traditional literary glosses in terms of Christian ethics and political philosophy offer the kind of explanation which literature exists to call into doubt. Renaissance intellectual history is, in some ways, not a proper background for Renaissance literature but an anti-background, not an explanation but the *explicandum*. It may even be that the very way we put our questions to the period reveals our positivist bias, the very ease with which we posit categories like appearance and reality may cast a Newtonian shadow. Style is, in its roots, the language of instinct, and

its workings are by nature no less real than the rational purposes
of positivist reality.

A rhetorical perspective may help, also, to sort out some confusions in Renaissance poetics, it may show how someone like
Sidney, for example, could in defending poetry confound its two
contradicting kinds. A serious reality will suggest a didactic
sugarcoating conception of poetry; rhetorical reality needs something more like Sidney's "golden" poetry, maker of a new reality. The rhetorical/serious dualism, that is, can clarify the relationship of moral to formal theories of poetry. Both finally
address themselves to behavior, as Sidney wanted to believe.
But the sugarcoating of conventional Renaissance didacticism
addresses itself to the central self and to a reality poetry can but
imitate. The golden poetic which he set over against such sugarcoating addresses itself to the rhetorical self, attempts to teach by
addressing the histrionic pleasures we draw on in remaining
ourselves. The Horatian _delectare_ turns out to be a _prodesse_ addressed to a different reality and thus speaking a different language. It is thus that formal and moral theories of poetry always
find their relationship. They refer to the two aspects of the self
and, like those two aspects, they can be held together in oscillation but never permanently unified. Sidney's confusion is an
archetypal one, then; perhaps this accounts for _The Defense of
Poetry_'s continued high reputation.

The seeming contradiction between Sidney's two themes falls
away when we see his attempt, more inclusive than he knew, as
an attempt to encompass two realities he did not fully discriminate. Surely just in this failure, in fact, lies his inability to finish
the _New Arcadia_. The _Old_ was built upon rhetorical coordinates,
but the _New_ was to be serious. The change in premises was too
much for both plot and character. Sidney was stymied, aware,
like Ariosto, Spenser, and Shakespeare, that the old epic seriousness would not do, but at a loss for something to put in its
place. He seems to have made a similar mistake in his life as well,
failing at critical junctures to discriminate between rhetorical
and serious reality.

Appropriate premises work their most radical change on a

writer like Lyly, that cynosure of Renaissance excess. As a rhetorical gesture, *Euphues* makes perfect sense, pure stylistic play on the one hand and pure advertisement for Lyly on the other. In both respects, *Euphues* most resembles Nashe's *Unfortunate Traveller*, another display gesture which makes its self-conscious stylistic excess into subject. And both come to grief in the same way. The freedom which an opaque style bestows liberates and expresses a self meagre, nasty, and sick. But it did not always work that way, witness *Venus and Adonis* and *Lucrece*. *Euphues* itself is finally less significant than its popularity, a popularity which reveals rhetorical attitudes toward style governing how we read a broad range of more important Renaissance texts. It is because *Euphues* has been felt as so indicative that it has been so much studied. Rhetorical coordinates show just what it indicates.

Don Quixote fits into the polarity I have been describing so naturally that the correspondence may seem prearranged. Cervantes sought to describe exactly the two kinds of self and motive I have been contrasting. *Don Quixote* juxtaposes the old and new realisms. The picaresque, serious realism of Sancho Panza was destined to inherit the earth for the next three centuries, but it is the realism of romance, the realism of Don Quixote's rhetorical motive, which finally prevails, which Sancho, along with the rest of us, comes to share.

Don Quixote's devotion to his fictional world persists total and absolute. He embodies the truth that Hamlet came also to understand, that the strongest motive is the most gratuitously artificial, the absolutely dramatic, sentimental motive. When, for example, Sancho objects that Don Quixote's grief over his lady's rejection is premature, since no rejection has in fact taken place, the rejoinder is swift and decided:

> Ahí está el punto—respondió don Quijote—, y ésa es la fineza de mi negocio; que volverse loco un caballero andante con causa, ni grado ni gracias: el toque está desatinar sin ocasión. . . . Así que, Sancho amigo, no gastes tiempo en aconsejarme que deje tan rara, tan felice y tan no vista imitación. [1.25]

"Ah, but that's the point," Don Quixote answered. "Just
here is the niceness of the business. For a knight to run mad
for a good reason is neither valuable nor elegant. The trick is
to go crazy for no reason at all. Don't, then, waste any more
time advising me to leave off so rare, happy, and unusual an
imitation."

The Don represents just that "Hotspur" point in the human
model for motive where sublimity falls over into pure play. He is
poised on the boundary between our two world views, a very
serious caballero who also embodies rhetorical motive, role playing par excellence. His rhetoric is always full-dress and fully
enjoyed and we banquet off it much as we relish the fustian in
Henry V.

It is hard not to think that Cervantes took these two fundamentally opposed ideals of life as his subject just because he felt in his
lifetime the one giving way to the other. His contempt for romances looks forward to the coming long interlude of naive
Newtonianism, but his fondness for them looks back to the older
rhetorical view, to a range of motive and kind of identity the
romances had come to represent. The two views oscillate with
the same kind of complexity we have found incarnated in *The
Courtier*, and lend to *Don Quixote* that characteristic epistemolog-
ical richness subsequent prose fiction was so often to lack.

Fielding tried to preserve it, using once again a self-conscious
rhetoric and narrative-speech-narrative pattern taken from the
classical historians. But the future belonged to Defoe's reality, a
serious, positivist reality to be seen through a transparent win-
dow of prose. Even when the subject of the fiction, as with
Clarissa, was the deep currents of rhetorical motive (is not
Lovelace motivated much as Shakespeare's Tarquin?), the technique moved in the other direction. There was enough rhetorical
zest left to propel *Tristram Shandy* to fame, but the Victorian
disapprobation that soon clouded Sterne's reputation showed
that high seriousness was taking charge. Fiction and its poetics
became serious and stayed that way until Joyce forced the return
toward rhetorical coordinates which still preoccupies us.

Yet, with both world views sharply before us, is it not possible to see the rhetorical view lurking even within the serious pre-cincts of Victorian fiction? Thackeray, after all, puts away his puppets in public. And that willingness to confess that a story is only a story which Henry James so deplored in Trollope—is this not rhetorical sincerity? Are there not rhetorical occasions aplenty in Dickens, oratorical set-pieces milked for sentiment to within an inch of their lives? There is more in Dickens than his relished public performances to remind us of Sterne. I don't see why such rhetorical elements ought to surprise anyone. The age and its thinking was indeed overwhelmingly purposive, but literature's business after all is to resist such disproportion and it has always done so, preserved both sets of coordinates. That is why the temptation to periodize on the basis of our fundamental dualism ought to be resisted. It would certainly make a nice pattern: Pagan rhetoric; Christian seriousness; Renaissance mix-ture; Scientific seriousness; finally, Modern play and—back to Pagan rhetoric again. But there are so many exceptions that the pattern cannot be sustained. That scientific materialism led to a preponderant seriousness from which we are only now recover-ing seems beyond doubt. The rest is conjecture.

What, for example, are we to say of the Middle Ages? Augus-tine laid down a method of literary interpretation wholly serious, yet he himself seems as preoccupied, indeed sometimes almost obsessed, with ornament as later medieval poetic. The problems of tone common in Renaissance texts crop up again and again in medieval literature, and not only in Chaucer or the *Second Shepherd's Play*. *Gawain* is now being read according to game coordinates, and *Pearl*, after all, is a poem *about* ornamentation and the kind of meaning it can express. Andreas Capellanus's tragicomic (in the sense used earlier for *Venus and Adonis*) set of Ovidian games testifies to a self-consciousness about rhetoric and connects that self-consciousness with role playing and a dramatic present in just the way our coincident spectrums would prescribe. In scriptural exegesis we find a play spirit which modern typological criticism is currently reviving. In the *ars dictaminis* we find the bizarre style of Boncompagno. The whole spirit of the Gothic was as much playful as sublime. You tried always to vault higher than your neighbor until, as at Beauvais, the whole arch collapsed. Medieval literature is full of the same ornamental ludic scoring.

So periodizing ought to be resisted. The central wisdom of Western literature lies in its basic structural pattern, its rich and contentious mixture of serious and rhetorical reality. It is this mixture which everywhere ought to be cherished. It turns up in the oddest places, in the juxtaposition of Odysseus and Achilles, and even in Achilles' dilemma itself—a long private life and a central self, or a heroic place in a rhetorical story. The self-correcting power of human expressivity seems perennially strong. Even the most compelling purpose—modern advertising, for example—turns into a game if it goes on long enough. The most emetic nonsense returns to laughter.

The self-corrective element seems especially obvious right now. In the ancient quarrel between the philosophers and the rhetoricians, we are again inclining toward the rhetoricians. This requires, finally, as we have seen, not a new theory of mimesis but a new theory of reality. We seem to be getting one.

This new theory of reality has only recently seeped down to the literary critic. It stems, obviously, from the changed status of the scientific proposition effected by nuclear physics. The realization that a scientific proposition makes true statements not about reality but about the symbolic universe in which it chooses to conduct its discourse brings with it a severe dislocation in human belief. The new emphasis on system rather than monad, on process rather than object, knower instead of known, affects us from the most abstruse theorizing down to our daily greeting, now no longer "Hello" but "What's happening?" It has been discussed brilliantly by Michael Polanyi in *Personal Knowledge: Toward a Post-Critical Philosophy*; it has led to the symbolist philosophy of Cassirer and Langer, to Owen Barfield's neo-scholastic effort to "Save the Appearances," to C. S. Lewis's biased but eloquent plea against abolishing man, to Whorf on language as a closed system, and to a great deal more besides. What it has done for rhetorical narrative is to free it from the paralyzing assumption that the primary purpose of prose is to describe objects, the primary purpose of narrative a sequential plot, the primary purpose of history fidelity to "what actually happened." Rhetorical styles are free to work in their own way. T. S. Eliot said, in a famous phrase, that a poem's "meaning" is like the piece of meat a burglar throws to a watchdog to keep him quiet. Well, the new nominalism now tells us there is no watchdog. This not only liberates Robbe-Grillet. It does a good deal for Gorgias and Ovid as well.

The change finds its major literary statement in the writings of Kenneth Burke. Ortega had posed the question in *The Rebellion of the Masses:* "But since it is impossible to know reality directly [*conocer directamente la plenitud de lo real*], we have no alternative to constructing our own arbitrarily [*construir arbitrariamente una realidad*], *supposing* that things are a certain way." Burke set himself the task of analyzing reality as a series of such suppositions, or frames of reference. He sought the master frame, the viewpoint in whose terms the others might be related. He found this in what he called the dramatic hub, a world not of one stage but of many. "The ultimate metaphor for discussing the universe and man's place in it," he argues in *Permanence and Change,* "must be the poetic or dramatic metaphor." Such a master metaphor not only made the whole rhetorical and critical vocabulary available for the analysis of society, it threw primary stress on rhetoric, rhetoric as the means of creating a frame of reference, and rhetoric as finally the substance of that frame. Comparative stylistics thus became at a stroke the central study, not simply for the critic but for the citizen. Style, from the periphery of attention, suddenly moved to the center. For if one accepts Burke's metaphor, style is all there is.

For the most part, we might note parenthetically, the world has begun to accept it. The new world picture, the dramatic one, is going to be—what a surprise—as literary as the old. The mathematicians have developed a quantitative analogue, game theory, and sociologists and philosophers have—following Huizinga in *Homo Ludens*—extended the philosophical implications of its closed-field thinking. Ortega described the game element in modern art in *The Dehumanization of Art* as early as

1925. The psychologists and analysts, Freud with the famous discussion of play in *Wit and Its Relation to the Unconscious,* Piaget's studies, today a book like Erikson's *Childhood and Society,* have charted the role of this kind of thinking—under the game/play rubric—as a technique of socialization. The implications for a new theory of identity, for man as actor, implicit so often in Burke, were made clear in Mead's *Mind, Self, and Society* (1934) and have been elaborated by Goffman, Berne, and others.

By the Second World War, and certainly after, the redefinition of the *Theatrum Mundi* metaphor which Burke had set in motion was pretty nearly complete. Virginia Woolf could write in *Between the Acts,* "He said she meant we all act. Yes, but whose play? Ah! *that's* the question!" It was indeed. Plotinus had premised a false outer life, a play, and a backstage inner reality, and this antithesis lasted long. But when you ask "Whose play?" everything changes. The tableau becomes a process, we become both actors and audience at once. It was only a matter of time before the theatre people rearranged dramaturgy to conform with the new metaphor, so that now we have happenings, participatory drama, and the theatre of the absurd, which I take to be the dramatic equivalent of a framed Campbell's soup can. When foreground and background become *choices,* there is no other way to go.

Since this system-thinking, this preoccupation with frame of reference, seems today to find its center in structuralism, we might spell out in these terms a few of the implications of the self-conscious, dramatistic world view which the structuralist critics have inherited. The two main targets of the literary structuralist attack, the traditional idea of mimesis and the "bourgeois" fictions it produced, both bear on our theme. Both aim to poison Eliot's watchdog. Instead of imitating the world, they aim to imitate wisdom, "the way in which knowledge is held." The structuralist aims to involve us in a process by which *we* make meaning, *we* write the novel. So Robbe-Grillet in *For a New Novel:*

For, far from neglecting him, the author today proclaims his absolute need of the reader's cooperation, an active, conscious, *creative* assistance. What he asks of him is no longer to receive ready-made a world completed, full, closed upon itself, but on the contrary to participate in a creation, to invent in his turn the work—and the world—and thus to learn to invent his own life.

So Ricardou's well-known chiasmus that the novel has metamorphosed from the writing of a history to the history of a writing. Writing becomes an allegory of the frame thinking that Burke encourages and thus, as Barthes says, the novel becomes criticism. Mimesis is an analogy of function not of substance. Since we not only invent a frame, but choose which one to invent, choice and invention are the only really serious subjects left. The novel's subject can only be the *process* of making sense and this by writing novels. The introverted thinking of the closed system can go no further. The process of designifying language (in the sense in which Barthes borrows it from Shklovsky) is both pursued and imitated. Or, as Burke said in *Counter-Statement* in 1931, "The hypertrophy of the psychology of information is accompanied by the corresponding atrophy of the psychology of form." The structuralists seem to have come to a position very like Milton's, when he selected the Fall of Man as the subject for *Paradise Lost*. They have selected the second Fall, modern man's irreversible acceptance of self-consciousness about what he knows and how he knows it, and for Milton's same reason. What else is left? Once you accept the circularity of language as a closed system (and, as Polanyi nicely observes, the existence of a dictionary proves this—words defined only by words), once you *speak* a language and thus commit your thought and self to its formal limitations, you simply have no choice.

The new, social construction of reality which, for literary critics at least, Burke began with the dramatic master metaphor, has led to a revolutionary stylistic position, now set forth as structuralist dogma: form without content, or rather form as content; style as thought; self-conscious personification rather than sincerity; surface rather than depth; conscious, deliberate unreality;

the writer as declared poseur. You will remember these not as creed of a fashionable *dernier cri* but as the catalog of charges traditionally made against rhetorical man and his opaque styles. Not altogether without reason did Barthes call the Sophist forebear. By whatever aperiodic ambages, the passion for formal rhetoric seems to have returned.

Bibliographical Note

Having excised from the text my agreements and disagreements with other commentators, I do not propose to reintroduce them here. The commentary on Plato is vast, on Rabelais and Castiglione extensive, on classical and Renaissance rhetoric nearly endless, on Shakespeare truly endless. Nor have scholars been idle on such topics as Western narrative, historiography, role theory, motivation, situational ethics, structuralism, and the like. The original draft of this book, by noticing only a small part of this vast corpus, was nearly twice as long as the present version and at least twice as hard to follow. An attempt to take full account of the relevant commentary—to mention Schiller every time he said something like what I say, and then to anatomize our areas of disagreement—would have made the book unwritable, unreadable, and probably unpublishable. Instead, I have chosen to develop a sequential argument as clear, and as clear of footnotes, as I could make it. I hope to return in much greater detail to each of the texts considered here. I will then be able to trace whatever pattern the commentary describes, much as I did for Sterne criticism in the first chapter of my *Tristram Shandy: The Games of Pleasure*. Until then, I am confident that no reader will think the argument I have pursued to exist in a cultural vacuum. And it is, too, a genuine part of my argument that the reader must see for himself what pattern the commentaries trace. If he finds the serious/rhetorical dichotomy to be fundamental there, he will have lent a substance to my case that I could never have supplied myself. If not, not.

I would like, however, to acknowledge some primary and long-standing debts. The first and predominant one, obviously, is to Kenneth Burke. I try to comfort myself, when I think how large this is, by reflecting that most current thinking in literary criticism, and by no means only in literary criticism, is coming to confess the same indebtedness. Even the structuralists must in time see how Burke, in the 1930s for the most part, thought through their major problems.

It was Werner Jaeger's one-sided praise of Plato in *Paideia*, and Karl Popper's equally one-sided, and equally serious, attack on him in *The Open Society and Its Enemies*, which first set me thinking about Platonic seriousness. Jaeger isolated all the main issues and, to see them clearly, one need only restate them in other terms. The book which most clearly begins to do this, as far as the attack on the Sophists is concerned, is Mario Untersteiner's fine *The Sophists*. For Ovid, it was L. P. Wilkinson and Brooks Otis who set down the main problems. Both posed them in a fundamentally wrong, totally serious way, and the revisions in Otis's second edition, where he begins to see this, make interesting reading.

For Chaucer, my primary debt is to a great scholar and teacher, Talbot Donaldson, who showed me, when I was both an undergraduate and a graduate student, that Chaucer was as fundamental to our own time as he was to his own.

Stephen Booth has, to my mind, written the major—and in a sense really the only—book on Shakespeare's sonnets and I cannot praise it highly enough. It was only because he stated the serious issues of the sonnets so clearly that I was emboldened to offer a rhetorical counterstatement. And I must recognize with equal gratitude, if not with equal indebtedness, two other outstanding studies, Michel Beaujour's *Le Jeu de Rabelais* and Nancy S. Streuver's *The Language of History in the Renaissance*. I came to both books after I had made up my own mind on the issues they so brilliantly analyze, but the sense of comradeship that they provided I am grateful for. That minds more learned and capacious than my own were thinking in the same way reassured me that there was indeed a road there to be traveled. Beaujour's book especially, in the striking originality with which it chronicles Rabelais's "victoire sur le serieux," seems to me, for all my disagreements with it, a genuine landmark in Renaissance studies.

I first began thinking about Shakespeare's history plays when studying them as a graduate student under Charles Prouty, and though, so far as I know, he never would have argued in print as I do here, it was from his thinking that my own began and the record ought to show this.

Perhaps it is with Huizinga as with Burke; the borrowing is now less personal than cultural. It is no weaker for that. The whole line of game thinking that led me from Caillois and Benveniste to Kenneth Boulding, to Laing and Barthes, to Gregory Bateson and Clifford Geertz, started with *Homo Ludens* and *The Waning of the Middle Ages*. To the work of George Herbert Mead, too, I find myself repeatedly returning. That I have not become more of a behaviorist than I have, I owe to a book now, so far as I can see, totally forgotten, Charles Horton Cooley's *Life and the Student*. "The study and measurement of behavior," Cooley wrote, "the outside of life, is a fruitful and promising method, but the idea of a human science consisting wholly of such study, without sympathetic observation of the mind, is, I think, only mystification. Outside and inside, consciousness and behavior, mutually complement and interpret each other. They cannot be disjoined without denaturing both." No one has ever put it better. Equipped with such wisdom, the student of literature at least scarcely needs, though he can make good use of, the sociologists like Erving Goffman who have followed out the implications of Burke's dramatistic thinking.

I must praise two more famous men, C. S. Lewis and Erich Auerbach. Both, to my mind, saw but did not see, told their stories greatly but got them essentially backwards and by so doing emboldened me to try turning things the other way round. From Auerbach, indeed, I can even borrow my apology for not having read all that I ought to have read. "If it had been possible," he remarks at the end of *Mimesis*, "for me to acquaint myself with all the work that has been done on so many subjects, I might never have reached the point of writing." So it has certainly proved with me, in trying to focus my own thinking through even these brief exploratory essays.

Works Cited in the Text

Auerbach, Erich. *Mimesis: The Representation of Reality in Western Literature*. Tr. Willard R. Trask. Princeton, 1953.

Bakhtin, Mikhail. *Rabelais and His World*. Tr. Hélène Iswolsky. Cambridge, Mass., 1968.

Barthes, Roland. "Science vs. Literature." *The Times Literary Supplement*, 28 September 1967, pp. 410–16.

Beaujour, Michel. *Le Jeu de Rabelais*. Paris, 1969.

Bebbington, W. A. "Soliloquy?" *The Times Literary Supplement*, 20 March 1969, p. 289.

Berne, Eric. *Games People Play: The Psychology of Human Relationships*. New York, 1964.

Booth, Stephen. *An Essay on Shakespeare's Sonnets*. New Haven, 1969.

Brault, Gerard J. " 'Une Abysme de Science': On the Interpretation of Gargantua's Letter to Pantagruel." *Bibliotheque d'Humanisme et Renaissance* 28: 615–32.

Buffon, Georges. *Oeuvres Philosophiques de Buffon*. Ed. Jean Piveteau. Paris, 1954.

Burckhardt, Jacob. *The Civilization of the Renaissance in Italy*. Tr. S. G. C. Middlemore. New York, 1954.

Burke, Kenneth. *Counter-Statement*. New York, 1931.

———. *Permanence and Change: An Anatomy of Purpose*. New York, 1935.

Caillois, Roger. *Les Jeux et les Hommes: Le Masque et le Vertige*. Paris, 1958.

Cassirer, Ernst. *An Essay on Man: An Introduction to a Philosophy of Human Culture*. New Haven, 1944.

Cooley, Charles Horton. *Life and the Student*. New York, 1931.

Curtius, Ernst Robert. *European Literature and the Latin Middle Ages*. Tr. Willard R. Trask. New York, 1953.

Delacroix, Henri. *Le Langage et la Pensée*. Paris, 1930.

Else, Gerald F. *Aristotle's Poetics: The Argument*. Cambridge, Mass., 1967.

Erikson, Erik. *Childhood and Society*. New York, 1950.

Freud, Sigmund. *Jokes and Their Relation to the Unconscious*. Tr. and ed. James Strachey. New York, 1960.

Goffman, Erving. *The Presentation of Self in Everyday Life*. New York, 1959.

Havelock, Eric. *A Preface to Plato*. Cambridge, Mass., 1963.

Huizinga, Johan. *Homo Ludens: A Study of the Play-Element in Culture*. Boston, 1950.

———. *The Waning of the Middle Ages: A Study of the Forms of Life, Thought, and Art in France and the Netherlands in the Fourteenth and Fifteenth Centuries*. London, 1924.

Jaeger, Werner. *Paideia: The Ideals of Greek Culture*. Oxford, 1944.

James, William. *The Principles of Psychology*. New York, 1931.

Kennedy, George. *The Art of Persuasion in Greece*. Princeton, 1963.

Laing, R. D. and A. Esterson. *Sanity, Madness and the Family*. New York, 1964.

Lewis, C. S. *The Abolition of Man*. London, 1943.

———. *English Literature in the Sixteenth Century*. Oxford, 1954.

Mead, George Herbert. *Mind, Self, and Society: From the Standpoint of a Social Behaviorist*. Chicago, 1934.

Ortega y Gasset, José. *The Dehumanization of Art*. Tr. Willard R. Trask. New York, 1956.

———. *La rebelión de las masas*. Madrid, 1929; 1968.

Otis, Brooks. *Ovid as an Epic Poet*. 2d ed. Cambridge, 1970.

Peckham, Morse. *Man's Rage for Chaos: Biology, Behavior, and the Arts*. Philadelphia, 1965.

Polanyi, Michael. *Personal Knowledge*. Chicago, 1958.

Popper, Karl. *The Open Society and Its Enemies*. 4th ed. rev. Princeton, 1963.

Ransom, John Crowe. "Shakespeare at Sonnets." *Southern Review* 3 (January, 1938): 531–53.

Robbe-Grillet, Alain. *For a New Novel: Essays on Fiction*. New York, 1965.

Robins, R. H. *Ancient and Mediaeval Grammatical Theory in Europe*. London, 1951.

Rose, Herbert Jennings. *A Handbook of Greek Literature from Homer to the Age of Lucian*. 4th ed. rev. London, 1950.

Sainéan, Lazare. *L'Influence et la Reputation de Rabelais*. Paris, 1930.

Speirs, John. *Chaucer the Maker*. London, 1951.

Streuver, Nancy S. *The Language of History in the Renaissance: Rhetoric and Historical Consciousness in Florentine Humanism*. Princeton, 1970.

Taylor, A. E. *Plato: The Man and His Work*. 7th ed. London, 1960.

Untersteiner, Mario. *The Sophists*. Tr. Kathleen Freeman. Oxford, 1954.

Whitehead, Alfred North. *The Aims of Education and Other Essays*. New York, 1929.

Wilkinson, L. P. *Ovid Recalled*. Cambridge, 1955.

Wölfflin, Heinrich. *Principles of Art History*. Tr. M. D. Hottinger. New York, n.d.

Index

Aleatory composition, 59, 113, 116–17, 175, 187
Alberic of Monte Cassino, *De Dictamine*, 24
Allegorizing (act of), 39–41, 59, 169–73 passim
Allegory: in *Gargantua and Pantagruel*, 171–86 passim; of style, 62, 64, 123, 124, 127, 162
Andreas Capellanus, 49, 218
Antique diction, 160, 173
Apollodorus, *Library*, 59
Apuleius, 16
Ariosto, Ludovico, 215; *Orlando Furioso*, 60
Aristophanes, *The Clouds*, 43
Aristotle, 6, 20, 65, 113; *Poetics*, 18, 111, 114; *Rhetoric*, 2, 26
Arnold, Matthew, 27, 28, 65–66, 67, 81, 195
Auerbach, Erich, *Mimesis*, 18, 227
Augustine, Saint, 218

Babble, 25
Bakhtin, Mikhail, 174
Barfield, Owen, 219
Barthes, Roland, 5, 222, 223
Beaujour, Michel, 185; *Le Jeu de Rabelais*, 168, 174, 226
Bebbington, W. A., 136
Bembo, Pietro, *Gli Asolani*, 163
Bergson, Henri, 159
Berne, Eric, 221
Boncompagno, 218
Booth, Stephen, 118, 226; *An Essay on Shakespeare's Sonnets*, 116
Bouillabaisse, 168
Brault, Gerard J., 179
Buffon, George Louis Leclerc, Comte de, 22–23
Burckhardt, Jacob, 161
Burke, Kenneth, 13, 220, 221, 225; *Counter-Statement*, 222; *Permanence and Change*, 220

Burton, Robert, 16

Caillois, Roger, *Les Jeux et les Hommes*, 187
Carroll, Lewis, 19
Cassirer, Ernst, 219; *An Essay on Man*, 58, 59
Castiglione, Baldesar, 24, 49, 186–87, 188, 212, 213; *The Courtier*, 13, 144–64, 207, 217
Central self, 6–8; denied by rhetorical man, 5, 27, 124, 137, 141, 203, 219; dynamic process, 156, 206–07, 210; and literary genre, 14, 19, 93, 112, 113, 124–27, 158; traditional concept of, 1, 36, 47, 52, 211. *See also* Sincerity
Cervantes, Miguel de, 109, 200; *Don Quixote*, 60, 216–17
Chaucer, Geoffrey, 24, 49, 94, 109, 188, 204, 212, 218; *The Canterbury Tales*, 65, 66, 67–76, 78, 80; *Troilus and Criseyde*, 13, 53, 66, 71, 76–81, 93, 163
Churchill, Sir Winston, *My Early Life*, 202
Cicero, 27, 211–12; *Consolatio*, 16; *De Oratore*, 144; *First Oration against Catiline*, 13
Cigars, 169. *See also* Allegory; *Merde*
Clarissa, 149, 217
Clarity, 1, 20–27 passim, 106, 160, 161, 187, 192
Coleridge, Samuel Taylor, *Biographia Literaria*, 89
Collingwood, R. G., 20
Comedy, 19, 56, 111, 158–60
Committee, The, 24
Cooley, Charles Horton, *Life and the Student*, 227
Criticism, New, 32
Curtius, E. R., 5

Decorum, 28, 90, 113, 159, 161

231